D1257350

LIBRARY OF
AND
MONEY BANKING
HISTORY

THE EVOLUTION OF MODERN MONEY

THE

EVOLUTION

OF

MODERN MONEY

BY

W. W. CARLILE

[1901]

REPRINTS OF ECONOMIC CLASSICS

Augustus M. Kelley · Publishers
NEW YORK 1969

First Edition 1901

(London: Macmillan & Company, 1901)

Reprinted 1969 by

AUGUSTUS M. KELLEY · PUBLISHERS

NEW YORK NEW YORK 10010

LIBRARY OF CONGRESS CATALOGUE CARD NUMBER

69-17029

PRINTED IN THE UNITED STATES OF AMERICA
by SENTRY PRESS, NEW YORK, N. Y. 10019

THE EVOLUTION OF
MODERN MONEY

BY

WILLIAM WARRAND CARLILE, M.A.

London

MACMILLAN AND CO., Limited

NEW YORK: THE MACMILLAN COMPANY

1901

Dedicated

TO

JAMES STEVENSON, Esq., F.R.S.E., F.R.G.S.

WHO HAS RENDERED A

DISTINGUISHED SERVICE TO MONETARY SCIENCE

BY HIS PUBLICATION OF THE

"CATALOGUE OF GREEK COINS IN THE

HUNTERIAN COLLECTION"

PREFACE

In the following pages an attempt has been made to treat the phenomena of money, from first to last, from the historical standpoint. As regards the money of antiquity I have been indebted for many valuable suggestions to Mr. George Macdonald, M.A., the editor of the recently issued *Catalogue of Greek Coins in the Hunterian Collection*, who also has been good enough to read the proofs for me.

In Chapters I. and II. of the first part I have drawn considerably on two articles contributed to the *Journal of Political Economy* (U.S.A.), as well as on a paper published in the *Transactions of the Philosophical Society of Glasgow for* 1898 ; and in Chapters V. and VI. of the second part on two articles contributed to the *Economic Review*.

A paper which was sent in, at the late Lord Farrer's suggestion, to the Indian Currency Committee of 1898, and printed in the Blue Book of 1899 (Appendix I. Class C. No. 21), is inserted as Appendix A., as illustrating the general principles of the work in their practical application. Appendix B. contains some variations which it seems necessary to introduce into Mommsen's theory of the reduction of the as, in the light of recent numismatic evidence.

I have to thank Mr. E. I. Carlyle, of the *Dictionary of National Biography*, for his invaluable assistance in looking up authorities in the British Museum, and Mr. S. Begg, of the *Illustrated London News*, for his excellent reproduction of the first denarius on the title-page.

CONTENTS

INTRODUCTORY

PART I

HISTORICAL TRANSITIONS OF THE MONETARY STANDARD

CHAPTER I

THE ENGLISH TRANSITION IN THE EIGHTEENTH CENTURY

CHAPTER II

THE TWO ROMAN TRANSITIONS

CHAPTER III

THE POSITION OF GOLD IN EUROPE BEFORE THE EIGHTEENTH CENTURY TRANSITION IN ENGLAND

CHAPTER IV

THE FRENCH CURRENCY IN THE MEDIÆVAL AND RENAISSANCE PERIODS

CHAPTER V

THE EMERGENCE OF THE MODERN SYSTEM

If the gold was already, in the seventeenth century and earlier, the true, though not the popular standard, then the transition in the eighteenth must be regarded as the climax of a process of development. Granting this, we have still to ask why the change came precisely when it did. Why did not the priority of gold, if already latent, assert itself earlier? The answer is to be sought in a yet closer examination of the details of the transition and the circumstances that immediately preceded it. The guinea rose to 30s. in 1695. Why did it not rise to 44s.? It is clear that the silver was already over valued, and already dependent for its monetary value on its convertibility into gold. The apparent reduction of the guinea was really

CHAPTER VI

THE CRITERIA OF STANDARD MONEY

The facts in the preceding chapters must be familiar to many, but their significance has been missed. In England it is universally assumed that silver was the standard up to the beginning of the eighteenth century. View of M. de Vienne He finds that gold since the fourteenth century was used in all large transactions. Yet he does not regard it as technically the standard. He holds to the principle that the standard is that metal in which computations are generally made. This principle seems at first sight obvious, but leads to difficulties. We had in England a popular standard that was plainly not the true standard. The " Bank Restriction." Case of Java. Harris's dictum, " The money in which wages are paid will always be the standard." Why not true? Because the value of that money itself may be dependent on something else. This is why silver is not regarded as the standard now. Money does not illustrate the democratic idea. Steuart's view, that large dealers are those who regulate prices. The rupee the " fixed point," yet illusory. Bagehot's view : " It is in the wholesale trade alone that prices are really fixed." The medium of wholesale trade will, therefore, become the measure of values. Tooke on large and small notes. Adam Smith on the two branches of the circulation. Diagram illustrating the course of the wholesale and retail circulation. It illustrates the manner in which currencies make their rounds within each country, while goods exported pay for goods imported. It indicates an unexpected degree of organic regularity. No room for those alleged variations in the " rapidity of circulation " which are often described as playing an important part in connection with the determination of prices. That theory examined. It owes its origin to Locke. What Locke meant by the rapidity of circulation. The diagram brings into a clear light the nugatoriness of the limitation in the legal tender of the silver. Mr. Leonard Courtney's evidence on that point. Reverting to the question of the criteria of the standard, the ubiquity of any money may be left on one side, also the fact of " thinking in gold " or " thinking in silver." There remain the questions : What is the money that passes by weight? and What is the money of external trade? In virtue of its possessing these two characteristics, gold is now reckoned the standard of England and of Europe. There is, however, an important difference between the state of things in which the principal metal is the current medium of computations and that in which it is not. In the one case it may be called the latent, in the other the overt and official standard. In both it is the only real money. Evidence that gold has passed by weight, throughout English history, since its introduction into the coinage. Rice Vaughan; Rushworth. James I.'s proclamation, 1617. Elizabeth's proclamation, 1587. Similar provisions in regard to silver in the reign of John. When a metal passes by weight, the equivalent of free coinage necessarily exists as regards it. How Mommsen treats the question, What was real and what was subsidiary money at various dates in Roman history? . . . . *Pages* 149—175

CHAPTER VII

THE ORIGINATING CAUSES OF TRANSITIONS

The subject-matter of this chapter bears necessarily a close affinity to that of the last. The proximate cause of a change of standard is ordinarily the influence of neighbouring countries. Illustrative instances. Germany adopted the gold standard in 1872 and the rest of Europe within the decade. Influence of England. London the centre of the world's finance. Mommsen's view. He prefaces his account of Roman money by an account of the Asiatic, Greek, and Sicilian monetary systems. The first denarii; significance of the image of the Dioscuri on the reverse. How the British-Indian rupee supplanted the native rupee as the money of Kashmir. A laboratory experiment illustrating the manner in which standards change. The change of standard there preceded all legislation with reference to it. A point that has interesting historical applications. Tendency to consolidation in the money of antiquity. Athens and her allies. Alexander and his successors. The Romans. The rationale of the connection between foreign trade and internal currency. Garrault. Every exporter is necessarily engaged in the propaganda of the standard of his country

PART II

CHAPTER I

THE ORIGIN OF MONEY

CHAPTER II

ORNAMENT AND MONEY

CHAPTER III

THE GROUND OF THE CONNECTION BETWEEN ORNAMENT
AND MONEY

ment. The struggle for existence not everything. Exertion
directed to the maintenance of "position in life"; not
necessarily selfish. Mill on "getting on." Instinct and
reason. Indirect beneficial results of the struggle for position
and distinction. Position in life to a great extent dependent
(1) on expenditure on superfluities ; (2) on the reserved
power of such expenditure. Identity at bottom between the
aims of the primitive and the civilised man. The impulse
presents itself most frequently in its negative aspect ; in the
fear of losing position rather than in the hope of improving it
Not a merely modern phenomenon. It accounts for the fact
that in so many countries, and since the most remote
antiquity, the metals of ornament have become money.

CHAPTER IV

THE NATURE OF THE STANDARD

The precise meaning of "acceptability." Synonymous with
"liquidity." Varying degrees of "acceptability." The
commodity which most approximates to invariability of value
possesses the highest degree of "acceptability." The law of
the origin of money is the same as the law of the transition
of standards. Homogeneity another requisite of the monetary
commodity. Homogeneity of substance is only important as
being essential to homogeneity of value. Dicta of Locke and
of Cernuschi. Xenophon on the *Revenues of Athens*.
"Silver never loses its value." Contrast between Xenophon's
theory of value and that of the Austrian school. The latter
takes men to be perfectly rational, while Xenophon recognises the vanity and frivolity of human nature. Necessity of
distinguishing between the causes that lead to the assumption
of the position of standard money by a commodity, and those
which maintain it in that position when once attained. It is
in regard to the former mainly that the frivolousness of human
nature comes into play. Connection between national wealth
and national self-preservation. Intimate connection between
the two desires which have made and which maintain the
metals of ornament as the monetary substances, the desire

for distinction in the present and the desire for security in the future. Liability to changes of fashion in regard to the precious metals counteracted by their association with the idea of wealth itself. In the practice of hoarding, Xenophon finds another cause of the maintenance of the value of silver. Compare Fullarton. Under modern conditions, for hoards substitute bank reserves. Remarkable passage in Mr. Fullarton's *Regulation of Currencies* on the necessary effect of the purchase by the Bank of England of all the gold brought to it, at a fixed price of £3 17s. 10½d. per ounce. He thinks this must entirely neutralise the effect on prices of fluctuations in the quantity of gold discovered. In other words, that so long as the system continues the value of gold must remain stable. He attributes the origin of the system of purchasing gold at a fixed price to the Act of 1844. It existed however in the eighteenth century. It was indeed a mere development of the system under which for many centuries gold had always passed by weight. It is not necessary to maintain that the standard substance does not in some real sense fluctuate, but only that in the universal belief of the practical world it does not fluctuate ; that is, while it remains the standard.

CHAPTER V

THE PHENOMENA OF REAL AND SUBSIDIARY MONEY CONTRASTED

It is certain that the absorption of all the gold brought to it at a fixed price by the Bank must operate so as to prevent any effect from being produced on general prices by increased supplies of gold, that is similar to the effect produced on prices by over-issued paper or depreciated silver. Tooke's line of reasoning in reference to the doctrine that an increase or diminution of money must be attended by a proportionate rise or fall of prices. "Compulsory government paper can act as an originating cause on prices, real money cannot." Mill's theory that it is the "actual supply" alone that determines the value of money examined. The "actual supply" is something that we can know nothing about till after the price is fixed and

CHAPTER VI

THE PLACE OF MONEY IN ECONOMICS

bility of our having the one without the other. The axiom
assumes that the commodities of one year are the *very same
substances* which formed the commodities of the previous year.
The line of reasoning of Mr. Wells, of Mr. Atkinson, and Lord
Playfair, which aims at showing that the fall of prices in the
last years of the past century was fully accounted for by other
causes than the appreciation of gold, really aims at showing that
the standard did not fluctuate. The axiom proves too much ;
it would prove that no one commodity could ever approximate
more to stability of value than any other. The axioms that
" any one commodity can measure the values of any and all
others," and that " there can be no general rise in values "
examined. If the latter were true, could there be any increase
in the national wealth ? Confusion between relations of value
that are contemporaneous and those that take time into
account. These "axioms" have a common source in the
detachment of the conception of value from its historical
foundation. The conception of value is based on the conception of price, and the conception of price is based on the
existence of money. The etymology of *aestimo*. General
tendency to invert the relations of the abstract and the concrete. Mill professes to leave the conception of money out of
account altogether in the first part of his work. The obscurity
of his discussion of international values is due to the fact that
he interpolates the ideas of price, &c., into a state of things
where there is, by hypothesis, no standard of value in existence.
Doctrine of the insignificance of money. It is true rather that
money is the pivot of everything in economics. Doctrines
that " money is of no use till it is spent," that what men really
want is always " commodities " and never money, that " the sole
benefit of foreign trade lies in the imports," &c. We find such
doctrines nowhere else but in treatises on economics. In the
practical world, if cheap imports are advocated, it is ordinarily
only as a means towards profitable exports. The aim of the
nations is still what it was in the days of the mercantile
theorists, to increase their command over the standard substance. View of modern Free Traders, such as President
Hadley, of Yale. They support Free Trade on the ground
that it is the export trades which are best worth fostering, and
that it is Free Trade which alone can foster them. There is

The Evolution of Modern Money

ERRATA

p. 14, l. 14, *for* overrated *read* underrated
p. 251, l. 4 from bottom, *for* necessaries *read* superfluities

THE EVOLUTION OF MODERN MONEY

INTRODUCTORY

THE all-embracing conception of growth, development, evolution, borrowed from biology, has, at this time of day, supplanted every other in the explanation of most social phenomena. It is no longer possible for any one to think of language as so recent and so great a philosopher as Renan thought of it, as having [1] "sprung at a bound from the genius of each race." The phase of thought which gave rise to the conception of civil government as having been established by a contract between king and people, entered into sometime at the dawn of history, is itself interesting now as a historical phenomenon only. With regard to the origin, growth and trans- mutations of money alone the case is different.

[1] *De l'Origine du Langage*, p. 16.

Even in regard to the money of antiquity we are still liable to speak of the "adoption" by Greece of silver as a standard, and of copper by early Rome ; and when we come to treat of modern developments it is, for the most part, taken for granted that we have given a fully adequate account of the recent changes of standard in continental Europe when we point to the legislation of 1872, 1873 and 1876, and of the change of standard in England when we have detailed the provisions of the Act of 1816. "In progressive societies," says Sir Henry Maine, "social opinion and social necessities are almost always in advance of law." That being so, any explanation of a change in a great national institution which stops short at giving us the clauses of the statute under which it was completed and ratified is equivalent to no explanation at all. What we want to get at in order to understand the course of events are the facts that bear on the development of the social necessities and the social opinion that were, in such a case, in advance of the law that was enacted. We recognise, for instance, that it is, at best, a merely superficial and quite unsatisfactory explanation of the manner in which bills of exchange and promissory notes became negotiable in England to point to the statutes of William and Mary and of Anne, which provided that they should be so, when we

know that they were already, in practice, continually negotiated, in the teeth of the principles
of the common law, for some centuries before
those statutes were passed. If, removing our
eyes from the mere fact of a statute being passed,
we inquire what it was that led up to it, the
whole subject ordinarily places itself before us in
an altogether altered light. To take an example
from very modern history, we find that when
silver became cheaper than gold in the seventies,
the French Government and the other governments of the Latin Union very shortly suspended
its free coinage. When, on the contrary, gold
became cheaper than silver in the fifties, and
when the new gold in consequence began to
supplant the ancient money of the country, so far
from there being any thought of suspending its
free coinage, the change was hailed with
universal satisfaction.[1] Why this difference in
public sentiment, or, indeed, in something more
than sentiment, in the two cases? It may be
answered in a general way, as indeed it has been
answered: "The commercial world believes
in gold, and prefers gold as a medium of
exchange whenever it can get it." That un-

---

[1] M. Chevalier says, with regard to the state of feeling in 1850 :
"The public applauded the introduction of gold in the place of
silver." M. Babelon, Prof. Laughlin, and Prof. Erwin Nasse, of
Bonn, might be quoted as bearing similar testimony.

doubtedly is true of the commercial world of the present day. There have been periods in the world's history however when gold was not the favoured metal. The Athenians never coined it except for one or two brief periods, under the stress of urgent necessity, and then it appears to have been in the highest degree unpopular. Our own ancestors, too, even got the length of agitating against Henry III.'s golden pennies. The explanation of the facts, it is evident, whatever it may be, is one that cannot be given apart from their historical setting. It was much more, of course, than a wave of sentiment, in the ordinary sense, that caused the closing of the mints to silver and the adoption of gold as the standard by the Latin Union in 1873. The nations belonging to it could not have continued to keep their mints open to the cheaper metal without incurring immense pecuniary loss for every day that they did so. Why was it that the unlimited minting of the cheaper metal in the fifties neither threatened nor was attended with any parallel evil consequences? The difference can be understood only if we suppose that gold had, somehow and in some sense, become the standard of Europe already in the fifties, and that silver had already become subsidiary. The very conception of "becoming" however, as applicable to such changes, is altogether foreign to the current line of thought, which seems to regard the choice of monetary standards as matters which are *ab initio* and throughout completely within the arbitrary discretion of kings and parliaments.

We will find, whenever we attempt to trace the development of money, either in ancient or modern communities, that the function of legislation, in so far as this legislation has been wise, and in so far as its results have been permanent, has been confined mainly to the consecration of facts that are already accomplished ; that the initiation of every great monetary change, as well indeed as the origin of the use of money itself, is traceable to the action of causes that have been in operation behind the scenes for centuries before this legal consecration took place.

Nothing is more certain than that the monetary standard has changed many times from substance to substance in the various nations of the East and the West during the course of the world's history. M. Babelon thus summarises the general trend of early changes in the Hellenic world and in ancient Italy :[1] "After barter pure and simple came cattle money, then utensil money, then iron, copper, gold and silver, estimated by weight, then copper and iron money. Finally we see copper and iron money giving place to money of silver and of gold." In dealing with the evolution of

[1] *Les Origines de la Monnaie*, p. 230.

money it might seem that the most natural line of procedure was to endeavour to pursue the course of these changes down the stream of history. That would indeed be the historical order; the most natural scientific order, however, would be the reverse.   The geologists have taught us that the best clue to the interpretation of the past is always to be found in the careful study of the present.   The existing generation has found the world in the middle of the yet uncompleted transition from silver to gold.   If we can gain an adequate comprehension of the manner in which that transition began, and in which it is running its course, we shall find then, perhaps, that we have the data available for interpreting both the origin of money itself and the course of transitions of the standard in the past.

PART I

HISTORICAL TRANSITIONS OF THE MONETARY STANDARD

Aera dabant olim, melius nunc omen in auro est ;
Victaque concedit prisca moneta novae.
—Ovid, *Fasti*, lib. I, v. 225.

CHAPTER I

If the question is asked: At what date must
we place the transition in England from silver to
gold as the monetary standard of the country?
we should perhaps receive the reply: In 1816.
The most cursory glance however at the conditions ruling during the eighteenth century is sufficient to show us that there did not then exist anything that even remotely corresponds to our
conception of a silver standard. We find Adam
Smith, for instance, speaking of gold as, in his
day, "holding up" the value of the silver coin, just
as we might speak of the sovereign as holding
up the value of the shillings and half-crowns now.
The fluctuations of the foreign exchanges, owing
to the state of the silver coinage had, when
Lord Liverpool wrote, already become a thing
of the remote past. For very many years they

had fluctuated only in conformity with the condition of the gold coinage and with that of the
balance of trade.   The mint price of gold too
had remained for very many years at the un-
varying figure of £3 17s. 10½d., as at present;
while the price of silver bullion fluctuated, at any
rate, as noticeably as it did during the earlier
years of this century.   Taking a survey of the
state of things, indeed, it is hard to say what
there is in it that is wanting to the complete
existence of the gold standard.   If to-day in
India we had a similar state of things established,
one in which the gold held up the silver to a
uniform value, and in which the exchange was
unaffected by anything but the balance of trade
and the condition of the gold coinage, we should
certainly have all the gold standard that any one
thinks of or aims at.[1]

Go back one hundred and twenty years, however, to the date of the great recoinage of silver,
and we find an entirely different state of things in
existence.   The guinea then rose and fell in
quotable value, like any other commodity; the
clipped and worn condition of the silver coinage
caused the dealings of internal commerce to be
attended with endless trouble and inconvenience;
and brought down the exchange with Hamburg

[1] Since the above was written this satisfactory state of things
may be said to have been realised.

and Amsterdam sometimes as much as four shillings in the pound. From 1695 to 1699 was the period of the recoinage of silver. Subsequent to that date history appears to be altogether silent in regard to monetary troubles, either in connection with internal dealings or with the foreign exchanges. Macaulay dwells with enthusiasm on the long years of immunity from such troubles that succeeded the recoinage, and which he, most naturally, regards as having flowed from it. The truth was, however, that it had hardly been completed before the new full-weighted silver began to leave the country again in a steady and unceasing stream. Eighteen years after its completion all the beneficial results which it was expected to secure had ceased to have any existence as far as the condition of the silver itself was concerned.

"In the reign of King William," remarks Lord Liverpool,[1] "when the silver coins were so very deficient, Mr. Locke had said,[2] 'It is no wonder if the price and value of things be confounded and uncertain, when the measure itself is lost.' To restore this measure the public had expended £2,700,000. But, notwithstanding so great an expense, this measure of property in the lapse of

[1] *Coins of the Realm*, p. 82.
[2] *Further Considerations concerning Raising the Value of Money.* Locke's Works, ed. 1823, vol. v. p. 158.

a very few years was a second time lost, and had
no existence, unless it had passed into the gold
coin."

Amid much that is uncertain and obscure there
are two facts that stand out clear and unmistakable.   First, there is the fact that while, in 1695,
silver was, at any rate, the apparently operative
standard of the country, it had by the middle of the
next century, probably by 1720, altogether ceased
to be so, and was merely a subsidiary coinage
held up in value by the gold.   Secondly, there is
the fact that this had all come about without any
action, or indeed any thought of action, on the
part of the legislature with the view of bringing
it about ; that it had come about indeed in the teeth
of statutory legislation that made both gold and
silver equally unlimited legal tender, and that
opened the mints to the free coinage of both.

In so far as the phenomenon has been recognised as one that calls for explanation, the current
explanation given of it is summed up in the well-
known formula of Gresham's Law.   Gold, we are
told, being overrated as compared with silver at
the mint, by Sir Isaac Newton in 1717, ousted
silver as the ordinary currency of the country.
The public having then come to use gold instead
of silver as money in the bulk of their transactions, gradually came to measure all values in
it, and eventually—a century later—adopted it

formally as their standard. The explanation is a rough and ready one, and is one, I think, that will not stand a careful scrutiny. To begin with, the statement that gold ousted silver as the ordinary currency of the country is a statement that is plainly enough not in accordance with fact. It stands to reason, on the contrary, that, with a state of things in existence socially in which the average working man was receiving wages of ten shillings a week or under, and was being paid weekly, the currency must, to a very great extent indeed, still have continued to consist of silver. If we want specific evidence on the subject, however, we have it from Harris.[1] Writing in 1757, he tells us that, in his time, "the great inland commerce of the country was chiefly carried on by silver," and that "laborers, handycraftsmen and manufacturers of all sorts" were paid their wages in that metal. Again, the statement that gold was overrated as compared with silver is one that, though strictly speaking correct, may readily mislead. Gold bullion was indeed overrated as compared with silver bullion, and the fact that it was so was one of much importance as bearing on the situation ; but the gold coin that was in circulation was not overrated as compared with the silver coin, but, on the contrary, came to be, by the middle of the century, very greatly

[1] *Essay on Coins*, part ii. p. 91.

underrated as compared with it. When this
ensued there were plainly two classes of money
in circulation, a worse and a better, and both were
unlimited legal tender. Why then did not the
worse, the worn silver, oust the better, the gold
coins, from circulation, as, by Gresham's Law, it
ought to have done? It is surely worthy of
remark that, in this case, Gresham's Law
altogether failed to operate, and that the worse
money, instead of supplanting the better, settled
down into a subsidiary currency alongside of it.
What happened—to trace the process, so far
as it can be traced in detail—was this. First, as
silver bullion was overrated as compared with gold
bullion, practically no fresh silver was brought to
the mints to be coined. The mints were thus
closed to silver as effectually as if they had
been closed by statute. Secondly, all the heavier
silver coins were picked out, melted down, and
exported. What were left, however, must have
been no insignificant quantity, if they were
sufficient to carry on all the inland commerce of
the country. They were, however, sufficiently
depreciated by loss of weight to be, at any rate,
not more valuable intrinsically than they were
nominally ; otherwise they too would have gone
to the melting pot. As time went on, they
continued to suffer from wear and tear, till, in the
end, they were found to have lost from a third to

a half of their weight. Their quantity being limited, however, by the impossibility of coining silver except at a loss, they came, by a natural process, to exemplify both of the two conditions that are, nowadays, laid down as essential for a subsidiary coinage ; their supply was free from the risk of unlimited augmentation, and they contained less metal than that which corresponded to their nominal value.

The state of things that thus came about was, it must be remembered, one to which the history of mankind up to that date could show no parallel. It seems to us so simple a matter to make the silver shilling circulate as precisely the twentieth part of the gold pound sterling that we do not readily realise the fact that the possibility of doing so had not so much as dawned on the minds of our ancestors in the seventeenth century. Locke was profoundly and justly impressed with the unsurpassable importance of making and keeping the monetary standard always absolutely uniform. He laid it down accordingly as self-evident that silver was the only substance that was suitable to be used as the standard money of any country ; as it was by the use of silver alone that that end could be attained, that the perfect identity of " the integer with its fractions," as Harris puts it, could always be insured. It had never apparently so much as occurred to

Locke, or to any one else in his day, that the identity of the integer with its fractions, as far as value was concerned—the only salient matter— could be perfectly maintained, while yet the standard money of the country consisted of a different substance from its subsidiary money. They might, no doubt, have found something of a precedent for such a state of things in the existence, in the past, of copper and billon moneys maintained at a value that was different from their intrinsic value. The inference may seem to us an obvious one that, if copper could be maintained at a parity with silver, then silver could be maintained at a parity with gold. Nothing is more certain, however, than that this inference was never drawn. It would be a gross anachronism, indeed, to represent to ourselves the Englishmen of the seventeenth century as on the look-out for such precedents. Silver was for them the inherited standard of the country, and the last thing they thought of or dreamt of was its displacement in favour of gold, or its reduction to a subsidiary position. Every step indeed in the transition from silver to gold, with all its momentous consequences, was evolved by the natural course of events, without forethought or intention on the part of any human being. In describing the origin of Cabinet government in England, Mr. Bagehot

says that "we blundered into it." It might be
said of the gold standard, in a similar manner,
that we blundered into it; the disastrous state of
the depreciated silver being itself converted by
an apparent accident into an essential feature of
the new system. It would, perhaps, be truer,
however, to say that, as the genius of the
English people in the political sphere, unaided
altogether by theory, evolved both the House of
Commons and the Cabinet, to be copied, when
the time was ripe, by the rest of civilised Europe,
so, in the monetary sphere, it evolved the system
under which, in the world of to-day, the standard
can remain one and uniform, while the currency,
as far as substance goes, can be as complex as
that of the United States is now.

Lord Liverpool's strongest point in defence
of the measures the adoption of which he advocated in 1805, and which were ultimately
adopted by the legislation of 1816, was that
they altered nothing, that, on the contrary, they
legalised in every respect the state of things
which *de facto* at the time existed. Practically,
there had been no free coinage of silver for
nearly a century; he proposed that the statutory
possibility of such free coinage should cease.
The silver coin in circulation had been protected
from the risk of being exported by the fact
that the natural process of attrition by use had

made it so light that it did not pay to export
it; he proposed that, in the issue of fresh
silver, this natural process should be artificially
imitated, that the weight of the new silver
coins, from the start, should be something
below that which represented their bullion value.
The mint price of gold had long remained steady
at £3 17s. 10½d. per oz., and the foreign exchanges had for many years been altogether unaffected by the state of the silver coinage. It was,
in Lord Liverpool's eyes, the one great recommendation of his proposals that, as he anticipated,
once they were adopted, this desirable state of
things would be stereotyped. All through,
nothing was altered, everything was continued.
It was a genuine stroke of genius, none the
less, to have grasped aright the true character
of existing facts, and to have shown how the
statutory law could be brought into conformity
with them.

This fact, that a change in the monetary
standard of the country, while it was actually in
process of accomplishment under their eyes,
could have escaped the recognition of contemporary observers, seems, at first sight, to be
one of so marvellous a character as to pass the
bounds of belief. Yet that it was a fact is
beyond all question. Harris, for instance, wrote
in 1757. In his day the whole state of things

which the legislation of 1816 found in existence
and stereotyped had already come into existence.
By his own account the foreign exchanges had
altogether ceased to be affected by the state of
the silver coinage. He, however, stoutly maintained that gold, in England, was then only a
commodity, and that silver was the sole true,
and, indeed, the sole possible measure of values
in the country. Wages were paid, he urged,
mainly in silver, and "enact what laws you
please,"[1] he said, "that which measures and pays
the price of labour will ultimately be the real
standard of the nation."

Sir James Steuart was another contemporary
observer, who wrote both voluminously and
acutely on the subject of the monetary standard.
The details of the transition indeed are to be
gathered more clearly from his pages than from
any other source. Writing in 1761, he refers to
it as a matter universally understood that " in
England[2] silver is the standard and the ruling
metal."

The view taken of the matter by Adam Smith
is a subject of still greater interest. It is of great
interest alike for what he saw and for what he
failed to see. He perceived in substance indeed,
and came very near to stating with perfect accuracy of form, the true relation which the silver

[1] *Essay on Coins*, part ii. p. 94.   [2] Works vol, v. p. 216

coinage bore to the gold in his day.   He saw that
the gold, not the silver, was even then the
regulative element in the coinage.   When we find
him putting forward and laying stress upon the
fact that the value of the existing [1] " worn and
depreciated silver coin was regulated by the value
of the excellent gold coin, for which it could be
changed ; " that the then recent reformation of
the gold coin had raised not only its own value,
but " likewise that of the silver "—it strikes us
that he seems to perceive clearly enough that the
shillings of his day were in truth to be looked on
merely as fractional parts of the guinea, just as
the shillings of our own are to be regarded as
merely fractional parts of the sovereign.   We
expect indeed to find him going on to the formal
conclusion that the gold was plainly the standard
money, and the silver, like the copper, merely
fractional and subsidiary.   That, however, he does
not do.   On the contrary, he is impressed with
the idea that it is silver which is still the standard,
the true measure of all values.   Dealing with the
subject generally, he remarks that the commercial
nations have ordinarily found it convenient to use
different metals coincidently as money.   One of
these metals they have always considered as more
peculiarly the measure of values than any of the
others, and this preference he says,[2] " seems

---

[1] *Wealth of Nations*, Book I. chap. v. vol. i. p. 60, ed. 1811.

[2] *Op. cit.*, p. 51 ff.

generally to have been given to the metal which they happen first to make use of as the instrument of commerce." Copper thus, he appears to think, remained to the end the standard money in Rome, and silver, up to his own day, had remained the standard money in England. In England he observed, " all accounts are kept and the value of all goods and all estates is generally computed in silver ; and when we mean to express the amount of a person's fortune we seldom mention the amount of guineas, but the amount of pounds sterling which we suppose would be given for it."

With regard to this line of reasoning, what will strike the most casual reader will be that if the fact that all computations were made in pounds sterling in Adam Smith's day could be taken as sufficient proof that silver was, at that date, the standard money of the country, then, on the same ground, we should be forced to the conclusion that silver is the standard money of England now. We all know now, however, that the words " pound sterling " have entirely lost, even in popular thought, their application to silver, and have become merely a synonym for the full-weighted sovereign. We have the key, I think, to the unconscious character of the English transition, as well as to the manner in which others of the historical transitions of the monetary standard in the world have effected themselves, in the fact that this change of application in these words from silver to gold had already taken place in the eighteenth century, unperceived even by its clearest-headed observers.   Lord Liverpool was the first to see distinctly the alteration of meaning.   He indeed remarks that, in his time, the words "pound sterling" no longer meant 1718·7 grains of fine silver, but instead 113 grains of fine gold.   In order to assure ourselves that the change of meaning was complete in Adam Smith's time, we do not need to go beyond his own pages.   In addition to the proofs already adduced we may take the simple fact of his stating as the result of a computation that "an ounce of gold coin is worth £3 17s. 10½d. *in silver.*"[1]   It is plain that if the computation had really taken account of the contemporary value of silver bullion, the ounce of gold would not have been found to be worth precisely this, its present mint price.   It is only because the computation is made in gold, the silver being regarded as bearing a constant fractional relation to the gold, that the ounce can be held to be worth £3 17s. 10½d.   We could not have a clearer proof that to Adam Smith himself the words "pound sterling" had reference no longer to silver but to gold.

In inquiring how such an unperceived transi-

_____
[1] *Op. cit.*, p. 55.

tion of meaning in such words could come about
it is necessary to advert to the wide divergence
of the principles which underlie respectively the
nomenclatures of economics and of physics.   The
things of the outward world depend, in the long
run, for their identification, and consequently for
their names, on the fact that we can lay our
fingers upon them, or, at any rate, can point them
out.   If we wish to explain to our neighbour what
gold, or lead, or iron is, we have the plain resource
of an object-lesson always open to us.   With the
things of economics, as of the purely subjective
sciences, the case is altogether different.   Before
we can identify and name them, we must know
what is the purpose for which human beings
intend to employ them.   The things of physics
take their names from their shape, their colour,
their weight, and so on.   The things of economics
take their names from the human aims that they
subserve.   If then two things subserve the same
purpose and subserve it equally well, a tendency
soon manifests itself to treat the two as absolutely
one and the same, and to sink and lose sight of
all distinctions that may continue to exist between
them, as being altogether irrelevant.   There is
little physical similarity indeed between five
sovereigns and a Bank of England five-pound
note, yet the words " five pounds " call up quite
indifferently the thought of either.   If, as Pro-

fessor Marshall justly remarks, a doctor's carriage
may be "capital" in the forenoon when he is
using it to visit his patients and not "capital" in
the afternoon when he is driving about in it with
his family for his own and their amusement, then
evidently its physical characteristics have to be
left very much out of account in its economical
classification.

The "money" of the money market, that
mysterious entity that is scarce to-day and plentiful to-morrow, without any corresponding change
having taken place either in the amount of bullion
in the Bank's coffers or in the amount of coin in
circulation in the country, can have no outward
resemblance either to shillings or to sovereigns ;
yet we call it "money," and we think of it as
money, because, like shillings and sovereigns, it
is the instrument with which we pay our debts
and make our purchases. The history of money
in all its varieties and in every age teems with
instances illustrative of this principle. Some of
them, indeed, are curiously enough paradoxical.
When we hear of a coin named the "Siliqua
auri" we should probably conclude that it was,
at any rate, a gold coin of some sort or other.[1]
It seems however, on the contrary, to have been
a silver coin which represented the $\frac{1}{24}$th part of

[1] Mommsen (Blacas), *Histoire de la Monnaie romaine*, vol. iii.
p. 83.

the gold solidus.   Similarly, in the Egypt of the
Ptolemies, we have a coin which is commonly
described as the copper *argenteus*, a large copper
that is to say, which was the equivalent in value
of the Attic obol.[1]   In the early Sicilian currency again we have the silver and copper *litrae*,
which were certainly not coins of silver and
copper respectively.[2]   Turning to the infancy of
commerce, when we find values stated in terms
of bullocks, slaves or caldrons, it is almost always
a question, and often a strenuously debated one,
whether it is actual bullocks, slaves, or caldrons
that the author or the inscription quoted allude
to, or whether, on the contrary, it is the value
of a coin or ingot of gold, silver, or copper
that had become the equivalent in value of
the slave, the bullock, or the caldron that is
meant.   With regard for instance to the oxen in
which the value of the armour of Glaucus and
Diomed is estimated in the *Iliad*, the better
opinion, I think, is that it was not actual oxen
that Homer had in his mind, but gold ingots with
which the value of the ox had become equated
and which thus, as in so many parallel instances,
took the name of "oxen."   It is inconceivable,
indeed, that actual oxen could have circulated as

---

[1] Babelon, *Les Origines de la Monnaie*, p. 385.

[2] Mommsen (Blacas), *Histoire de la Monnaie romaine*, vol. i.
p. 104.

money among the soldiers of a besieging army. The expression seems to be a survival from a state of things not then existent. The early Attic proverb that ran to the effect that when a man's silence had been purchased " an ox had passed over his tongue," as Pollux and Plutarch tell us, refers to a coin or ingot that had become known as an " ox," not to the actual animal itself.[1]

Lenormant urges in opposition to this view that no such coin as a *bous* is known, and that no coins at all had been issued at the early period when the proverb originated. If the *bous*, however, were not a coin, there is no reason why it should not have been an ingot of a given weight, originally the equivalent in value of the ox. The shekels that Abraham paid for the cave of Macpelah were not coins, but ingots, as were the pieces of silver paid for the threshing floor of Ornan the Jebusite, and the pieces of silver which Job's friends presented to him, which, curiously enough, the Septuagint translates as *amnada*, lambs.[2]

Professor Ridgeway, in his very suggestive work on the *Origin of Currency and Weight Standards*, attempts to prove the proposition that, over the whole known world, from the

---

[1] See Ridgeway, *Origin of Currency and Weight Standards*, p. 4.

[2] Ridgeway, *op. cit.*, p. 270.

Euphrates to the Bay of Biscay, and over a period of many centuries, the ox bore a constant relation of closely approximate equivalence in value to the gold weight or gold piece of 130 to 135 grs. When we know that an ox which is worth perhaps something under £2 on the plains of Texas now, is worth nearer £10 in New York, it is hard to believe that the valuation of cattle in metal or metallic money in the ancient world effected itself on principles so amazingly different from those which it follows in the modern world. In the neighbourhood of Nineveh or Babylon there can be no doubt that the ox must have been worth many times the amount in gold that it was worth on the steppes of Scythia. It is not, however, in the least necessary for the support of Professor Ridgeway's more general view as to the original connection between the value of the ox and the coins which he describes as "ox-units" that so incredible a proposition should be sustained. He himself indeed recognises that it is not so. Skins of animals, as he remarks, became the unit of account in the Hudson Bay Territory, in dealings between the Indians and the traders, as they did in the earlier periods in Esthonia, in Lapland, and in many other parts of the world. The beaver skin, when the traders went there in the first instance, was worth two English shillings. Subsequently its value rose to many times that figure.

A denomination of value, however, still remained in existence that did not follow the fluctuations of the actual beaver skin.   It may be called the beaver skin of account.   It was nothing else but a synonym for two shillings.   A beaver skin in the flesh might thus be sold for ten to twenty beaver skins of account.   The transition of standard from skins to metallic money had, in short, been effected in precisely the same manner as the transition from gold to silver had been effected in England in the eighteenth century. The words " beaver skin " had, more or less unconsciously to the Indian users of them, changed their application from furs to silver, just as the words "pound sterling," in the eighteenth century, changed their application from a given weight of silver to a given weight of gold ; and the change, in both instances, had arisen from causes that were, in their nature, the same.

Other instances illustrative of a similar principle of transition will readily present themselves to those whose reading has made them in any degree familiar with the phenomena of early money. [1] In the Greek colony of Olbia, for example, on the northern shores of the Black Sea, salt fish was the principal article of export, and thus, like the tobacco money of Virginia, became the local medium of exchange, as it did

[1] Ridgeway, *Origin of Metallic Currency*, p. 317.

in Iceland in the Middle Ages. Subsequently
we find the place of the actual fish taken by a
bronze coin made in a shape that bears a rough
approximation to that of a fish, and inscribed θυν
for θύννος, tunny, and by a larger coin inscribed
ἄριχο [= ἄρριχος],[1] a basket, it being apparently
the equivalent in value of a basket of the fish.
Among the Irish Celts, again, as among so many
primitive peoples, cattle and slaves were both
used as media of exchange. After the ninth
century A.D., gold and silver by weight are
found to have supplanted them, and then the
words for female slave, *cumhal*, and for horned
cattle, *set*, are, curiously enough, found to be used
to designate the metallic ingots that have taken
their place. In the *Book of Armagh*, for instance, a nun is recorded as having sold a horse
for a female slave (*cumhal*) of silver.[2] In the
Cretan inscriptions found at Gortyn, says Professor Ridgeway,[3] certain sums are counted by
kettles and pots—*lebetes* and tripods. Recently
M. Svoronos[4] has advanced the hypothesis that
the *lebetes* and tripods of the inscriptions refer
not to a currency in the kettles and pots of the

---

[1] *Zeit. für Num.*, x. p. 145. This derivation, it must be said, is
not undisputed.
[2] Babelon, *Les Origines de la Monnaie*, p. 86.
[3] *Origin of Metallic Currency and Weight Standards*, p. 314.
[4] *Num. Chron.*, 3rd series, ix. 242.

old Homeric times, but to certain Cretan coins which are marked with a stamp which he recognises in many examples as a *lebes*, and in at least one case as a tripod. As people were occasionally condemned to pay in fines from 50 to 100 "kettles" it seems improbable that it was literal kettles that were in question. In all these cases, the popular apprehension evidently failed to draw any distinction between the original unit and the metallic one that supplanted it. If a man had to pay a fine or tax of 50 or 100 tunnies, slaves, or kettles, it would evidently be quite the same thing to him whether he paid it in literal or in metallic tunnies, slaves, or kettles, so long as the old units and the new were certainly and readily exchangeable at par. In all such cases, for the transition of meaning to take place at all, there must have been a "bi-metallic" period of longer or shorter duration, in which the old unit and the new, as far as value was concerned, meant one and the same thing.

CHAPTER II

THE TWO ROMAN TRANSITIONS

COMING next to the period when metallic money had begun to establish itself in the ancient world, we find the same principle at work in respect to the transitions of standard from one metal to another that we had seen in operation in regard to the money that consisted in cattle, slaves and utensils. It seems beyond doubt that copper was the earliest metallic money of ancient Hellas as well as of ancient Italy. The first obol appears to have been a copper bar or spike (ὀβελός), six of which made a (δραχμή) or handful.[1] Subsequently we find the places of both the drachm and obol of copper taken and held during many ages by the famous coins which were their silver equivalents. This however in Greece all took place before recorded history begins. With the Italian transitions the

[1] Plutarch, Lysander, cap. xvii.

case is different.   Thanks to the fact that the
history of Roman money has been dealt with
by a man of genius of the first rank, it is
possible for us to follow the course of the
transition from copper to silver in Rome in
the third century B.C., as well as the course
of the subsequent transition from silver to gold
during the Empire, with a degree of intelligent
comprehension greater than that with which we
can follow any other change of standard in the
world up to the last great change which has
been gradually accomplishing itself among us.

Amid much that is disputed in connection with
the first of these transitions, it is well, perhaps, to
set down what there is that is clear and definite
beyond all possibility of controversy.   There is,
in the first instance, the bare fact of the transition.
It is beyond all question that, up to the beginning of the third century B.C., copper had been
for some hundreds of years the standard of value
in Latium and throughout Italy.   There the very
word for " to value " was *aestimare* ;   their
treasury was known as the *aerarium*.   During
the latter part of the period, no doubt, the silver
of Magna Grecia, of Sicily, and of Etruria circulated more or less in Rome, though it is remarkable that very little of it has ever been found
there.   Copper formed, at any rate, the great
bulk of the circulation.   Penalties were fixed,

taxes were imposed, and all accounts were kept in copper. If we come to the time of Sulla, again, we reach a period when copper had ceased to exist as any part even of the subsidiary circulation, and when there was not an ounce of copper in the treasury, though it still retained the name of the *aerarium*. Such a fact, it is plain, is quite irreconcilable with Adam Smith's view that copper remained the monetary standard in Rome to the close of its history. All that did remain in Sulla's day and after it was a terminology derived originally, no doubt, from the use of copper, but which, by that date, had long become applicable to silver only, except, indeed, in as far as it was applicable to gold.

It was about 268 B.C. that silver was first coined in Rome, and, about the same time, what is called the first reduction of the as took place. The amount of this reduction, its causes, and its consequences, are all still, more or less, in controversy. We shall probably not go far wrong in following, in the main, Mommsen's account of it.[1] He regards the two events, the issue of silver and the reduction of the as, as part of the same operation, and does not look upon the latter as anything

---

[1] Mommsen, *Histoire de la Monnaie romaine*, vol. ii. pp. 67 ff. Numismatic facts recently come to light, I find, make it necessary to modify Mommsen's account in some important details. The matter is dealt with in Appendix B. The general principles in question remain unaffected.

in the nature of an act of bankruptcy. What is certain is that, before 268 B.C., the word "as" was the name first for a copper ingot, and then for a copper coin a little under one pound in weight, and the equivalent of one pound of raw copper in value, which was the universal unit of account in all computations ; and that, after 268 B.C., it was made the name for a coin of, at first, four ounces, and, afterwards, much less in weight. In such circumstances it was, perhaps, natural to suppose, as Pliny does, that even the first reduction was made with the view of paying off national creditors with the equivalent of six and eightpence in the pound. The remarkable fact, however, is—and it is one that appears to be quite irreconcilable with such a view—that, though the old *as libralis* ceased to exist as coined money, it remained in continual use as money of account. There were thus, in a sense, two asses contemporaneously in existence, the libral or one pound, and the triental or four ounce as ; and as so many of the one must have been exchanged every day for so many of the other, it seems impossible that the last can be regarded as a reduction of the first, in the sense, say, that the pound sterling of the 37th of Henry VIII. was a reduction of the pound sterling of the 18th of Henry VIII. How so confusing a terminology ever came to be resorted to has not, I think, been satisfactorily explained. It is remarkable, however, that it had its prototype in Sicily, where there were two litrae contemporaneously in existence, the heavy and the light, the first of which bore the name of the silver and the second of the copper litra. The Roman monetary system, indeed, is manifestly throughout modelled on the Sicilian, and it appears to have adopted this feature of it with the rest.

The *as libralis* then, as a coin, was done away with before the triens, or four ounce as, was used. Mommsen, however, as observed above, has established beyond all doubt the fact that, though it ceased to exist as a copper coin, it remained in existence as money of account, and has further established the fact that, even as a coin, it immediately came into being again, in silver, under the name of the sestertius or nummus. The diobol of Tarentum, weighing about a scruple of silver, had, apparently, in the course of commercial transactions, equated itself in value with the pound of copper,[1] just as the beaver skin of Hudson Bay equated itself temporarily with two English shillings, or as the pound sterling, in the eighteenth century, equated itself with 113 grains of fine gold. Accordingly a coin weighing a scruple was issued in Rome, and was called the *nummus* (from νόμος) on account of its equivalence with the old

[1] *Op. cit.*, vol. i. p. 256.

standard, the *as libralis*. Like the Sicilian litra, which had also been called the *nummus*, it represented the unit of account. For the moment the money of Rome was bimetallic. Every transition of the standard, indeed, as we have seen, implies necessarily a bimetallic period of shorter or longer duration. "Thus," says Mommsen, "fines for injuries which the law of the Twelve Tables fixed at 25, 150, or 300 asses, were payable in so many sesterces,"[1] precisely, indeed, as fines fixed by the old English law in so many pounds sterling of silver are payable now in so many sovereigns. "What is certain," he observes elsewhere, "is that the *as libralis* was retained as money of account, and that it survived, long after its suppression, in the sesterce or num-mus of silver, which had the same value ; only in keeping accounts care was taken to add the words *aeris gravis* to distinguish the old as from the new. Indeed, there was no difference between the silver nummus, weighing two and a half new asses of four ounces each, and the old as, which weighed ten ounces."[2] We could not, it will be seen, have a closer parallel to the English trans-ition. The copper *as libralis* survived in the silver sesterce, precisely as the pound sterling of silver survives in the gold sovereign.

The undisputed reign of silver as the standard

---

[1] *Op. cit.*, vol. ii. p. 31.   [2] *Op. cit.*, vol. ii. p. 16.

money in Rome was of short duration. The
period of bimetallism that rendered possible the
transition from copper to silver had hardly ended
before a second period of bimetallism began, which
prepared the way for the second transition, that
from silver to gold. Very little gold money,
indeed, was struck during the republican period,
and what there was was struck not in Rome but
by the generals on campaign, in virtue of their
imperium militare. Gold, for all that, was not
without its importance in the monetary circulation,
taking that expression in its wider sense. It was
already largely in circulation in the shape of ingots,
which probably, though not certainly, bore the
stamp of the State guaranteeing their purity.
Their purity was, at any rate, a matter of concern
to the authorities, as evidenced by a law of Sulla,[1]
which ordained the punishment of the adulterators
of the gold ingots with the same severity as the
coiners of false silver money. A legal ratio, too,
must have been fixed between the two metals, as
it was at an early date provided that 5 per cent.
of the tax on enfranchisements was to be paid in
gold, and as the generals, in sending for gold,
ordinarily named the amount required in sesterces.
In the first and second centuries before Christ,
from four-fifths to one-half of the treasure in the
aerarium consisted of gold. Thus there is reason

---

[1] Mommsen, vol. ii. p. 110 *et seq.*

to believe that, even earlier than Cæsar's day, gold had already supplanted silver, to a large extent, as the money of wholesale trade and large operations generally.

The value of gold, as measured in silver, in the early days of the Republic ranged as high as 1 : 17. The discovery of the mines of Noricum about 150 B.C. caused, we are told, a fall in its price of one-third in the Roman market.[1] Shortly after that date the pound of gold was worth 4,000 sesterces, the ratio thus being 1 : 11·91. After Cæsar had brought to Rome the rich spoils of Gaul the pound of gold fell to 3,000 sesterces, thus showing a market ratio of 1 : 8·93. When, however, Cæsar commenced the regular issue of the aureus, the ratio of 1 : 11·91 was maintained in the coinage and was subsequently continued under Augustus. This fact must be taken into account in connection with the immense issue of gold in the early days of the Empire, as abundantly evidenced by the discovery of buried hoards. In the treasure of Brescello alone were discovered 80,000 gold pieces, all struck between the years 46 and 38 B.C.

The phenomenon of this great issue of gold is one apparently of a similar character to the large issue which succeeded the fixing of the ratio in England in 1717, or the more recent pheno-

[1] Mommsen, vol. ii. p. 112.

menon of the great issue in bimetallic France
which succeeded the Californian and Australian
gold discoveries of the fifties.   Such phenomena
are commonly spoken of as instances of the
operation of Gresham's Law.   Assuredly, however, they are phenomena of a very different
character from the supplanting of good money by
base coin or over-issued paper.   In the latter case,
industry and commerce are thrown into confusion,
and the reform of the coinage becomes, sooner or
later, the subject of an urgent popular demand.
In the former case, on the contrary, as was found
by the experience both of England and of France,
there is nothing but general congratulation at the
change.   So far as it is possible to judge, the
same was the case in Rome in the era of Augustus.
Gold had already become the most important
medium of wholesale trade.   Its new abundance
made it now also the great medium of the internal
circulation, and relegated silver to the second place.

   In this second Roman transition, again, the
characteristic remarked on above, both in connection with the first Roman transition and with
regard to the English transition of the last century,
viz., the retention of the old terminology, made
applicable, more or less unconsciously, to the new
standard, is observable.   Mommsen himself, indeed, is struck by the English parallel.[1] " Accounts

[1] *Op. cit.*, vol. iii. p. 45.

continued," he says, " to be kept regularly in
denarii and sesterces, just as accounts are kept at
the present day in England in pounds and shillings
of silver ; but these denominations of value were
no longer represented by a fixed quantity of
silver, but by the quantity of gold that corresponds
to it.   So the denarius signified less a denarius of
silver than $\frac{1}{25}$th of the aureus."   The Senate, as
he remarks, in this case as in so many others,
avoided, where it could, calling things by their
names.

The feature of the English transition and of
the two Roman transitions that has, so far,
engaged our attention, was their emergence and
completion without conscious intent or forethought on the part of any one, together with
the conditions which rendered such a series of
events possible.   In all three transitions we
found the same principle in operation, the retention of the old terminology, while the thing
that it signified had changed.   The correspondence with each other which their leading features
present, however, is worthy of notice in some
others of its aspects.   It was not only the
transitions themselves that were unconscious and
unperceived by the contemporary world.   The
emergence of subsidiary money that accompanied
them partook also of the same character.   We
know that after the edict of 1717 in England, by

which the guinea was fixed at twenty-one shillings, what happened to the silver coinage was
this, that it became of its own accord a subsidiary
money, circulating as such alongside of the gold,
and that it went on thus circulating for the best
part of a century, until, indeed, the Act of 1816
ratified and continued the state of things already
in existence. In the more modern changes of
standard in Europe the adoption of silver as
token money has been something that was done
of set purpose from the first. We have thus come
to think of the establishment of a subsidiary
coinage as a change that is always effected by the
conscious act of the central authority. It is an
unwonted conception to think of money which
has been the principal measure of values as
becoming of itself subsidiary. In Rome, however, we find that both in the case of the first
transition, from copper to silver, and in that of
the second, from silver to gold, the old standard
money, when displaced by the new, experienced
the same fate as it did in England. If we regard
the state of things existing in Rome immediately
after the first reduction of the as, the reduction
to the triens,[1] and the issue of the sesterce as the
silver equivalent of the old *as libralis*, we find
copper still retaining its value in the monetary
circulation. The first reduction, however, was

[1] Following Mommsen.

very shortly followed by a second, and it is with this second reduction, the substitution of the quadrantal or three-ounce for the triental or four-ounce as, that the intrinsic and the monetary value of the copper coinage unmistakably part company. Then, for the first time, the copper is found to be circulating at a conventional value. Thenceforward, the process of degradation was rapid. From three ounces the as presently fell to two, then to one, and so even to fractions of the ounce. The utmost carelessness, too, soon crept in in regard to the relative weight of the various pieces. In the uncial series, as it is called—that is to say, the series issued when the weight of the as was at one ounce—pieces which in value were reckoned as the third or the quarter of the as were now and then found to be heavier than the semis, or half-as piece. The number of globules marking the value is alone of importance. The size of the coin, as Mommsen remarks, had evidently come to be looked upon as of no more moment with regard to the determination of its value than would be, with us, the special size of a bank note. Its value had plainly come to depend exclusively upon its exchangeability, at a fixed rate, for sesterces and denarii, just as our shillings depend for their value on their exchangeability with the sovereign at the rate of twenty to one. In this fact, indeed, we have the explanation of its rapid degradation. The underlying cause which had led the Roman state to issue silver was to be found in the fact that silver had already become the money of its wholesale trade. The denarius was modelled on the drachma, the great unit of account in the Hellenic world. It was in denarii and drachmas, or in some other form of silver, that what we would now call the international balances were settled. The asses, therefore, so long as they were exchangeable in fixed proportion for denarii, served perfectly well the purpose of the internal circulation, no matter what their weight might happen to be. It soon appeared, accordingly, that neither debtor nor creditor gave themselves any concern in regard to the question of the weight of the copper. The worn and light coins were seen to serve every purpose which the full-weighted ones served, and, when fresh issues were needed, the state found its profit, as our own government does at present, in the margin between the intrinsic and the nominal value. It had thus every inducement to make this margin as wide as possible. Such a profit is, of course, not necessarily illegitimate. It can be secured by civilised governments at the present day without any mischievous result whatever ensuing. When, however, the underlying principle of the distinction between reductions in the weight of the subsidiary money, which may be innocent when coupled with a rigid limitation of its quantity, and reductions in the weight of the principal money, or of the subsidiary money combined with unlimited issues, which are among the most dangerous of public crimes, had not even begun to be understood, it was undoubtedly fraught with much danger. With the ancients all the monetary metals were *ipsae opes*, and the reduction in the weight of one sort of money no doubt seemed to them very much the same kind of operation as the reduction in the weight of any other. We thus find that the same confusion of thought which has generated free silverism in the United States appears to have generated a movement of a closely similar character in ancient Rome.

After the reduction of the copper had been an existing fact for upwards of a hundred years without any one apparently being much the worse for it, there supervened a period when democratic sentiment in the Republic reached its high-water mark. The unit of account up to that date had never been altered. It had been from the first and still was the *as libralis*, represented in silver by the sesterce, or rather practically by its multiple the denarius. The aim of the new movement was to alter the unit of account. The coined as of the later date weighed only a fraction of the coined as of the earlier. It was still, however, the as, and in some sense, in the eyes of the Roman popular party, no doubt it was "the as of their fathers." A proposal accordingly came to be put forward in favour of enacting that all debts for the future should be payable not in asses of the earlier date or their silver equivalent, but in asses of the later date or their intrinsic equivalent. This took shape finally in the Lex Valeria of 86 B.C.,[1] which thus substituted the second as for the first. Sallust remarks of the measure *Argentum aere solutum est*, and one cannot fail to be struck by its similarity to the modern proposal for paying gold debts in silver. The quaestors affixed to the temple of Castor— the bourse of Rome—a tabulated statement showing the reduction of debts effected by the new enactment. It amounted to 75 per cent. ; and to this the public were authorised to conform their payments, and did, as a matter of fact, conform them while the law remained in force. The change however was too violent and too arbitrary to last. Sulla repealed the Lex Valeria and re-established the original method of computation.

If we turn again to the second transition in Rome, we find the silver money following the same course which, in the earlier period, had

[1] Mommsen, vol. ii. p. 74.   See also footnote on same page.

been followed by the copper. Up to the time of Nero the denarius was found to contain 99 per cent. of pure silver. A process of depreciation then began.[1] The denarii of the latter part of this reign contain from 5 to 10 per cent. of alloy. Under Trajan and the Antonines—the golden age, it must be remembered, of the Empire—the proportion of alloy rises markedly to something between 20 and 25 per cent. Under Severus, again, the silver becomes mere billon money, consisting, to the extent of at least one half, of copper. The real reason of this depreciation is again, no doubt, to be found in the fact that gold had now definitely taken its position as the principal measure of values, and that, consequently, the intrinsic value of the silver coinage had come to be, to a great extent, a matter of indifference to the general public, so long as it continued to be exchangeable for gold in fixed proportions. The depreciation, at any rate, was consistent with a high degree of national prosperity. It caused no tumult, and, apparently, attracted very little notice.

The immunity, however, from the danger involved in such a depreciation, it would have been safe to predict from the first, could not endure indefinitely. If the state could issue billon that circulated at the gold price of silver, while

---

[1] *Histoire de la Monnaie romaine*, vol. iii. p. 28.

the principle of limitation so familiar to us
now had hardly even begun to be dimly
recognised, the emperors of the second century
were perhaps hardly to be blamed if they began
to fancy that they had, in the power of issue,
a Fortunatus's purse without bottom. It is not a
matter of surprise, at any rate, that the depreciation of the denarius, which under the Antonines
was, or at any rate seems to have been, innocuous,
led up, when accompanied with unlimited issues
by Caracalla and his successors, to the great
crisis of the third century, which was one of the
main factors in producing the political anarchy
that prevailed in the Empire for more than a
generation.

The denarius, which had become half copper in
the reign of Severus, continued its course of depreciation, and had become nothing but pure
copper by the time of Gallienus. Thus not only
was the silver standard then a thing of the past,
but silver itself as currency had completely disappeared. At the same time, the aurei had become
so irregular in weight that the use of the balance
was necessary in all transactions where gold
changed hands. This period of monetary anarchy
was ended by the reforms of Aurelian and Diocletian. At length, under Constantine, the new
system was placed upon a basis which remained
unshaken for many centuries. Under it the

recognition of gold as the standard metal was definite and complete.

The pound of gold was taken as the point of departure. The solidus aureus was struck as the $\frac{1}{72}$nd part of it, and we know that it remained unaltered in purity and but little altered in weight far down into the Middle Ages. At the same time, the principal silver coin took its name, the "milliarense," from the fact that it was the $\frac{1}{1000}$th part of the pound of gold in value. Silver, however, never regained an important place in the circulation of the Western Empire. By the end of the fourth century it had once more disappeared completely from circulation. Thenceforward the money of Rome was gold and bronze exclusively, as was the earliest money of the leading barbarian nations who served themselves heirs to her possessions. The Burgundian laws make no mention of silver, and the Franks coined little or none of it before the era of Pepin and Charlemagne.

CHAPTER III

In the preceding chapters I have endeavoured
to show how it was possible for a transition of
standard to effect itself unconsciously, and for a
metal which had been the standard metal to sink,
in a manner which escaped the recognition of the
contemporary world, into the position of subsidiary
money. A question which will have to engage
much of our attention presently will be the question of the ultimate originating causes of these
transitions. In the meantime, it may be said that,
to us who have lived in the midst of the last
change from silver to gold in the modern world,
and have seen Germany adopt the gold standard
in 1872, and the Latin Union, together with
practically all the rest of Europe, adopt it a few
years afterwards, one seemingly obvious agency

in connection with changes in any given country must appear to be the influence of neighbouring countries : "the impulse from without," as Mommsen puts it.   Even this, however, has been denied, and somewhat strenuously.   In connection with the Indian currency question it had come to be urged that India should bring her monetary system into conformity with that of the principal countries with which she dealt.   In reply to this contention we find Sir Robert Giffen arguing that[1] "the foreign trade of a country is hardly a thing to be considered at all in connection with its internal money."   If the case were otherwise, he remarks, "we as a great trading nation would never have adopted a gold standard.   When we began such a standard last century we were almost alone in so doing.   The rest of the world, the most important countries with which we traded, had silver."   There is no doubt that, as regards the facts of the case, Sir Robert Giffen here reflects the view that is very generally current.   It seems almost universally taken for granted, indeed, that up to the close of the seventeenth century silver was beyond all question and in every sense the standard money of every European country.   I notice, at the same time, that a different view is taken by M. de Vienne, one of the leading contributors to the

[1] *Economic Journal*, Sept. 1898, p. 305.

Revue Numismatique.[1]   I shall have occasion in
a subsequent chapter to return to the consideration of his line of reasoning.

If the current view were the sound one, we
should certainly, in the case of the English
transition, be in the presence of a capricious
volte face of which no intelligible explanation
could be given. The truth is, however, that a
very little inquiry is quite sufficient to satisfy
us that the opinion that silver was in any exclusive sense the standard of the rest of the world
outside England in the beginning of the eighteenth century is not one that can for a moment
be accepted. If we were to imagine that silver
occupied, in the Europe of that day, a position
analogous to that which gold occupies in the
Europe of our own, we should be very greatly
indeed in error. Sir James Steuart had occasion to write, when at Tübingen in 1771, "a
dissertation upon the doctrine and principles of
money applied to the German coin," in which
he reviews the monetary position in several
European countries. From that treatise we can
gather that gold, in the beginning of the eighteenth century, instead of occupying a secondary

---

[1] See *Revue Numismatique*, vol. x. 3me series, p. 100, where a
paper of M. de Vienne's entitled "Des anciens prix et des difficultés inhérentes à leur évaluation actuelle" is reviewed.

position in the wholesale trade of Europe, was
in all countries at least co-ordinate with silver,
if it had not indeed in all already distinctly
taken the first place. In Holland,[1] the Bank of
Amsterdam was in the way of issuing, from time
to time, " what regulations they thought fit as to
the rate at which they would receive the different
species of coin. These regulations were formed
according to the fluctuations of the value of the
metals. When silver rose with respect to gold,
then the silver species was received at a higher
rate than formerly ; when gold rose in respect to
silver, the gold coins were received at a higher
rate than formerly." In the Netherlands therefore it is clear that gold was at any rate as
acceptable as silver in the settlement of international balances. There is good reason to
believe, however, that both there and elsewhere
in Europe it was already more acceptable.

Russia, no doubt, was not a factor of prime
importance in European commerce in those days ;
still the fact is worthy of notice that, as a recent
writer tells us,[2] Peter the Great forbade his
subjects to accept payment for their merchandise
in their national currency of silver, and not

---

[1] Steuart, works, vol. iii. p. 411.

Peter the Great, by K. Walinzewski (English translation), p.
463. Steuart also mentions that in 1761 France was sending
ingots of gold to Russia. Works, vol. iii. p. 103.

without effect, as Russia "towards the year 1723
gained several tons of gold yearly on her foreign
exchanges." In regard to France Sir James
Steuart[1] says that the bullion in the Paris market
consisted mainly of foreign coin. These coins he
remarks incidentally were " Spanish and Portu-
guese pieces, ducats, guineas, carolins, et cetera,"
all of them gold.[2] It was this bullion that
France bargained for and received in settlement
of the debts that were due to her from abroad ;
and it was with this bullion, in turn, that she paid
her foreign debts. " The Italian trade again,"
he remarks,[3] "is carried on with zechins," also,
of course, gold.

As to the state of things in Germany his information naturally is more detailed. By the
regulation of Leipzig,[4] in 1690, the florin, the unit
of the German money of account was, he says,
"attached to the gold as well as to the silver coin.
Debtors were thus authorised to acquit the obligations they had contracted either in the gold or
in the silver species." The ratio fixed at Leipzig,
like the English ratio in 1717, over-rated gold as
compared with silver even from the beginning,

[1] Works, vol. v. p. 246.

[2] Within French territory remittances were made by preference
in gold. Silver was only used when gold was not available. See
Cantillon, *Essai sur le Commerce*, p. 332. Cf. Garrault, see below
p. 116.

[3] *Op. cit.*, vol. v. p. 248.   [4] *Op. cit.*, vol. v. p. 214 *et seq.*

and over-rated it still more markedly after the rise in silver that characterised the earlier years of the eighteenth century. It is interesting to inquire why it was that in these circumstances the gold did not assume the principal place in the German currency, as it did in the English. The reason is not far to seek. In England the mint edict fixing the ratio was a reality. It was of course rigidly adhered to. In Germany it was a mere dead letter. " Had the mints in Germany been under as fixed regulations as in England," says Sir James Steuart, "and had all the princes been obliged to coin silver as well as gold at the rate of the Leipzig regulation, or not at all, it would have happened that the coinage of silver would have been absolutely interrupted, as is the case in England." [1] What did happen, however, was that the "mints not being under certain regulations, the silver was melted down and recoined below the rate fixed at Leipzig." It was coined indeed " even below the proportion of the gold." [2] The result was that the cheap silver ousted the dearer gold as the currency of the country. Did that make silver the standard ? Assuredly it did not. Steuart's account of what happened is worth quoting. " Debtors," he says, " will now no more pay in gold at the Leipzig regulation, because they

[1] *Op. cit.*, vol. v. p. 215.
[2] *Op. cit.*, vol. v. p. 216.

can pay cheaper in the new coined silver ; and as
the value of such silver is determined by no settled
regulation, and that it is yet lawful money, the value
of the florin is daily debasing ; the consequence
of which is to raise the value of the conventional
currency of the gold, which has not yet been falsified.   This has obliged merchants, who never can
be made the dupes in money matters, *to stipulate
the payment of their florins according to a deter-
minate proportion of the gold coin.*"[1] He shows, in
a manner which it is not necessary to follow, how
the confusion of the silver coinage caused the
emergence of two different sorts of florin, one
worth one-eleventh of a carolin,[2] the other worth
ten seventy-sevenths of the same coin.   Neither
it seems had an independent value ; both were
mere fractions of the carolin.   "When bills are
drawn in such florins," he says, " referring to the
latter class, it is stipulated that payment is to be
made in carolins at 9 florins 42 kreutzers per
carolin."[3]   The true standard of value in the
German Empire was thus in Steuart's time beyond
all question gold, and had been so at any rate
since the beginning of the eighteenth century.

[1] *Op. cit.* vol. v. p. 217.

[2] This coin is more usually called the carolus.

[3] *Op. cit.*, vol. v. p. 217.   That is to say, at the particular date
at which Steuart was writing.   As the florin depreciated the number
of florins per carolin would be increased.

The fact that the currency was mainly silver was no more a proof that the standard was silver than it is a proof that the standards of India and of Java are silver at the present moment.

So much for the eighteenth century. It will be worth while next to inquire what were the relative positions of gold and silver in England and in Europe generally in the seventeenth. Sir Thomas Mun, in his remarkable booklet, "*England's Treasure in Foreign Trade*," which, though first published by his son in 1664, was written probably some twenty years earlier, has occasion to remark that the "late[1] raising of the gold 10 in the 100 did bring in much store thereof," the reason he gives being that such a modification of the ratio gave "advantage to the merchant to bring in the Kingdom's yearly gain by trade in gold rather than in silver." Whatever the cause was, the interesting fact is that we have here the contemporary testimony of a highly qualified witness to the fact that in 1640 or thereabouts the international balance due to England was settled mainly in gold. Mun speaks of this modification of the ratio in favour of gold as if it were a fact of an isolated and more or less accidental character. The case, however, I think was otherwise. We get a glimpse of the true operative cause of such modifications in a report of the

[1] *England's Treasure in Foreign Trade*, p. 42.

committee of Charles I.'s Council in regard to a
proposal for an alteration in the value of the coin
made by the officers of the mint in 1626.   The
proposal, if given effect to, would have coined the
pound sterling into 70s. 6d.—instead of 62s. as
established under the regulation of the 43rd of
Elizabeth—and would thus have altered the ratio
very markedly in favour of silver.   The committee
thus express themselves :

"If then we desire our silver to buy gold, as it
of late hath done, we must let it be the cheaper
and less in proportion valued, and so contrary, for
one equivalent proportion in both will bring in
neither.   We see the proof thereof in the unusual
proportion of gold brought lately to the mint by
reason of the price, for we rate it above all other
countries, and gold may be bought too dear.   To
furnish the mint this way with both is altogether
impossible." Elsewhere they observe, " We further
conceive that the raising of the silver to the gold
will, upon some sudden occasion beyond sea,
transport our gold and leave the state in scarcity
of that as now of silver." [1]

We are accustomed to think of the legislators
of the seventeenth and preceding centuries as
continually in search of the intrinsic ratio between
the precious metals, and as continually attempting
to adjust the monetary ratio to it.   Their true

[1] *Cottoni Posthuma*, p. 306.

attitude was altogether different.   We find them
here expressing the curious opinion that if they
did succeed in striking on the precise intrinsic
ratio, then neither metal would come to the mint.
They were continually embarrassed between the
choice of two evils, the scarcity of gold and the
scarcity of silver ; but it is plain enough from the
general course of their action that the two did not
loom equally large in their estimation.   The truth
was that the vital necessity of protecting the
nation's store of gold from being depleted by its
exchange for the continuously cheapening silver
appears to have been just as strongly, if less con-
sciously, felt in the England of the Stuarts as it
was on the continent of Europe thirty years ago.
The method that had to be adopted to protect it
was of course different.   In modern Europe this
was done by closing the mints to the silver.   In
the seventeenth century in England it was done
by steadily over-rating gold in the coinage.   Between the accession of James I. and the Revolution silver fell by successive stages nearly forty
per cent. in value.   Each successive fall threatened
to carry away the gold, and would have done so
but that it was met by an alteration in the ratio
in favour of that metal.   One of these alterations
was " the late raising of the gold 10 in the
100 " that Mun speaks of.   Looking back at it
from our present point of view, we can see that it

was not anything isolated or accidental, but was
rather, it may be said, organic.   The close of
Elizabeth's reign saw the ratio at 11 : 1.   The
2nd of James I. put it over 12 : 1.   The 9th
of James I. at over 13 : 1.   The 17th of James I.
and the 9th of Charles I. saw it again markedly
raised, and finally the 15th of Charles II. brought
it close up to 15 : 1.

As the result of these continual alterations in
favour of gold, we hear, all through the period,
of silver being scarce, of 2*d.* perhaps having to
be given to change a 20*s.* piece, of the heavy
silver being all melted down and exported, and of
what remained being much under its due weight ;
and we hear consequently of proposals to remedy
this state of things by putting back the gold to a
lower monetary value ; but we do not hear of any
of these proposals being accepted.   The statesmen
of the period had, on the contrary, evidently a
wholesome dread even of bringing the ratio in
the coinage very close to the intrinsic ratio, lest
some "occasion beyond seas" should cause their
gold to be transported.   The general result is
that the condition of things which we noted in
the eighteenth century, seems to have been, to
a great extent, anticipated in the seventeenth
century.   Wages were paid and the retail trade
of the country was carried on by the light and
worn silver coins which circulated at a conven-

tional value, and which never went, and in the nature of things never could go, outside the country, while the external commerce was carried on in gold. McCulloch says of the silver of that period: "The coins were in a bad state. This arose principally from gold being over valued as compared with silver, which, by making it the interest of people to pay their debts in gold, occasioned the melting down and exportation of the silver coin of full weight."[1] The contemporary testimony of Rice Vaughan on the same point is more important and more interesting.[2] Owing to the raising of gold 2s. in the pound in the ninth year of Charles I., silver not being at the same time raised, great quantities of gold were, when he wrote, being coined and little or no silver, so that "a man may go into a great many shops before he can get a 20s. piece to be changed, for the greatest part of the paiements is now in gold, contrary to the former times." It seems thus that gold was not only the medium of external trade, but was taking the first place in regard to internal payments. The silver too,[3] Vaughan tells us, was usually light, seldom "up to the King's ordinance." The gold, on the contrary, was ordinarily of full weight. It could not be other-

---

[1] *Literature of Political Economy*, p. 156.
[2] *Discourse on Coyn and Coynage*, p. 70.
[3] *Op. cit.*, p. 72.

wise. "It was continually weighed and rejected if not weighty." It begins to be very clear, I think, that the gold standard in England, instead of being a thing of yesterday, dates back at any rate to the days of Charles II.

What then of the period yet preceding? The remarkable fact is that, in the days of the Tudors and of the later Plantagenets, the predominance of gold, as the medium of all important transactions both in England and in Europe generally, is more and not less conspicuous than it was in the days of the Stuarts. We had occasion to notice the system adopted by the Bank of Amsterdam of giving credit for either gold or silver at the ratio of the day and then issuing their "bank money" in return for deposits of either. This system seems to have had the effect of making silver more available than it would otherwise have been as a medium of wholesale transactions. The bank's system was, however, only a further development of the system antecedently in use in the Netherlands. It had long been the practice of the authorities there to issue "plakaats" at frequent intervals, stating at what rate in florins and stivers—their own currency—the currencies of every neighbouring country, gold and silver alike, would be accepted in the settlement of obligations. The Dutch, being a community of merchants, and

Holland, as it was said on our side of the water,
being "a perpetual fair," their continual changes
of ratio did not cause the same mischief and
inconvenience that they would have caused in
England.   Certain it is, at any rate, that with the
rise of the great Netherland cities, first Antwerp,
then Amsterdam, to the position of centres of
European finance, there was a general tendency
manifested for silver to assume a parity of function
with gold as a medium of international trade,
which certainly had not been so conspicuous
during the previous period, during which Venice,
Genoa and Florence had held the leading
positions in the commercial and financial world.

Gold, we know, was the undisputed standard
money of the Western Empire in the fifth century,
as it was, to the last, of the Eastern, and probably
the tradition of it as being money, in a sense in
which nothing else was, never altogether died out
in the south of Europe.   However that may be,
we seem to hear of nothing but gold in connection
with the great transactions of the Italian bankers
of the Middle Ages and the Renaissance.   Referring to the state of things existing in the fourteenth century,[1] an early French historian,
Mathieu, tells us that "gold was then very scarce
in France, nor had they plenty of it afterwards,
but by their traffic with Italy, which last named

---

[1] See Anderson, *Annals of Commerce*, vol. i. p. 190.

country had by its traffic, in a manner, stored up all the gold of Europe, insomuch that, whilst the kings of France could give at most £6,000 sterling of portions with their daughters, a Duke of Milan (Visconti) gave 200,000 crowns (gold florins it should be) with his daughter to Lionel Duke of Clarence, son to Edward III. of England." "There are several instances," says Anderson, referring to the same period, "of treaties made between princes and states of Europe, wherein it is expressly stipulated that the money contracted to be paid shall be in the gold florins of Florence."[1] He instances for one the treaty made between Pedro of Castile and the Black Prince, where the payment to be made to the latter, as the price of his assistance against Henry, Pedro's rival, is stipulated to be made in florins. If such payments are not stipulated to be made in Florentine gold, we may reckon at any rate with almost absolute certainty on finding them stipulated to be made in gold of some other description.

In the north of Europe, the English noble had a wide use in transactions of the kind. In 1398, for instance, the island of Gothland was handed over by the Grand Master of the Teutonic order to Eric X. of Denmark, in consideration of the

---

[1] *Op. cit.*, p. 196. The historical instances that follow are drawn, unless where otherwise noted, from the same source, and will be found there under their date.

payment of 9,000 gold nobles.   Under the treaty
of Bretigny, A.D. 1360, John of France agreed to
pay to Edward III. a ransom of 3,000,000 gold
crowns.   In 1402, Brandenburg was sold by its
elector to a neighbouring potentate for 400,000
(gold) florins.   In 1407, we find an English
indemnity for injuries inflicted on the shipping of
the Hanseatic League computed and paid in
nobles.   In 1492, Henry VII. withdrew his forces
from France, and allowed Charles VIII. to annex
Brittany unopposed, for a payment of 745,000
gold crowns.   In 1527, Henry VIII. exacted
from Francis I. a stipulation to pay him an
annuity of 65,000 crowns in consideration of his
making a treaty of perpetual peace with him.   In
the same year, Charles V. resigned his pretensions
to the Moluccas in favour of Portugal for a payment of 35,000 ducats ; and, in 1550, we restored
Boulogne to France for a payment of 400,000
crowns.

We may be quite certain that such payments as
these were really in gold, as the usual mode of
reckoning in England was in pounds or marks
sterling, and in France by livres.   When gold is
specially mentioned, therefore, actual gold, and
not silver at a gold valuation, must be meant.
On the other hand, if we come across a payment
which is mentioned as being made in sterling, or
in livres, we cannot, by any means, assume that

it was not also, in truth, in gold.   A noble was
6s. 8d., and three nobles were often spoken of as
a pound sterling.   In 1406, for instance, Henry
IV. granted leave to Philip d'Albertis, a Lombard
residing in London, to give a bill of exchange on
his partner in foreign parts for 2,500 marks
sterling, to the Bishop of Bath and Wells or his
attorneys, for the first fruits of the Bishopric of
Durham, on condition however, " that *neither the
said gold* [received for the bill of exchange] nor
any other gold or silver, either in bullion or in
coin, be transported beyond sea."   It is very
interesting and very significant to observe that
the phrases " pound sterling " and " mark sterling "
were used as applicable to gold no less than to
silver, so long ago as the beginning of the fifteenth
century.

In the event of royal marriages, actual or
contemplated, during the Plantagenet and Tudor
period, we are sure to find the dowry of the
princess, and the settlement to be made on her,
stipulated in terms of nobles, crowns or florins.
What is still more significant is the fact that the
state loans, such as those of Edward III. from
the Bardi and Peruzzi, of Edward IV. from
Cosmo di Medici, of Edward VI. from the Fug-
gers, and of Philip II. from the bankers of
Genoa, are all of them always in gold.   With
regard to the latter, De Mailly, the Genoese

historian, tells us that his countrymen had taken such advantage of Philip's necessities "as to have made 11, 12, and sometimes 18 per cent. interest on the said loans, whereby the ancient nobles had drawn annually from Spain a revenue of fifteen millions of gold." It will be remembered too, how, by an operation on gold, Sir Thomas Gresham and some other English merchants, instigated and probably backed by Walsingham and Elizabeth's government, caused all Philip's bills of exchange drawn on Genoa in 1587, for the victualling of his fleet, to be protested, and thus delayed for a year the sailing of the Armada.   Burnet tells the story : " A merchant of London," he says, " being very well acquainted with the revenue and expense of Spain, and of all they could raise, and knowing also that their funds were so swallowed up that it was impossible for them to victual and fit out their fleet, but by their credit on the bank of Genoa, he undertook to write to all the places of trade and to get such remittances [? demands] made on that bank that he might have as much of the money in his own hands as there should be none current there equal to the great occasion of victualling the Spanish fleet.   He reckoned that the keeping of such a treasure dead in his hands until the season of victualling was over would be a loss of £40,000, and he managed the matter

with such secrecy and success that the fleet could
not set out that year.   At so small a price (says
the Bishop) with so skilful a management was
the nation saved at that time."   Has finance no
laureate to celebrate worthily so remarkable an
achievement?

One very important factor in securing for
gold at a very early date the first place as
international money lay in the fact that it was
the official money of the Roman Curia. We
know that it was so at any rate as early as 1331,
thirteen years before Edward III.'s coinage of
gold in England.[1]   Professor Rogers has repro-
duced an account of a journey to Avignon made
in that year by a representative of Merton College, with the object of obtaining from the Pope,
John XXI., the ratification of the transfer to
the college of a church which had been given to it
some sixty years before, by Edmond of Lancas-
ter, the younger brother of Edward I.   The
currency, we are told, "is three times changed
on the road, and the payments at the Curia are
made in gold."   Considerably fuller details are
given of a mission,[2] also to Avignon, with a

[1] *Hist. of Agriculture and Prices*, vol. i. p. 135.   It was probably because the Florentines were bankers to the Pope that they
came to strike gold before Venice, Genoa, or Pisa. The same
fact also helps to account for the rapid assumption by their florin
of the position of international money. See Prof. Villari's *Hist.
of Florence*, vol. i. p. 329.   [2] *Op. cit.*, vol. i. p. 136.

similar object—the appropriation of a rectory—
from Queen's College in 1363. Whitfield, the
emissary, began his journey by exchanging his
"viaticum," £23, at the London "cambium" into
florins at the rate of 3s. 1¼d. per florin. Arrived at
Avignon, he finds it necessary to consult three
lawyers, Englishmen as it happened. "The
expenses of legal advice at the court were
enormous," and it is noteworthy that they had,
like the official charges, all to be met in florins.
In 1350 we find Edward III. granting licences
to a great number of people going to Rome—it
was the jubilee year—to take with them in gold
what was requisite for their reasonable expenses.
In 1532 it was found that during the previous
half century 80,000 gold ducats had gone to
Rome in payment of the annates or first fruits of
archbishoprics and bishoprics,[1] and thereupon all
further payments of every sort to the See of
Rome were finally forbidden.

In 1429 we have a very significant Act
(8 Henry VI. cap. 28), prohibiting merchant
aliens from bargaining to be paid in nobles.
That such an Act was necessarily futile is obvious,
but the fact of its being passed speaks volumes
in reference to the contemporary estimation of
the two metals. All through these centuries it
was the fixed policy of every European govern-

---

[1] Ruding's *Annals of the Coinage*, vol. ii. p. 82.

ment to make its subjects bring in as much gold as possible in return for their merchandise, just as it had been the policy of the Roman Empire nine hundred years before. We find the code of Justinian forbidding Romans from parting with gold to barbarians in return for their wares, and naively enjoining them, on the contrary, to get as much of it out of them as possible (*subtili ingenio*).[1] We have seen the same policy cropping out, long afterwards, in the action of Peter the Great. An instance of some interest illustrating it is recorded in the days of Henry VIII.[2] One of the English merchants at the Calais Fair, writing to that monarch, says : " Your subjects will bring back above £3,000 sterling in angels and ducats. We seek all the angels here, and give a penny in the piece to have them to carry home." It is not, perhaps, without significance, again, that Chaucer tells us of the Clerk of Oxenforde, that " He had but little gold in cofre." If we wish to know what was the true standard money at any given epoch, the first inquiry we should make is : What is the money that was by preference hoarded ?

Such being the general sentiment in regard to

[1] Lib. iv. tit. lxiii. par. 2. " Non solum aurum barbaris minime praebeatur, sed etiam si apud eos inventum fuerit, subtili auferatur ingenio."

[2] See Shaw, *Hist. of Currency*, p. 120.

gold, it is not surprising to find that on several occasions and in various countries of Europe steps were actually taken to establish it as the formal and legal standard. So far back as 1343 it was proposed by Edward III.'s advisers that, by an arrangement with the Flemings, the same gold coinage should be adopted in England and Flanders,[1] that "all gold money should be taken at bullion value, and all silver money to be reckoned thereby." In 1534, in Florence, Mr. Shaw tells us,[2] "all contracts and payments were commanded to be made in gold *scudi*." This was done by the Florentine authorities, " in order to defend themselves from a flood of cheap and cheapening silver." The new system how- ever broke down, he says, because the custom was then universal in Europe of allowing the coins, both gold and silver, of every country to circulate within every other, and the custom was too strong for the statute.[3]

[1] *Op. cit.*, p. 42.   [2] *Op. cit.*, p. 94.

[3] *Hist. of Currency*, p. 22. Mr. Shaw however, I find, writes under a complete misconception as to the nature of this measure. His information is apparently based on a decree of Alessandro di Medici of 1534. A copy of this decree is in the British Museum. It is headed in the catalogue " Decree with reference to the issue of a silver coinage," and its whole scope and aim from beginning to end is to secure the currency of the new silver which was then about to be issued at a fixed ratio with the gold. Under these circumstances the description of it as a measure " of pure gold monometallism " is, to say the least, somewhat eccentric. At the

By far the most important and interesting attempt however at the official establishment of a gold standard during the Middle Ages or Renaissance periods was that made in France in 1577 ; but what has to be said in regard to it had better be left till we reach the subject of the French currency.

Up to the close of Edward I.'s reign we hear, from the chroniclers and in the records, of nothing but silver. Of the Angevin period Henry of Huntingdon says specifically that the English exports were paid for in silver, and that silver was, in consequence then more plentiful in England than in Germany. The treasures left by William the Conqueror, by Henry I. and Henry II., the ransoms of Richard Cœur de Lion and of William the Lion, the proposed dowry of the Maid of Norway when her marriage with the Prince of Wales, afterwards Edward II., was in contemplation, and the dowries of the other princesses mentioned during the period, are all in undoubted silver. Edward I.'s subsidies to his Continental

same time, if the seventh clause were alone to be regarded, this description would, at first sight at any rate, seem to hold good. It is there certainly provided that all exchanges are in future to be made in nothing but scudi d'oro. In about half a dozen passages, however, throughout the decree we find it laid down quite explicitly that a scudo d'oro is to be taken to mean either a literal gold scudo or else seven lire—or seven lire some odd soldi, as the case might be— of the new silver coinage.

allies appear to have been also all in silver. At the very close of his reign, 1307, we find him laying an injunction on the Pope's Nuncio, "that neither the English coin nor *silver in mass nor in bullion* shall be carried out of the kingdom to the Pope ; but that the sum so raised (by Peter's pence) shall be delivered to merchants in England to be remitted to the Pope by way of exchange." It is interesting to compare this injunction with the next official reference that we find to the same burning question. It comes about seventy years later, in the reign of Richard II. We find the parliament then passing an Act to remedy the "great mischief that the realm suffers because of *gold and silver* as well as money, plate and jewels .... being carried out of the realm." It is therefore enacted that foreign payments shall only be made by bills of exchange. "The merchant so exchanging to make an oath that he shall not transport any manner of gold or silver under color of that remittance." How the merchant was to meet his bills in such conditions Parliament did not stop to inquire. The significant thing for our present purpose of course is that, while Edward I. mentioned silver only as the treasure that must not be carried out of the realm, Richard II.'s Parliament mentioned both "gold and silver." This marks the transition. Thenceforward, all the great transactions, sales of territory, Kings' ransoms, princesses' dowries, state loans and so on, which, in the first period, were stipulated and negotiated in silver, are now found to be stipulated and negotiated in gold, and in gold only. Now too, accordingly, commences the series of depreciations of the secondary metal.

Mr. Keary, in his introduction to the *Catalogue of English Coins* [1] in the British Museum, remarks : " From the time of the introduction (or the definite establishment) of the penny coinage, the numismatic history of England continued almost uniform. There was no break in continuity made by the Norman Conquest, subsequently to which pennies continued to be issued of the same size, weight and general appearance as those which preceded it. There was, indeed, in later reigns a gradual diminution in the weight of the penny ; but *until after the appearance of a gold currency* [2] (A.D. 1343 or 1344), and the issue of the groat and half groat (A.D. 1351), this diminution was very slight. After that date it became much more rapid. This continuity of numismatic history is undoubtedly significant of a stability in the fiscal and financial condition of the country." Two facts are here, in a striking manner, brought into conjunction : the coinage of gold in England by the 18th of Edward III., and the rapid depreciation of the silver currency in the period that

---

[1] Page xxvi.   [2] The *italics* are mine.

followed, as contrasted with the previous five or six centuries of remarkable stability. The question can hardly fail to suggest itself : Was there a causal connection between the two ? The "gradual diminution of the weight of the penny in the later reigns," to which Mr. Keary alludes, can only refer to the fact that Edward I. coined twenty shillings and threepence, instead of twenty shillings only, out of the Tower pound, then a synonym for the pound sterling. There was no other legal diminution, and this was so minute that it probably passed altogether unperceived. The coinage was often, no doubt, in the earlier period, impaired by clippers and sweaters, and was much debased during the anarchy of Stephen's reign, when every powerful baron issued a coinage of his own. But always, both in Saxon and Norman times, the Crown, on the restoration of its authority, directed its first energies to the restoration of the silver coinage, and always brought it back both to its original weight and its original standard. Glance, again, at the period that followed. The legal weight of the sterling penny, which had not varied by more than half a grain since the days of Offa, had come down, by the end of Edward III.'s reign, from 22 grains to 18. By the end of Henry VII.'s it was down to 12 grains, and by the end of Elizabeth's it was down to $7\frac{3}{4}$ grains.[1] Mr.

---

[1] Ruding's *Annals of the Coinage of Britain*, table, vol. i. p. 22.

Keary remarks that the continuity of numismatic history during the former period is significant of stability in the fiscal and financial condition of the country, and it may be admitted that it was, so far, a satisfactory symptom. But will any one contend that a period, the commencement of which takes us back to the semi-barbarous potentates of Mercia, and which embraces the invasions of the Vikings and the Norman Conquest, was one characterised, on the whole, by a greater degree of fiscal and financial stability than that great period during which England asserted for herself a position second to that of no other nation in Europe, whether in arms, in letters, or in science ? If John, or Ethelred the Unready, in their direst straits, did not depreciate their coinage, while Edward III., in the full tide of his prosperity, did, are we forthwith to rate their honesty and wisdom above his, or does it not seem more probable that we have to look in the monetary conditions of their respective ages for the cause of a contrast so remarkable ?

Scotland, too, it is worthy of note, introduced gold about the same time as England did,[1] and presently she also began her career of deprecia-

---

[1] Ruddiman's introduction to *Anderson's Diplomata*, p. 132. Ruddiman thinks no gold was coined in David II.'s reign (1329-70). That however is an error, cf. *Coinage of Scotland*, Ed. Burns, F.S.A. Scot., vol. i. p. 267.

tions, in which indeed she rapidly outran the sister country. Up to 1328, at any rate, the money of the two nations had remained indistinguishable, that of both being to all intents pure and of full weight.[1] In that year negotiations were afoot for the marriage of Robert Bruce's son to Edward III.'s sister, and it is noticed with regard to the proposed portion of the princess that it is stipulated to be so many pounds simply, derived from lands in Scotland, it being quite unnecessary to specify these pounds as "pounds sterling," in order to distinguish them from the "pound Scottish." This occasion was the last however in which, in any state document, when money was in question, that distinction was omitted. Within a few generations we know that the pound Scottish had become only a fourth part of the pound sterling, and that it ended by becoming only a twelfth part of it.

If we look generally at the period ranging from Edward III. to George III., and apply to the money of that epoch the same tests as those which Mommsen applies to the money of Rome, when he is endeavouring to decide which metal was, at any given date, the true standard of value, and which was merely subsidiary, we shall, I think, be led to the conclusion that, throughout the whole of it, the position of the real though

---

[1] Anderson's *Annals of Commerce under Year* 1328.

latent standard must be accorded to gold.   We
saw, in following Mommsen, that shortly after
268 B.C., when silver was first coined, the copper
coinage entered on its course of depreciation, and
finally, by the time of Sulla, disappeared as money
altogether.   We saw again how, shortly after the
coining of the aureus by Julius Cæsar, the debasement of the silver set in.   Gold then at once
assumed the first place, though the contemporary
world had not realised the fact, and the denarius,
even so early as Nero's day, had rather to be
regarded as the 25th part of the aureus than
as possessing an independent value in silver.
It took several centuries, however, before this
latent priority of gold obtained distinct official
recognition.   It was in the system of Constantine,[1] first, that the pound of gold was used as
the unit of account, and that the milliarense was
coined in silver as the one-thousandth part of it.
So in England the coinage of gold dates from
the middle of the fourteenth century.   The rapid
depreciation of the silver together with its displacement as the principal measure of property
immediately followed.   It took another five
hundred years, however, before the change of
standard, already in a sense effected, received
its official ratification by the Act of 1816.

[1] *Hist. de la Monnaie romaine*, vol. iii. p. 81.

CHAPTER IV

IN glancing at the history of the English and
Scottish currency we found the coincidence between the introduction of gold and the commencement of depreciations of the silver very
conspicuous. If we turn now to the currency in
the thirteenth and fourteenth centuries on the
other side of the Channel, we find that its history
also goes to confirm the opinion as to the causal
connection between the introduction of a second
and more precious metal and the depreciation of
the first. At the same time, the case of France,
it must be said, is a more complicated one than
that of England. Nicholas Oresme, the famous
Bishop of Lisieux, writing in 1373 his treatise
De Mutatione Monetarum, certainly remarks
significantly :[1] "*Mutationes hujusmodi sunt noviter
adinventæ. Nunquam enim sic factum est in*

[1] *Capitulum*, xviii.

*civitatibus aut regnis olim prospere gubernatis, nec
unquam reperi historiam quæ de hoc faceret men-
tionem* " ; and Le Blanc [1] so far confirms Oresme
in that he tells us that Philippe le Bel was
the first French king who used the depreciation
of the currency as a means of raising revenue.
This would place the commencement of depreciations in France half a century or so earlier than
their commencement in England ; and, as the
introduction of gold was also by so much earlier,
this would tally perfectly with the theory in
question.   The statements of Oresme and Le
Blanc, at any rate, both point to the existence of
a considerable period of stability in the weight
and standard of the French silver immediately
before the introduction of gold in the thirteenth
century, and we know how completely this
stability vanished almost immediately after it.
Le Blanc,[2] however, cannot have meant that
Philippe le Bel's was the earliest depreciation of
the French currency, as he gives us some details
of a much earlier one, as far back, indeed, as the
reign of Philippe I. ; and Oresme's knowledge
with regard to the history of his country, no
doubt, did not extend to a very remote period.

---

[1] *Traité Historique des Monnoyes*, ed. Amsterdam, 1692, p. 179.
Eighteenth century writers, such as D'Aguesseau, treat of the series
of French depreciations as beginning with Philippe le Bel.

[2] *Op. cit.*, p. 148,

By Mr. Shaw's account,[1] gold, after having disappeared completely as money in Western Europe for about six hundred years, reappeared in 1252, at which date, following Villani,[2] he asserts that the florin was first coined by the Republic of Florence. Such earlier coinages of gold as undoubtedly took place were merely, he thinks, for purposes of display, and the pieces are rather to be regarded as medals than as money. This view, however, cannot be sustained. At the fall of the Western Empire, as we know, gold was the

---

[1] *Hist. of Currency*, p. 1.

[2] The origin of the gold florin presents a problem on which further light is desirable. G. Villani states that it was first issued n Florence in A.D. 1252, and this seems to be pretty generally accepted, as, for instance, in Murray's " New English Dictionary." Le Blanc, however (ed. Amst. 1692, p. 147), emphatically asserts that the florins are much more ancient than Villani thought, and quotes, in proof of this, a mention of gold florins made in a deed of gift to a Confrérie des Clercs at Pontoise dated MLXVIII. He quotes another authority, too, which, however, is entitled to less weight. Apart from these authorities, there seems to be unmistakable evidence of the early existence of the gold florin in France. De Saulcy's collection of mint documents begins with 1180, and the second of them (vol. i. p. 115) contains instructions in regard to the weight and standard of florins which were then about to be issued. The presumption is that if any earlier mint documents could be found, florins would be mentioned in them also.

[Since the above was written I have ascertained, through M. de Vienne, that the true date in the Pontoise document—which is in the archives of the town—is 1368. De Saulcy's dates too are apparently not much to be relied on. See *Notes and Queries*, 9th s. vii. p. 7 and p. 151.]

principal money of Rome, and what other money
there was was copper, not silver.   Silver, at the
same time, had been chiefly in favour with the
Germans as money since the days of Tacitus,[1]
and it continued to be so.   The old denarii of the
Empire, when displaced within its bounds by the
base issues of Caracalla and his successors, found
their way into free Germany, and there circulated
as the principal medium of exchange among the
" barbarians."   This state of things in its general
features perpetuated itself into the early mediæval
period.   The use of pure silver as money became,
indeed, a note of Teutonic nationality.   While,
on the other hand, the issue of gold, or copper, or
billon coinages, as in London and in Northumbria
in the days of the Heptarchy is,[2] Mr. Keary
thinks, some evidence of Roman influence not
yet extinct.

The money of the Merovingian Franks was, at
any rate, we find, a continuation of that of the
Roman Empire, consisting mainly of gold, though
the *solidus aureus* was, for the most part, replaced by its third part, the *tremis*.   With the
accession of the Austrasian House all this was
changed.[3]   Silver then became the principal

---

[1] Keary, Introduction to the Catalogue of English Coins in the
British Museum, vol. i. p. v.   Cf. Mommsen, *op. cit.*, vol. iii. p. 132.

[2] *Op. cit.*, pp. xx. and xxi

[3] E. W. Robertson, *Historical Essays*, p. 42.   See also *Rev. Num.*,
2 ser. vol. iv. p. 65.

money of the country.   From Charlemagne, as
every one knows, dates the adoption of the *libra
denariorum*, with its divisions into 20 silver *solidi*
and 240 silver pence, as the standard money of
the greater part of Europe.

The countries south of the Alps were, however,
much less affected by Charlemagne's reform than
those to the north of them.   Spain was outside
its range altogether.   There the reckoning in
libræ, solidi and *denarii* of silver was quite
unknown, and in Castile, Borghini says, the
gold solidus of Constantine was current up till
1487.[1]   In Italy, though the silver standard was
introduced, and was nominally in force for many
centuries, the Bezant, under the various names of
the " Augustale," the " Michalate," the " Scy-
phate "[2] and others, continued, all along, to have
an important circulation, and served probably
almost, if not quite, without intermission as the
money of all but retail transactions.   Even in the
fourteenth century, Muratori says, " the Bezant "
was a familiar word in Tuscany.   If any one asked
in his prayers " *l'aver di buoni bizanti*," no one
would be at a loss to know what he meant.[3]   Borghini, it is worthy of note, looked at the issue of
the Florentine florin in 1252 as significant, not as

[1] *Discorsi della Moneta Fiorentina*, vol. iii. p. 320.
    See *Muratori Antiquitates Italiæ*, vol. ii. p. 770 ff.
    Op. cit., vol. ii. p. 790.

being the resurrection of gold after it had hiber-
nated for several centuries, but merely as having
ousted the "imperiale" from circulation.[1] He
appears to think that several of the Italian cities
were eager to issue gold in the thirteenth century
on account of the prestige that would have accompanied it, but that none of them ventured to do
so at an earlier date than Florence, the issue of
gold being then regarded as a prerogative of "the
great princes of the world,"[2] that is to say, of the
the two empires. Frederick II., we know, issued
an Augustale in Italy in 1230.[3] Borghini refers
to an opinion that was current in his time, which,
however, he regards as erroneous, to the effect
that the privilege of coining gold was obtained,
in the first instance, by the Italian cities from the
Emperor Rudolph in 1280.[4] It is significant that
the issue of the florin in Florence followed almost
immediately on the death of Frederick II., a date
which may be fixed upon as that of her achievement of complete independence. The prestige
attaching to the striking of gold is illustrated by
the story that Villani tells us of the negotiations
of the Pisans and Florentines with the King of
Tunis. The former endeavoured to belittle the
latter in the eyes of that monarch, but were

[1] *Discorsi*, vol. iii. p. 188.   [2] *Op. cit.*, vol. iii. p. 304.
[3] Muratori, *op. cit.*, vol. ii. p. 788. Muratori says in 1222.
[4] Borghini, *op. cit.* vol. iii. p. 277.

covered with confusion when it appeared that they themselves struck silver only, while the Florentines struck gold.

As, then, gold appears to have been the principal money earlier in Italy than in the more northerly portions of Charlemagne's empire, it is interesting to inquire, Was that fact accompanied in Italy also with an earlier depreciation of the silver? It appears to have been so. We learn from Villani [1] that when the florin was struck in 1252, it was the equivalent in value of the lira of silver. We know further that the double florin issued by Edward III. in England, a century later, was something less than the third part in value of the pound sterling, then the same thing as the Tower pound. It thus seems evident that, by the middle of the thirteenth century, the Florentine silver had already been depreciated so as to have fallen to one-sixth of its original value. [2]

To return to Charlemagne's reform, we have in it another important historical transition of the monetary standard. It reverses, however, in one salient characteristic those previously commented

---

[1] *Cronica*, lib. 6, cap. 54.

[2] That the Florentines of the thirteenth century understood all about the depreciation of the currency is evidenced by the fact referred to by Orsini (*Storia della Moneta della Republica Fiorentina*, p. xiv.), that in 1296, they reduced the standard of their silver to raise funds to pave the bridge of S. Trinita.

on, inasmuch as it is a transition from a more precious to a less precious metal. It has been frequently said that sooner or later an epoch arrives
in the industrial expansion of progressive nations
when a medium of exchange of enhanced value
becomes necessary to them, and that, in such
circumstances, the dearer medium somehow or
other comes to be adopted as the money of the
country. This, we are told, is the true explanation of all transitions of the standard. Taken
very broadly, the principle contains, no doubt,
a certain element of truth. It is open to so many
quàlifications and exceptions, however, as to be
of little value for practical application. Here, at
any rate, we have an undoubtedly progressive
nation relinquishing the dearer for the cheaper
medium. Similarly it may be remarked that the
semi-barbarous kingdom of the Cimmerian Bos-
porus used gold very largely for many years, and
that, in the first and second centuries before
Christ, while such states as Rhodes, Massilia
and Rome itself were using silver mainly or
exclusively as their money, the north of Gaul and
the south of Britain were using an indigenous
gold coinage imitated from the staters of Philip
of Macedon. The first monetary metal of any
country is likely to be the metal found beneath
its soil. The silver ore in the German mountains
had probably a good deal to do with the Teutonic

preference for silver, and the displacement of gold in its favour towards the end of the eighth century in France, puts in a strong light the Teutonic ascendency which appears to have caused or accompanied the accession to power of the House of Heristal.

The Merovingian coinage presents one of the very few instances that we find in history of a gold currency that had become to a large extent debased, and that remained debased for a considerable period. Le Blanc thinks that its debasement was not due to the action of the Crown, but to the frauds of the moneyers. M. Babelon regards the state of things then existing as a return to the condition of private coinage, a condition through which, he believes, that most primitive money has passed. It is noteworthy that, long before Pepin's reform, the gold coin had lost one of the most important attributes of money, that of being available, as it stood, for the payment of taxes. [1] It appears from a passage in the life of St. Eligius, who lived as far back as the reign of Dagobert I., and who was himself a moneyer or mint official, that all the money which was paid in tribute to the treasury was melted down and refined before it was finally deposited. It would in these circumstances of course be accepted only for what it was worth

[1] Le Blanc, *op. cit.*, p. 40.

intrinsically.   The kingdom of the Franks must
therefore for a long period have been practically
without a currency at all, a fact which certainly
makes the introduction of the silver coinage more
comprehensible.

In Pepin's time the pound of silver was divided
into 264 pence.   It was Charlemagne who first
made the weight of the pennies such that their
number to the pound came down to the famous
figure of 240.   Why did he raise their weight?
A wise ruler would no doubt sedulously avoid
their depreciation, but the actual raising of their
weight would seem at first sight to involve just as
great an injustice as its lowering, and at the same
time to involve a description of injustice to the
perpetration of which there was no readily comprehensible temptation.   A perfectly adequate
reason no doubt is to be found if we suppose that
gold was still an element of importance in the
monetary system.   It might then obviously have
been necessary to readjust the relations between
the metals.   A couple of generations later we
find Charles the Bald fixing the ratio between
pure gold and the coined silver at 1 : 12,[1] and his
object then was plainly to prevent the country's
store of gold from leaving it.   The edict of
Pistoia runs : " Throughout the kingdom the

[1] Le Blanc, *op. cit.*, p. 121.   See also Ducange, *Gloss.*, art.
" Moneta " ; sub-heading, " Moneta Decima."

pound of fine gold must not be sold except for
twelve pounds of silver in new deniers." It seems
beyond doubt that Charlemagne's increase in the
weight of the penny was a step taken with the
same object.   It was a measure analogous to
those raisings of the gold which occurred at such
frequent intervals in England during the rapid
fall in the value of the silver in the Stuart period.[1]

We are thus led to the conclusion that it is an
exaggeration to speak of gold as having at any
time completely disappeared from the monetary
system of France.   It can hardly be said to have
completely disappeared from the monetary system
of Britain, much less from that of her southern
neighbour.   There is scarcely any period in which
we do not find certain payments made to the
exchequer in gold by weight as well as in silver
in both countries.   There was however, beyond
doubt, a considerable period in France as well as
in Britain when it disappeared from the coinage,
though the period was very much shorter in the
former country than in the latter.   It embraced,
at the same time, even in France, the whole of
the Carolingian epoch as well as the earlier part
of the Capetian.   Charles the Bald's edict makes
no mention of any coin but silver coin, though it
legislates carefully and expressly with regard to

---

[1] Under Charlemagne's immediate successors the weight of the
penny was still further greatly increased.

the maintenance of the purity both of uncoined
gold and uncoined silver.   Le Blanc indeed
quotes several cases in which, during the period
of the second race of kings, payments are mentioned in various deeds as having been made in
so many solidi of gold, and he is of opinion consequently that a gold solidus was in use all through
the Carolingian period, though, as it chanced,
none had come down to his day.   It appears
however now to be established that the word
"solidus" was in the cases which he cites used
as the denomination of a weight—the twentieth
part of the pound—not of a coin ; and with this
view of course the numismatic evidence corresponds.

Towards the close of the eleventh century however we come upon unquestionable evidence of
the circulation of gold in coin.   Some gold
coins of Louis VI. (1108–1137) are preserved,
being the earliest French gold after the close of
the Merovingian epoch still extant.   There is
known further to have been at this period an
important circulation of gold in the south of
France—the Marabotin currency ; so important
was it indeed that the opinion was general in
Le Blanc's time, though he did not share it, that
the Marabotins were French coins.   There is now
no question as to their Spanish origin, though
there is still some controversy as to the derivation

of their name.   They used to be regarded as
having been the coinage of the Al Moravid
caliphs,[1] who ruled in Spain from 1056 to 1146.
The better opinion, however, now appears to be
that the word Marabotin or Maravedi, which in
Arabic also means "sacred," is used as signifying
"the money" *par excellence*, and that the Marabotin can trace a lineal and uninterrupted descent
from the solidus of Constantine.[2]

Such an extensive currency of foreign gold
circulating, as no doubt it did, at tariffed rates
along with the coin of the country would obviously
be calculated to produce effects precisely similar
to those which would be produced by national
issues of gold, and it is surely not a little singular
to find that this reappearance of gold in the
French currency is followed very shortly by the
earliest of the French depreciations of the silver.
An old chronicle[3] has the following record with
regard to the year 1103, somewhere about the
end of the reign of Philippe I. : "*Fuit magna
tribulatio, et nummi argentei pro aeris* (sic)
mutati et facti sunt," and, as a matter of
fact, some of Philippe I.'s deniers are found

---

[1] E. W. Robertson, *Historical Essays*, p. 56.

[2] *Résumé Historique de la Monnaie Espagnole*.   M. de Vienne,
Revue Numismatique, 3me series, tome xi. p. 375.   Gold under
the Romans was "sacra moneta."   See Sabatier, *Monnaies Byzantines*, vol. i. p. 48.

[3] Le Blanc, *op. cit.*, p. 148.

to be about one-third copper. Again the same
chronicle tells us, with regard to the year 1112 :
"*Iterum nummi mutati sunt et cum granis* (sic)
alii facti," and again of the year 1120 "*mense
Novembre mutati sunt nummi.*" Thus in the
course of seventeen years there were three
affaiblissements, as they came to be called, of the
silver, and their net result was to bring the
French penny down to one-fourth of its former
value, and to one-fourth likewise of the value
which the sterling penny still retained.

About the middle of the twelfth century, however, another influence came into play. Henry II.
of England was then the real ruler of the greater
part of the country, and, with the English rule,
the English money appears to have attained the
predominance. We have an edict of Henry II.,[1]
issued in 1158, fixing the value of the mark of
silver at "13 solidos et 4 denarios sterlingorum
de custodia, vel 53 solidos et 4 denarios Turon-
enses." One English penny was thus made the
equivalent of four deniers Tournois, and this
relation varied little if at all for about a century
and a half, when we reach the era of Philippe le
Bel and his depreciations.[2] It became the basis
of the famous "standard of St. Louis," the restora-

---

[1] Le Blanc, *op. cit.*, p. 153.   But see below.
[2] Le Blanc, *op. cit.*, p. 166. St. Louis tariffed 1 sterling at 4
deniers Tournois.

tion of which was always the popular demand during the debasements of the thirteenth and fourteenth centuries. It is very interesting to find that, at this early period in European history, the English pound sterling—though so different a pound sterling from the present one—was, as it is now, the true international money of a great part of the Continent. In 1289, we see it thus used in a contract entered into between Philippe le Bel and the King of Castile, and in 1295 in another contract between the same prince and the King of Norway. In 1248 we find the Prior of Lansac, in the diocese of Cahors, making a bargain in sterling money with Count Raymond of Toulouse for his protection. The price offered and accepted seems a moderate one ; it is an annual payment *dimidiae marchae sterlingorum*—the ever famous six - and - eight-pence. M. de Saulcy, I observe, is of opinion that the edict quoted above, which Le Blanc attributes to our Henry II., is really an edict of Philip Augustus of the year 1204. If that attribution is correct, the use of the words " sterlingorum de custodia " ("sterlings of the treasury") would seem to indicate that the sterling had attained at this period in France a position not far removed from that of the official standard. The fact too that the denier Tournois was an exact subdivision of the sterling penny made the Tournois money part of the same system, and was apparently the operative cause in making it supplant the denier Parisis.

Whatever the cause may have been, at any rate the fact remains that the 150 years that extended from the middle of the twelfth century to the end of the thirteenth century were not an era of depreciations in France. We found Henry II. of England or Philip Augustus—whichever it was—tariffing the denier Tournois at one-fourth of the penny sterling, and again we find St. Louis tariffing it at precisely the same figure. The sterling had not changed in the interim, nor had, apparently, the denier Tournois.

The period too appears to be essentially a silver period. The state transactions between John of England and Philip Augustus were all in silver, and the vast treasure left behind by the latter also consisted exclusively of silver. By the time of St. Louis however the gold period, or at any rate the bimetallic period, is found to have fairly begun. His coinage indeed might best be called trimetallic. It comprised, in pure gold, the Mouton; in fine silver, the Gros Tournois; and in billon, the Denier. These were all in circulation together. With such a currency, in an age which had its experience yet to gain, it would have been safe to predict from the beginning that the depreciation of the coins of the inferior metal could not be long delayed, and accordingly in the time of Philippe le Bel, the grandson of St. Louis, the depreciations came, and in no stinted measure.

Dante has handed this prince down to posterity with a mark of infamy against his name for

> . . . . The woe he worked
> With his adulterate money on the Seine.[1]

and it would not be easy to exaggerate the mischief which the continued pursuit by himself and several of his immediate successors of the monetary policy which he instituted in 1295 inflicted on his country from first to last. At the same time, it is necessary to endeavour to apportion fairly the blame between himself, on the one hand, and his age and his circumstances on the other. After the battle of Courtrai the exigencies of his unsuccessful war with the Flemings rendered it necessary to raise fresh funds somehow or other. State loans were then hardly as yet invented, and most of the various forms of taxation which at a subsequent period would have been resorted to, would have been looked upon as highly obnoxious innovations, if indeed the levy of such taxation would have been at all possible. Oresme who, nearly a century later, after much experience had been gained,

---

[1] *Paradise*, cant. xix. v. 117 (Cary's translation).

wrote in vigorous condemnation of the depreciations, does not nevertheless deal with his
subject at all as a writer of the present day would
deal with it.   He treats the arguments in favour
of the depreciation of the currency as arguments
that require to be seriously considered and
carefully answered.   It appears to have been
contended that such depreciations were both the
surest and readiest methods by which a prince
could raise revenue for the conduct of his wars,
and not only that, but also that they were the
fairest, as the burden of them fell upon no
particular class, but was distributed equally over
all.   This he does not deny, but points out
where the danger lay.   The prince, he says,
having made a fair sum of money by his first
depreciation without difficulty, and perhaps
without apparent injury to any one, would be led
to conclude that, by a second and yet greater
depreciation he would similarly make a second
and yet greater sum of money, and would thus be
led on to a third and a fourth, till in the long run,
as had been seen in their late experience, disaster
would overtake both him and his country.
Tom Paine remarks on the analogy between
the resort to stimulants by the individual and the
resort to depreciations of the currency by a state,
and here practically Oresme anticipates him.

This whole method of dealing with the subject

is a method which, it seems to me, we could only expect to see made use of at a time when the dearer metal had already supplanted the cheaper as the medium of large transactions, and when it had become possible consequently for the cheaper metal to be, for a time at any rate, maintained at a conventional value much above its intrinsic value by its exchangeability at a fixed ratio with the dearer. No prince or state has ever made much out of the falsification of the money which was the principal measure of property in the country at the time, and few have even seriously attempted it.

It must be said, at the same time, that the French King learned very rapidly the dangerous lesson which Oresme describes for us. In Rome the depreciation of the denarius began with Nero, and it was half copper by the time of Severus ; yet Mommsen thinks that there is nothing to indicate that even at the latter date its old value in the monetary system was not perfectly maintained, nothing to indicate that it had fallen to a discount as measured by the gold. With Philippe le Bel, on the contrary, the variation from the standard of St. Louis began in 1295, and the issue of the debased money was apparently so reckless and so unrestrained that, by 1301, three of the new deniers were worth intrinsically only one of the old.

One agency in bringing about the rapid fall of the denier, which did not come into play in the strong, well-ordered bureaucracy of Rome under the Antonines, was the coinage not issued by the crown. The right of coinage had been usurped by many of the barons and prelates in or about the period of Charles the Simple, and now, for some centuries past, had become fully established and recognised. Philip did not attempt to call it in question, though, at the same time, it is curious to observe that he claims that the right of " debasing and diminishing the money " was a royal prerogative exclusively. The bishops and barons however did not look even at that matter in the same light, and, accordingly, the result of Philip's debasement, says Le Blanc,[1] was " to give an opportunity to his neighbours and subjects to launch qnantities of false money throughout the kingdom." The King got Clement V., with whom he had then established an *entente*, to issue a bull excommunicating them. This he did with all his heart. The terms of the excommunication however were general, and the culprits, says Le Blanc, *n'en faisaient grand cas*. The rigid limitation of quantity which alone could have maintained the monetary value of the depreciated coin became of course, in such circumstances, impossible.

[1] *Op. cit.*, p. 195.

If however the barons and prelates contributed thus to the aggravation of the mischief, they were themselves the first to feel the pinch. As the denier fell the gold money rose in value, and with it, just as in modern days when gold is allowed to go to a premium, the price of all produce rose too. The villain who had commuted his feudal services for a money payment was then in an extremely fortunate position. The money obtained by the sale of a few septiers of wheat, when reckoned in livres and sols, was sufficient to acquit obligations which, some years before, could only have been acquitted by the sale of several times the quantity.[1] There must have been large classes with whom the "cheap money" was in the highest degree popular, and it played its part, beyond question, in rapidly breaking down the power of the feudal nobility. We hear a great deal from Le Blanc about the impoverishment of the nobility, and to this cause M. Villani, a contemporary writer, even attributes the disaster at Crécy. It seems certain however that the loss to one class must have been, to a certain extent at any rate, offset by the gain to another.

In 1303 we find the prelates very much alive to the injury which the circulation of base money was inflicting on the interests of their own order, and of that with which they were closely con-

[1] Le Blanc, *op. cit.*, p. 239.

nected.   It is noteworthy however that they
neither question the king's right to mix the silver
with copper, nor dispute the necessity for exercis-
ing such a right in certain circumstances.   What
they do is to make him an offer of one-tenth of
their revenues, provided that the moneys were for
the future left undebased, unless it could be shown
that " there was an indispensable need for the
debasement, certified to by the grand council,
and endorsed by an assembly of the seigneurs." [1]
The offer seems liberal and the conditions reasonable, but it was not accepted.

By 1306 the loss of real revenue, not only to
the barons and prelates, but also of course to the
crown itself, had reached such a height, and the
cry for remedy and redress on the part of the
classes injured had become so overwhelming, that
a return to *forte monnoye*—the first of many such—
was decided upon.   Then, probably for the first
time, the mass of the population realised what for
them a depreciation of the currency and its inevitable consequences could mean.   The standard
of St. Louis was to be restored.   The new deniers
accordingly were rated officially at the amount
only which they were worth intrinsically, which was
one-third of the sum for which they had up to
that date been passing.   If a man had the equivalent of a shilling in his pocket, he found all at

[1] *Op. cit.*, p. 186.

once that, owing to a royal proclamation, it was now only the equivalent of fourpence. The result was general turmoil and confusion in trade, and a serious sedition in the capital. The masses of the poor were reduced to despair, and, as Le Blanc sententiously observes,[1] "having nothing else to lose, they lost the respect due to the king's majesty," and even besieged him in the Temple where he was then residing, and overturned the dishes that were being brought for his dinner. They wrecked at the same time the magnificent house and luxurious gardens of Stephen Barbette the master of the mint, who was supposed to have been the true author of the reform.

All through history we find that it is the reform, the return to sound money rather than the depreciation itself, that first rouses popular discontent. It is only when the mass of the people learns that depreciations must be followed sooner or later by such remedies that they begin to entertain a salutary dread with regard to them. The mysterious "war of the moneyers" in Aurelian's day, in which, as the Emperor writes to his friend, he lost 7,000 of his best troops, may possibly be explainable as a widespread insurrection caused by the return to sound money.

The duration of the "forte monnoye" was very short In 1310 we hear of a second *affaiblisse-*

---

[1] *Op. cit.*, p. 190.

ment, succeeded in 1314 by a second *renforce-ment*. Then followed a period which lasted well into Charles VII.'s reign, during which these alternate *affaiblissements* and *renforcements* succeeded one another almost uninterruptedly every few years. There was an interval indeed of seventeen years of stable money during the reign of Charles V., the sagacious pupil of Oresme, and a few other intervals while perhaps Charles le Bel, or Philippe de Valois, or John, was repenting of his folly and making promises of amendment. After a time too the return to *forte monnoye* became less and less complete ; and thus by the date of Louis XI.'s accession the "livre" had become a name for about one-fifth of the amount of silver of which it was the name in 1295.

It would be a profitless task to attempt to follow out the history of such a period in detail. It will be sufficient to glance at a few of its general features. The contrast with the state of things in contemporary England is a remarkable one. Not only were the English depreciations less in degree than the French, they were different in kind. Up to Henry VIII.'s time the English kings never resorted to depreciations with the object of raising money. Ruding's[1] tables of the seigniorage show that the Crown made no more out of the silver coinage when the sterling penny

---

[1] *Annals of the Coinage*, vol. i. p. 182.

was at 18 or even at 12 grains than it did when it was at 22. These depreciations seem to have been forced upon the country, as the later French depreciations were, by the necessity that was felt for protecting the stores of the precious metals. There was always up to the close of the seventeenth century a large amount of foreign coin in circulation in both countries. Very frequently the rate at which the foreign coin was allowed to circulate was tariffed, and, when it was not, its monetary value was often fixed almost as effectively by trade custom. Depreciations in one European country thus tended to throw the monetary system of neighbouring countries into confusion. One of Clement's bulls denounces Philippe le Bel's depreciations on account of the injury that they inflicted, not only on France itself, but also on its neighbours. England thus was obliged to protect her money occasionally against Scotch or French depreciations by counter depreciations of her own.

The remarkable thing was how firmly our ancestors during the Plantagenet period adhered to the principle of sound money. The French kings in the thirteenth century were unfortunate no doubt in having a billon coinage to begin with, inherited from the earlier depreciations of Philippe I. and Louis VI. It was our boast in England up to the close of Elizabeth's reign that,

with one short interval, we had never had anything
but pure gold and silver in circulation, and it was
with the greatest reluctance that the coinage even
of copper halfpence was at last permitted.

This sentiment in favour of the precious metals
only, as money, though we have now outgrown
its necessity, was in its day a most important
safeguard. When the denier was already half
copper it became a much easier matter to adulterate it still further than it would have been to
adulterate a coin which had always from time
immemorial been practically of pure silver.

The depth and persistence of the English sentiment is placed in a striking light by the fact that
in France itself, during the English sixteen years
occupation,[1] neither Henry V. nor the government of Henry VI. issued anything but the best
and soundest money, though at the same time
"*Charles qui se dit Dauphin,*" as an English
ordinance describes Charles VII., was pursuing the
usual French course of issuing "double deniers
of less weight and baser metal than those of our
dear grandfather King Charles VI." Such a
memory is hardly less gratifying to our national
pride than the memory of Crécy or of Agincourt.

The morality of the French kings in monetary matters had, indeed, in this period, sunk
surprisingly low. Philippe de Valois and John

[1] Le Blanc, *op. cit.*, p. 244.

are the kings who exhibit themselves perhaps
in the least enviable light. The former in 1350
having diminished the amount of silver in one
of his coins, the "double Tournois," makes
the officers of his mint "swear on the holy
Gospel" that they will keep the alteration a
secret from the merchants who bring billon to
be coined. An instruction issued by John to his
mint officials in similar circumstances is even
a trifle more shameless. The "blanc" had been
reduced so that in future it would contain only
about one-fourth of pure silver and three-fourths
copper. "Keep the matter secret,"[1] says the
ingenuous sovereign, "and if any one asks you
what is the standard of the blancs, tell them that
it is one-half silver" (*six deniers de loy*).

The main interest of the period for our present
purpose, however, lies in its bearing on the
evolution of the gold standard in Europe. On that
point Le Blanc's own words are worth quoting[2]:
"When Philippe le Bel," he says, "debased the
silver money he did not touch the gold. The
people finding that there was no certainty in
contracting in that sort of money, of which the
value changed so often, ceased making their bargains in livres and sols, and used for that purpose
the species of gold which were not changed, and
of which the value was stable, particularly the

[1] Le Blanc, *op. cit.*, p. 218.   [2] *Op. cit.*, Prolegomena, p. xix.

florins of Florence and the gold moutons of St.
Louis." On this Philippe legislated to forbid bargains in gold, as so many of his successors did
after him ; but, as might be expected, with little or
no effect. All such bargains indeed had afterwards
in the reign of John not only to be condoned, but
also to be validated. Thenceforward gold came
more and more to loom before the popular mind
in France as the true standard of value.

We have a significant indication of the light in
which it had come to be regarded in an ordinance
of John issued in 1355.[1] Froissard tells us that,
on St. Andrew's day in that year, the Estates of
the Realm being assembled, the king set forth
the condition of his wars and asked a subsidy.
He promised to make the money " forte et
durable" if they furnished him with funds to
carry on his operations. They agreed to the
levy of a tax on all commodities of eight deniers
in the livre, about three per cent., and to a tax on
salt. The two together were estimated to be
sufficient to place 30,000 men in the field. Thereupon the king issued the ordinance referred to.
Le Blanc gives the text in full. Some of the
phraseology is technical and intricate, but the
following is its general tenor. The king promised
that thenceforth nothing but good and stable
money should be issued in the kingdom. The

[1] *Op. cit.*, p. 219.

"denier" of fine gold, that was to say, the
mouton, was to be struck at the rate of fifty-two
to the mark, and to be made to pass current for
twenty sols in silver. The effective currency of
the two metals together, at this rate, was to be
secured by maintaining the weight and standard
of the silver at the figure necessary for the
purpose. The standard was to be two-thirds fine,
and the weight was to be such that the silver
would readily exchange at par with the gold.
This is expressed in the words "*afin que l'on n'ait
cause de haucier la monnoye d'or.*" Throughout,
it will be seen, the gold piece is the point of departure; the silver is that which is to be made
and kept conformable to it. The provisions of
the ordinance, all through, are drafted on that
presupposition.

The above arrangement, however—the king
went on to explain—was to be regarded only as
provisional. Once his wars were over, and his
finances in such a position that it would be
possible for him to return to a *régime* of *très forte
monnoye*, then he would improve the quality of the
silver to such a degree that it would pass current
along with the same gold piece, no longer however at the rate of twenty sols, but at the rate of
thirteen sols four deniers, the ratio of eleven to one
between gold and silver being thus established.

This figure, thirteen sols four deniers, is a

curious and significant one to find in such a connection.   It appears to indicate that the tradition
of the sterling standard was not yet extinct.   The
distant, perhaps never attainable, ideal which both
the king and the Estates of the Realm, who were
parties to the bargain, seem to have had dimly
in view was the coinage in gold of the mark
sterling.

Even the more modest ideal of making the
silver current at the rate of twenty sols, or one
livre, to the mouton was never attained.   Five
years later, however, after John's return from his
captivity in England, a smaller gold piece, one of
which there were sixty-three to the mark, was
struck, and was made current at that rate.   This
currency was maintained for about twenty years,
a period which included the whole of Charles V.'s
reign, and this fact was not without importance in
connection with the discussions, two centuries
later, on the proposal to adopt the gold crown as
the official standard.   It enabled those who
favoured that proposal to represent it as being,
in a sense, not an innovation, but a return to
a time-honoured system.   Gold pieces representing one livre, it must be said, also appear
transitorily in the French coinage in subsequent
reigns.   These latter pieces of course were
not struck at sixty-three to the mark, but
varied between ninety-six and sixty-eight.

This attempt at the maintenance of a coincidence, or aliquot proportion, between the silver "pound," or the silver "livre," and the gold coin is a point worthy of note both in regard to the French and English money. Edward III.'s first gold coins bore no aliquot proportion to the pound sterling. They were unpopular and were recalled in the course of the year in which they were issued. The "noble" was then coined at 6s. 8d., one-half of the mark, or one-third of the pound sterling, and had a great vogue, not only in England, but all over Europe. Eventually[1] the depreciation of the silver sent the value of the noble up to 8s. 4d. Then however the "angel" was struck at 6s. 8d., and when it in its turn went up to 7s. 6d. and 8s. we find yet another coin, the "George noble," taking its place as a gold piece of 6s. 8d. The pound sterling and mark sterling thus had always, or almost always, their representatives in three and in two respectively of these gold pieces.[2]

Le Blanc claims that with the final departure of the English in 1454 the period of monetary disorders in France came to an end. The sub-

---

[1] See Table of the Gold Coins, Ruding's *Annals of the Coinage*, vol. i. pp. 23 and 24.

[2] Similarly the Florentine florin of 1252 was the lira of silver coined in gold. See Borghini, *Discorsi*, vol. iii. p. 266. Villani, *Cronica*, lib. 6, cap. 54.

sequent depreciations, he thinks, were due either
to fluctuations in the intrinsic value of gold and
silver, or to the necessity of protecting the
national money against the debased coin of foreign
nations.   This view cannot be accepted without
modification.   Louis XI. certainly, whatever he
was in other respects, as regards his monetary
policy, appears in the light of a wise and careful
administrator, and the same may be said of
Charles VIII. and Louis XII.   During these
three reigns there was nearly half a century of
fairly stable money.   With Francis I. however
the case was different; and, with the wars of
religion, we enter a period that recalls the days
of Philippe le Bel, Philippe de Valois, or John.
With regard to the beginning of the reign of
Henry III., Le Blanc himself says:[1] "The disorders of the state continuing, the evil of the
'raising of the money' increased every day."
That was to say, the depreciation of the silver
made itself manifest in the continuous rise in the
gold. "In 1574 the gold crown was worth
58 sols.   In 1575 it had to be rated at 60 sols.
The people, putting any value on the moneys
that they pleased, and raising their price according to their own caprice, sent up the crown to
68 sols."

In the contemporary literature on the subject

[1] Le Blanc, *op. cit.*, p. 271.

there is a good deal of railing similar to this of Le Blanc's at the audacity of the public in putting what price they pleased on the gold, instead of conforming themselves in the matter to his majesty's ordinances. At the same time, the true nature of the case was beginning to be understood. The situation was regarded as being very grave. A contemporary official document says, with some exaggeration, that the disorders, unless remedied, threatened infallibly the entire ruin of the kingdom. Several assemblies of experts were convoked to discuss the matter and consider what remedy was possible. Finally, in December 1575, the States General having assembled at Blois, the "Cour des Monnoyes" laid before them and the king a project of monetary reform of a very interesting and remarkable character.

Their memorandum on the subject, while its quaint citation of the views of Plato and Aristotle and the policy of Agesilaus gives it a mediæval flavour, has in other of its aspects a surprisingly modern sound. The Cour point out to the king the heavy loss of revenue caused to the state by the ceaseless rise in the value of the gold, just as our Indian finance ministers up to 1895 were continually pointing out to our government the loss of revenue caused by the steady "fall in the rupee"—another expression of course for the

rise in gold, in India.   In 1561, they observe, the
sol was one-fiftieth part of the crown in value.
It had since depreciated so as to become only
one sixty-fifth part of it, and thus the government
were now losing every year one-quarter of the
amount that should have accrued to them.

The Cour go on to point to another cause of
loss, which has also occupied an important place
in Indian despatches of recent years. "You, sire," [1]
they say, " as regards your special interest, lose
enormously by this *surhaussement des monnoyes*"
[the context makes it perfectly clear that by
" monnoyes " the gold crown is meant], " not only
because the greater part of your receipts are in
livres, while at the same time your foreign
payments, to a large extent, must be made in
actual gold crowns, but also because pressure is
continually being brought to bear on you to raise
the salaries of your military and civil officials,
it being no longer possible for them to maintain
themselves on their former incomes, so great has
been the rise in the price of food and of the other
necessaries of life owing to the depreciation of
the coinage."

So much as to the interests of the sovereign
and the manner in which they were affected by
the monetary disorders.   Elsewhere the Cour
draw attention, in a manner that would have met

[1] Le Blanc, *op. cit.*, p. 275.

with the cordial approval of Ricardo and the
Bullion Committee of 1810, to the injustice which
the same disorders were inflicting on every one
engaged in commerce throughout the kingdom.
" To pay in sols," they say, "that are worth one-
sixtieth only of the crown, a debt that was contracted when they were worth one-fiftieth, is to
cheat the creditor of one-sixth of what is due to
him. It is precisely as if a merchant who had
sold 100 ells of cloth, the ell being then three
and a half feet in length, were to measure his
cloth with an ell which was two feet and four-
fifths only, in order that he might only have to
deliver eighty ells." Such a passage makes it very
clear that to the mind of the " Cour des Monnoyes " and of course of the commercial classes
generally in France at this period, gold had
already assumed the position of the true standard
of values and measure of wealth. It is clear
that a man, even then, was considered so much
richer or so much poorer, just as he is all over
the world to-day, precisely in accordance with the
amount of gold which he held, either in immediate
possession or practically at command. Another
passage from the same memorandum which
makes this fact very clear is the following : [1]
" It will not do to conclude—when the crown
has risen in value—that a man who has made

[1] Le Blanc, *op. cit.*, p. 279.

a bargain in livres, when he gets the number of livres he has bargained for, gets all that is due to him. Though he has his livres, he has not got his due, inasmuch as the livres depreciate just in proportion as the specie rises, ... and the merchant who, as regards his foreign trade, cannot stop at what we call a 'livre,' but must consider the quality and the intrinsic value of this 'livre,' is obliged to raise the price of his goods to you in proportion as the current medium of payment depreciates. Otherwise he could not come out square."

In such a passage as this I think we may trace the hand of François Garrault, Sieur des Gorges, Conseiller du Roy and " General " in the " Cour des Monnoyes," who was probably the true originator of the whole project for the formal adoption of the gold standard. He has published separately a very striking dissertation on the subject,[1] in which his anticipation of the solution of modern monetary problems is, in a high degree, remarkable. The manner in which the depreciation of the ordinary currency and the consequent rise in gold operates to make a general rise of prices inevitable, I have not seen so well described by any modern economist.

[1] It is bound up along with Jean Bodin's *Discours sur le rehaussement et diminution des Monnoyes*. Paris, 1578. It is not paged, but is very short.

There are two sorts of traffic, he points out, internal and external (*régnicolle et étranger*), and with respect to each the functions of money, to some extent, differ. The man who is engaged in foreign trade pays little attention to the value imposed by the state on its money, but regards alone the intrinsic value, which is the same everywhere; he must place therefore such a price on the merchandise that he imports from abroad that he may be able to obtain for it the same amount of gold or silver that he has had to send away in exchange for it, together with his expenses and profit.

For example, he says, suppose a merchant engaged in the Italian trade buys three ells of velvet at the price of three [1] pistolets per ell, at a time when the pistolet stands at 2 livres 18 sols. In order to get back his principal alone, he must sell the velvet for 8 livres 14 sols; but if in the meantime the pistolet has gone up to 4 livres, then, to come out square, he must get 12 livres for his velvet. In other words, he must raise the price of his velvet by about 25 per cent.

Some think, he says, that such adjustments only apply to large transactions and have nothing to do with retail sales, but that is not so. The merchant who buys wholesale in order to sell

[1] The Spanish gold crown, which then had a large international circulation.

retail must take into consideration the value
which the people from whom he buys place on
the money which is the medium of exchange in
the transaction, and must adjust his selling price
accordingly.   He goes on to show from other
instances how rises in wholesale prices, due to
the rise in the gold coin, as measured in livres,
must react through every department of retail
trade.   Even the charge for a man and horse
for a day must go up, in the long run, as the gold
crown goes up.

Garrault, however, was something of a courtier,
and, in spite of the lucidity of his demonstration
of the inevitableness of a rise in prices when the
money was depreciated, he concludes by saying
that he does not at all mean to justify the public
in ignoring his majesty's ordinances in the
matter.   It was still, indeed, both their duty and
their interest to conform themselves to them.

There is one passage in his dissertation that
has a strikingly modern sound, and at the same
time that is of much importance for the information it contains.   After dwelling, according to the
fashion of the time, on the fact that the transactions
of Abraham with the Hittites, and of Tobit with
Gabel of Rages, were in silver by weight, he goes
on to observe that " the same principle," the
principle, that is to say, of the delivery and
receipt of money by weight, was acted on now—

at the time he wrote—by those public merchants who are called "banquiers," "*who make their payments and remittances of money to every place in marks, ounces, pennyweights and grains of gold*, reckoning so many coins to the mark of gold in accordance with the intrinsic value of these coins, and without paying any attention to their price, their nominal value (*estimation*), or their form." This surely goes a long way to make it clear that gold was as truly the international money of Europe in the sixteenth century as it is to-day.[1]

To return to the memorandum of the "Cour des Monnoyes," having described the nature of the disease, they next proceeded to prescribe the remedy. It was nothing else but this : to make an end, once for all, in all computations, of all mention of the sol and the livre, which had already become "imaginary money," and which were, moreover, continually varying in value, and to adopt in their place, as the standard of reckoning in every bargain and contract henceforth to be made in France, "the gold crown,[2] an unchanging money which now for a hundred years past, since it was first issued, had always

---

[1] The only early bills of exchange with regard to which information appears to be available are made payable in gold coin ; the silver exchange being also mentioned. See *Notes and Queries*, 9 S. v. iii.

[2] Le Blanc, *op. cit.*, p. 278.

remained, within a trifle, identical with itself in intrinsic value."

A royal edict gave effect to the recommendation.[1] "The only means of preventing in the future such monetary disorders as had ruled in the past," it set forth, "was to establish the value, price and estimation of everything on a solid foundation, firm and stable, and not variable . . . . . namely, on the Crown of the Sun, which has always remained sound and whole in its weight and standard without having up to the present ever suffered any alteration." The king promises at the same time, both for himself and his successors, "to maintain and preserve for ever the said crown at its present weight and standard," which were respectively 2 dwts. 15 grs., and 23 carats. This gold crown was to be worth 60 sols, and at the same time a silver piece of 15 sols, to be called the "*quart d'écu,*" was to be struck, to circulate along with it, and, as a matter of fact, was struck in 1580. Gold was then, in theory at any rate, taken as the basis of the monetary system, and silver was relegated to the second place.

The reform seemed a very promising one. How was it, it will be asked, that so little came of it? It was from the first a failure, as Le Blanc admits; and eventually in 1602 it was repealed

[1] *Op. cit.,* p. 282.

by Henry IV.'s government, and the reckoning in sols and livres was reverted to.

The reason of the failure is not indeed far to seek. The edict of 1577 is interesting now on account of its aim only. The most cursory glance at its wording is sufficient to show that it did not and could not carry out that aim. The memorandum of the " Cour des Monnoyes," after recommending the adoption of the crown as the standard of all computations, goes on to recommend that " nevertheless every debtor shall be held to have discharged his debt if, for each crown due to him, he shall pay 4 testons and 2 sols, or 3 francs of silver, or 60 sols in pieces of six-blancs, three-blancs or Karoluses." This recommendation—except indeed as regards the Karolus, a Netherlands coin—was embodied in the edict, and the result of course was to convert the whole measure from beginning to end into a solemn absurdity.[1] The government began by adopting the solid and unchanging gold crown as their standard money, and then went on to alter the meaning of the word " crown," making it signify not only so many grains of gold, but also so many testons or francs of silver, and even so many blancs of low billon. The edict thus became merely an edict to reduce the value of the crown from 65 sols to 60 sols, and, as might

---

[1] As in the Florentine measure of 1534. See *supra*, p. 70, footnote.

be expected, met with no better success than other similar edicts in the past had met with. It is true that some limitation was placed on the tender of the billon—a fact in itself of considerable historical interest—but, allowing for that, it remained the case that a debt the payment of which was specially stipulated in gold might, under the statute, be acquitted by the payment of the whole in silver, or, for that matter, of two-thirds in silver and one-third in billon. In such circumstances, it is abundantly plain that no adoption of a gold standard had taken place. The fact of the attempt at its adoption and the discussions that accompanied it are however, on that account, none the less interesting for the light that they throw on the relative positions of gold and silver in Europe at that date.

CHAPTER V

OUR survey of the state of things in England
and in Europe generally, as regards the monetary
circulation before the beginning of the eighteenth
century, has led us to the conclusion that even
then the first place has to be assigned to gold ;
that it was, even then, the principal medium of
foreign trade, and the true, though not the
popular, standard of values. If we may regard
that conclusion as at any rate provisionally
established, then the so-called transition of the
eighteenth century, completed in the nineteenth,
will have to be looked upon rather as the climax
of a series of events which brought the already
latent priority of gold out into the light of day,
and secured for it official recognition, than as an
event which, all at once, displaced silver from the
position of real money and set up gold in its

stead.   The true displacement of silver, I think, took place, not in the reign of Anne, but in the reign of Edward III.

Granting all this, we have still to ask : How was it that this priority of gold, if already latent, did not openly assert itself sooner, and what change of circumstances was it that led to its doing so eventually?   Our likeliest method of finding the clue to the solution of these questions will be by examining yet further the circumstances that attended the transition.

There are some of these circumstances which Lord Liverpool frankly owns himself altogether at a loss to explain, and which writers who have succeeded him have apparently failed to recognise as standing in need of explanation.   Lowndes tells us that in 1695 he had sample bags of the silver money then in circulation weighed, and that he found it, on the average, deficient in weight by about 47 per cent.   Five hundred and seventy-two bags, which ought to have weighed 221,418 oz., weighed only 113,771 oz.[1]   It must have been deficient in intrinsic value much more than this, as there appears to have been a considerable admixture of base money circulating with it.   Dryden, it may be remembered, found forty brass shillings among the money sent him on one occasion by his publisher.

[1] *Report on the Silver Coin*, p. 159.

In these circumstances,[1] as Lord Liverpool points out, "the price of silver bullion should have risen to about 10*s.* per ounce, and the guinea should have risen to nearly twice the value at which it had hitherto passed in currency, that is, to almost 44*s.*, but neither of these consequences happened. The price of silver in bullion rose to no more than 6*s.* 5*d.* per ounce, and the guinea rose only to the value of 30*s.*" 'It is true," he adds, "that the further rise of the guinea was prevented by orders given to the officers of the Exchequer and to the receivers of the public revenue not to receive it in payment at a higher rate, and, some time afterwards, the value of the guinea was still further limited by two Acts of Parliament," reducing it by similar orders, first to 26*s.*, and then to 22*s.* The problem remains to be solved, however: How was it that these orders to the receivers of the revenue exercised any control over the value of the guinea? At the time of the Bank restriction, the premium on gold was found to be something that it was entirely beyond the power of legislation to affect. In our day, it is a familiar enough fact that no internal legislation on the part of such states as Spain or Chili or the Argentine Republic—except, indeed, legislation to reduce their issues—could do anything to limit the

[1] *Coins of the Realm*, p. 77.

premium on their gold. Mr. McLeod appears to think that the English legislation had not, in reality, any effect on the value of the guinea, that what brought down its price was the substitution of the new full-weighted silver for the old. This however does not correspond with the facts. The recoinage was not completed for five years from its commencement in 1696; and the guinea was brought down, through all the successive stages mentioned, before the recoinage had fairly begun. The Acts of Parliament that Lord Liverpool refers to were, both of them, Acts of the 7th and 8th of William and Mary (1696–97); and there is not the smallest doubt that they were immediately effective What then is the explanation?

We know that, in Adam Smith's day, the light and worn silver was entirely dependent for its monetary value, which was quite double its intrinsic value, on the fact of the limitation of its quantity and the consequent convertibility of it at a fixed rate into guineas. The problems that puzzled Lord Liverpool become soluble if we suppose that this state of things was anticipated already in 1696, that the silver was, even then, dependent for the value that it possessed in the monetary circulation on its convertibility into gold. There can be no doubt indeed that it was already divorced from its bullion value, and that this divorce was due to the very same cause which recently brought about the divorce between the monetary value of the rupee in India and its bullion value, and which, in the eighteenth century, brought about the divorce between the monetary value of the light silver of Adam Smith's day and its bullion value—the fact, namely, that the mints were practically closed to its free coinage. In the cases of the silver of Adam Smith's day, and of the silver of 1696, no doubt the mints were not closed by statute, but they were quite as effectually closed, in both, by the existence of a ratio that would have made it a losing game to bring silver to be minted. The relations of value between the gold and the silver being thus already conventional, it becomes comprehensible how the legislature could control them. It must be remembered, again, that a reduction of 10 or 20 per cent. in the value of the guinea, as measured in the current silver, would be precisely the same thing as a rise of 10 or 20 per cent. in the value of this silver as measured in guineas. What then the Acts reducing the guinea—first to 26s. and then to 22s.—really did was, in truth, *not to pull down the guinea, but to raise the silver.* It was thus raised some 30 per cent. by two successive stages. The value of the gold was, in a very true sense, all the time, altogether immovable and unmoved. It was the real move in the value of the silver that caused an apparent move in the value of the gold.

These circumstances bring into prominence the central significance of one fact in connection with the relations of standard and subsidiary money which we shall find quite universally operative ; that is, the efficacy of receipt, at a given rate, of the two moneys, principal and subsidiary respectively, in the payment of taxes, in raising and, generally speaking, in controlling the value of the latter. Sir Dudley North, in 1696, was very much alive to the importance of receipt at the Exchequer as bearing on the character of the circulation. His suggested remedy for the deficiency of the silver coin was a simple one, and no doubt would have been an effective one. " Make it receivable only by weight," [1] he recommends, " in the payment of taxes." " If that were done," he says, "all men would refuse clipped money in common payments." [2]

He records too a fact of some significance in the present connection, the fact that the milled half-crowns, of which the edge was just clipped, would not pass current, while old hammered ones "clipped to the quick" would. This could have been due, I conceive, to no other cause except the usage of the receivers of the revenue in accepting the latter while they refused the former. What

---

[1] *Discourse on Trade*, p. 20.   [2] *Ibid*, p. 19.

precisely their rules and usages were and how, as the course of events developed, they were modified is a matter on which our information is deficient. Consequently there are several points in connection with the transition in regard to which hypothesis has to take the place of definite information. How was it for instance that the evils connected with the depreciation became all of a sudden acute in 1690 or thereabouts? Macaulay speaks of them as being the gradual growth of many years, and so no doubt in a sense they were. At the time of the recoinage not a shilling, it seems, of the milled money issued by Charles II. was in circulation. All the silver consisted of the hammered money of Charles I. and his predecessors. It is quite certain therefore that all through Charles II.'s reign the silver was already much below its statutory weight. That this was the case indeed is proved by an abundance of independent evidence. Even earlier, in 1626, Sir Robert Cotton says that it would have taken more than 65—instead of 62—of the shillings then current to make a pound sterling. At the same time it is certain that the lightness of the silver at the time of the Revolution was not producing the turmoil and confusion in trade that it produced very shortly afterwards.[1] " It all took place in three years," says Sir James Steuart.

[1] *Works*, vol. ii. p. 376.

"At the Revolution the guinea was 21s. 6d."
The silver then, he thinks, must have been of the
standard weight. That it certainly was not. At
the same time the public do not seem then to have
experienced any serious inconvenience from its
lightness. Its exchangeability for the gold appears
to have held it up for all the purposes of internal
trade. In Rushworth's day, though even then
light, it was occasionally at a small premium.[1]

There was one great difficulty connected with
the use of overrated silver in the seventeenth
century which was not to anything like the same
extent applicable to it in the eighteenth, and which
has not been so since, viz., the facility of imitation.
The illicit coinage of money, such as the old hammered money, did not present the same difficulties
to the coiner as the forging of the milled money
did, and of the milled money there was at the
Revolution, as we have seen, none in circulation.

It is possible that the activity of the coiners
may have forced on the receivers of the revenue,
about 1690, the adoption of fresh regulations or
practices in connection with the receipt of the
light money, as the result of which the proportion
of it which was refused at the Exchequer under-
went a great increase. If that were so then the
sudden rise of the guinea to 30s., and the sudden
confusion into which the whole internal trade of

[1] Lord Liverpool, *Coins of the Realm*, p. 62.

the country was thrown, would be quite explicable. Certain it is that the first Act passed in connection with the preparation for the recoinage was one to the effect that " all taxes and debts due to the Crown for excise, customs, &c., and the whole year's land tax might be paid to the collectors at any time before the 4th May, 1696, in the clipped coins, and that all loans of money borrowed on the authority of Parliament might also be paid in clipped coins, as if the same were good and lawful money, unless otherwise specially directed." [1] This Act appears to have at once completely rehabilitated the conventional value of the silver. It then became possible to bring down the guinea 30 per cent., or in other words to raise the silver in that same proportion. Probably the Act simply effected a return provisionally to the mint regulations that had been in force three years previously, when the guinea, as we are told, was still at 21s. 6d.

In connection with monetary questions which have recently emerged in America, the Monetary Commission of the Indianapolis Convention, following the lead of its most distinguished member, Professor Laughlin, has drawn attention to what it describes as the " quasi redemption " or " indirect redemption " of the silver money there by its receipt in payment of taxes in lieu

[1] Ruding, *op. cit.*, vol. ii. p. 400.

of gold, and at a fixed ratio to gold. Professor Laughlin himself, in his history of American Bimetallism, has occasion to remark that it has been a great puzzle to many people to understand how it was that the silver dollar and the silver certificates based on it, which were not redeemable in gold, were nevertheless maintained at par with United States notes which were.[1] It was such a puzzle indeed to the celebrated " Andy " Johnson that he regarded it, in anticipation, as something quite incredible—just as incredible, he said, as the discovery of the Philosopher's Stone. This raising, however, of the value of the subsidiary currency without any legal provision for its direct convertibility is now, in almost every country in the civilised world, a most conspicuous fact. Professor Laughlin's explanation of the phenomenon as applicable to the American silver and the silver certificates based on it is this : that the statute ordains that they shall be " receivable for customs, taxes and all public dues," and that this " quasi redemption " of silver in gold is effective in keeping the internal circulation at par with gold. It is that indeed which, at the present moment, keeps our shilling, which has not sixpence worth of silver in it, and which moreover is not legally redeemable in gold, up to its present value as the twentieth part of a sovereign. It is to the same fact that the

[1] *Hist. of Bimetallism in the United States*, p. 84.

maintenance of the value of the French five-franc piece, the Dutch guilder, and all the other over-rated silver of Europe and America, is due. In Turkey, owing to its influence, without any action on the part of the government of the country, except the cessation of coinage, the silver medjidie is maintained at par with the gold, its conventional value being thus raised to about double its intrinsic value.

It seems indeed that it is not possible to provide an unlimited or practically unlimited outlet for any article at one price immovably fixed, no matter how worthless the article may be in itself, without at once making it suitable to serve as currency. Postage stamps are an instance in point. For some reasons, real or fanciful, it is thought undesirable to encourage their use as small money, and so artificial difficulties have to be created to prevent it. The reason for their suitability for currency is of course this, that they too are, in a sense, redeemable in gold ; not indeed in actual gold, but in services that are indispensable to every one, and for which the fixed gold price that is charged is by every one readily paid.

When we find a principle so conspicuous in its operation at the present day, we may be sure that, if we look for it, we shall find it also widely operative in history. We find in it indeed the explanation of the stealthy and surreptitious character that has ordinarily marked the progress of historical depreciations. They have probably been universally, in the first instance, up to a certain point, successful, and, for a time also, free from effects that were obviously injurious. Why, indeed, should they not be so? Working under scientific conditions, we in England were able in 1816 to effect a depreciation of our shilling—to coin sixty-six of them to the pound instead of sixty-two as formerly—without any one having been, either sooner or later, in the least the worse for it. If Charles I. had ordered such an increase —as indeed he did, though the order was subsequently rescinded—we should have reckoned the step as among the universally condemned depreciations of history.

What is technically a depreciation of the currency, thus we see may, in the nature of things, be both successful and innocuous. The prince or the government, however, which has effected the depreciation, having thus made some money easily and without apparent bad results, ordinarily goes on to argue, as Oresme puts it, that if, by one change in his money, he can make a certain profit, by parity of reasoning he ought to be able by a second and greater change to make a still greater profit, and so on *ad libitum*. When this sort of reasoning is put into practice, the scheme necessarily in the end breaks down, and the trade of the country is thrown into confusion. The break-down may come from more than one cause. Most frequently no doubt it has come from the cause suggested, the over-issue of his money by the prince himself. The meaning of over-issue, in the last resort, is the issue of a greater quantity of subsidiary money than that for which there is in the normal course of things an outlet in the payment of taxes. The supply being greater than the demand, or the "vent" as the older writers graphically express it, the value is no longer maintained. The money accumulates in the hands of traders, and not being available for use abroad, people become willing to give more of it than the statutory quantity for such money as is available for use abroad, say for gold bullion. Thereupon follow the general rise of prices and all the familiar phenomena of a depreciation.

It may be, however, that the state has become too experienced and too wise to tolerate over-issues of such money. The English nation had become so by the close of Elizabeth's reign. Still the situation may not be free from danger. If a large margin is left between the nominal and the real value of the subsidiary money, then the illicit coiner may come in with the anticipation of reaping his share of the profit, and he thus may unduly increase the issues. The real risk, thus

again, comes from the production of an excessive
quantity of the conventional money. Let the
quantity be kept within such bounds that the
amount issued will not bear an undue proportion
to that which the community require for the payment of custom dues and other taxes, and there
will be no fall in its value.

The introduction of the milled money was therefore a most important preparatory step towards
the establishment of the modern system. It
would have been of little avail for the government
to restrain its issues, so long as the coiners could
practically enlarge them without limit. The recoinage of 1696 did not do all that has been
claimed for it. It did not prevent the silver from
becoming again, in a very few years time, as
light as it had been before the Revolution ; but
it effected an alteration of great practical moment
in substituting for the money formerly in use a
description of money which it was very much
more difficult to imitate. The shillings and sixpences that were current in Lord Liverpool's day
often bore hardly any impression. Both the
king's head and the coat of arms on the reverse
were, in many cases, almost completely worn
away. Lord Liverpool believed that coins like
them could be, and probably were, made in any
quantity in Birmingham. In that there is no
doubt he was wrong. If they had been largely

counterfeited, they would never have become so scarce as they did undoubtedly become. He tells us himself that they were, in spite of their lightness, now and then at a small premium. Sir James Steuart, and Harris, the master of the mint and the author of the *Essay on Coins*, investigated the question with some care, and both came to the conclusion that there was little or no counterfeit silver current. Harris had a considerable quantity of it assayed, and found that its composition corresponded so precisely with the mint standard as to negative the supposition of counterfeiting. Sir James Steuart[1] gives us an interesting account of the tests to which he subjected it. " I put a handful of the coins," he says, " into a coal fire, and taking them out when red hot and throwing them on the hearth, I plainly discovered on many of them some part of the arms of Great Britain appearing in the cross upon the reverse, in a different colour from the ground of the coin. In others indeed nothing could be seen. This was owing to the degree of wearing. How then can any die strike an impression upon a coin that will answer all these appearances? I communicated to Mr. Harris the trials I had made and he was perfectly satisfied, upon the whole, that no shilling had ever been counterfeited at Birmingham."

[1] Works, vol. iii. p 133, footnote.

The opinion of Mr. Bagehot that the attempt
to maintain the rupee at a conventional value in
India must fail, an opinion which has now been
so signally falsified by the course of events, rested
on the belief that illicit coinage would render any
effective limitation of the quantity of the currency
impossible. If it paid, he urged, to forge coins
of the same quality of silver as those which the
state issued, nothing could prevent the whole
coinage coming down very shortly to its bullion
value ; and he was fully satisfied that it would
pay to forge, if any considerable margin was left
between the monetary and the bullion value.
Experience, however, has now proved abundantly
that the state, under modern conditions, can
exercise a much more effective control in this
matter than had been anticipated.

When the old hammered money was in use,
any one individual if moderately ingenious could,
working on his own account, manufacture passable
imitations of the current coins. Now, considerable capital is needed for the enterprise.
Expensive machinery has to be purchased, and
there must therefore be the prospect of issuing a
large amount of coins before it will pay to
purchase it. The industry is thus handicapped
by the fact that capitalists have usually a healthy
dread of spending some years out of their lives in
gaol. The machinery too is noisy, and the risk

of detection is thus greatly increased. At any rate, when we ask why was it that the modern system of gold monometallism with silver as manifest subsidiary money did not establish itself anywhere in the world before the beginning of the eighteenth century, although gold had for long already been the principal medium of commerce, we have one patent reason in the fact that the introduction of the mill had not before that date come in to make the counterfeiting of the coinage on a large scale practically impossible.

Another obstacle which, in the seventeenth century and the centuries that preceded it, stood in the way of the emergence of our modern system was the fact of the circulation, ordinarily at tariffed rates, within every European country, of the coins of every other. Certainly, as long as foreign silver circulated freely along with our own, it would have been quite impossible for us to have controlled absolutely, as we do now, the amount of the silver in circulation ; and foreign coins circulated and were tariffed in England even as late as the middle of Charles II.'s reign. By the time of the Revolution, however, Lowndes [1] tells us, there were none in circulation. The abolition of seigniorage by the 18th of Charles II., together with the existence of unfavourable

[1] *Report on the Silver Coin*, p. 76.

tariffs, brought all such coins to the mint, or in one way or another caused their disappearance.

These indeed were but secondary causes. The true root cause was to be found in the gradual growth of wiser counsels and truer economical conceptions. The earlier practice of European governments had frequently been to tariff the coins of their neighbours at more favourable rates even than their own, in order to draw them into their territories, their one idea being the acquisition of as much treasure as possible. Few or none of the economists of that epoch thought of calling in question the desirability of the end to be achieved, but many of them pointed out that the encouragement of the circulation of foreign coins was not the way to achieve it. Mun,[1] for instance, pointed out that if the advantage given were a decided one the foreign coins would, under the operation of what is nowadays called Gresham's Law, 'carry away all our sterling money." If the advantage were not great enough to do this, it would be ineffective either way. He thought it worth while also to observe that it was unfair to foreigners to put high tariffs on their coins. It was a breach of " the laws of intercourse," and if we did it they could do it as well.

The discussion throws an interesting light on

[1] *England's Treasure in Forraigne Trade*, p. 45.

the mode of viewing such questions then in vogue. Mun and the rest of the mercantile school were of course never tired of pointing out that "all the ways that force treasure into a kingdom do not make it ours," and consequently do not make it stay there. The only way, they contended, for the nation to grow richer, to acquire in the aggregate a greater command of treasure, was to spend less than its income, to sell more to the foreigner than it bought from him for its own consumption. If the nation did that it might keep its mind at ease, the balance must in the long run come in in treasure ; and that doctrine, in spite of the issues with which it is complicated nowadays by the phenomena of the movements of accumulated capital, contains an impregnable truth, and one moreover which is as fully alive and operative in the councils of the world at the present moment as it was in the seventeenth century.

There was yet another and indeed much more important way in which the gradual growth of sound opinion prepared the way for the modern system and made its eventual adoption inevitable. The English nation at the close of the seventeenth century had not learnt, it is true, the right remedy for the monetary confusion of the preceding epoch. They had however gone a long way towards learning what suggested remedies were false and mischievous. The minting of sixty-two instead of sixty shillings from the pound of standard silver, ordained by the 43rd of Elizabeth makes the last of the series of depreciations that had brought down the pound sterling to one-third of its original weight. When, in the early part of Charles I.'s reign, the maintenance of a rate favourable to gold had caused the heaviest of the silver to be culled out and melted down, the proposal was made to coin seventy shillings to the pound sterling. It was however vigorously, and, as it turned out, successfully assailed by Sir Robert Cotton. Seventy years later, a similar proposal gave rise to the famous controversy between Locke and Lowndes, in which happily Locke's principles triumphed.

It would be a mistake, at the same time, to assume that Locke was altogether and unquestionably in the right, and that Lowndes was altogether in the wrong. The same problem, whether, in effecting the readjustment of a depreciated currency, we ought to go back to the original value of the currency before the depreciation began, which was Locke's view, or whether we should adopt the market rate of the day as the basis of the readjustment, which was Lowndes's, has come up on many occasions since in monetary history, and it has not always been Locke's principle that has been followed.   In recent years, for instance, in India, we have not endeavoured to reinstate the rupee at its original value, but have instead maintained it at the market value of the day.

It was, indeed, it may be said, in a manner by accident that Locke's principles led up to a satisfactory result.   They certainly would not have done so if at the same time the necessity of maintaining a ratio which was decidedly favourable to gold had not also, by that date, strongly impressed itself on the mind of the nation.   We saw Charles I.'s Council, in 1626, showing itself much alive to this necessity.   Not only must their ratio, they said, be such as would keep the gold in the country while things remained in *statu quo*, but it must also be such as would prevent it from being transported "by any sudden occasion beyond seas."   The same consideration undoubtedly weighed with Sir Isaac Newton in the final rating of the guinea at 21s. in 1717. The heavier silver was found to be leaving the country.   The subject was referred to Newton, then master of the mint, and he reported "that the principal cause of the exportation was that the guinea, which then passed at 21s. 6d., was generally worth no more than 20s. 8d., according to the relative value of gold and silver at the market."   He thus acknowledged that 10d. or 12d. ought to be taken from it "in order that gold might bear the same proportion with the silver money in England which it ought to have done by the course of trade and exchange in Europe." He did not however recommend taking 10*d.* or 12*d.* off it, but only 6*d.* "That great man,"[1] as Lord Liverpool remarks, "appears to have been apprised of the fluctuation which frequently happens in the relative value of the precious metals, and he was probably apprehensive that if the rate at which the gold coins were to pass had then been reduced in full proportion compared with the value of the silver coin, there would be the greatest danger that these gold coins, which were at the time almost the only instrument of commerce remaining in the kingdom, might in their turn be melted down and exported." Our greatest theoretical man of genius thus showed himself a true Englishman in his dread of too complete subservience to theory.[2]

---

[1] *Coins of the Realm,* p. 83.

[2] Similarly, the committee of 1798, on whose recommendation the guinea was reduced from 22s. to 21s. 6d., and of which it is interesting to note that Locke was a member, expressed themselves in the following terms : "That the bringing down of the guinea to 21s. 6d. would make the value of our gold coin very near as $15\frac{1}{3}$ to 1 in proportion to the rate of our silver money, which, though not quite so low as in Holland, would be sufficient to correct the error" (Ruding, ii. p. 427). Similarly also, in France, in 1641, Louis XIII.'s government, having ascertained that the German and Italian ratio was 12 to 1, the Flemish and Dutch $12\frac{1}{2}$ to 1, the English $13\frac{1}{4}$ to 1, and the Spanish $13\frac{1}{3}$ to 1, made their own $13\frac{1}{2}$ to 1 (Le Blanc, *op. cit.,* p. 307).

If the ratio was to be maintained at a figure rather more favourable to gold than the respective value of the metals elsewhere in Europe warranted, and if, at the same time, the lesson that there must be no more depreciation of the silver was at last fairly learnt, nothing else could result but that which did result, that the country should make shift as best it could to carry on its wage payments and retail trade with what remained of the silver, no matter how light or scarce it became, leaving to gold, which, with increasing wealth, flowed in in ever larger measure, not only the settlement of international balances but the internal wholesale trade as well. This makeshift position, as we know, lasted for about a century, and fortunate it was for us that it did so. It gave time for monetary theory gradually to adjust itself to facts as they stood.

Adam Smith,[1] if he failed to recognise that gold was already the true standard, recognised at any rate that, in substance, it was the regulating metal. He even suggested Lord Liverpool's reform, of rating the silver above its value and limiting its legal tender power.[2]

We find Sir James Steuart, too, in spite of his vigorous advocacy of monetary reform on bi-metallic or symmetallic lines, recognising that

[1] *Op. cit.*, vol. i. p. 58 (B. 1, chap. v.).
[2] *Op. cit.*, vol. i. p. 58 (B. 1, chap. v.).

the shilling and sixpence had become " nothing else but tokens." [1]

It was of no small importance in connection with the development of scientific legislation with regard to the silver that the country had become already accustomed to the conception of " token " money in connection with the copper. If copper coin could circulate without inconvenience as tokens, the inquiry became an inevitable one—why should not silver ones ? It seems to us so obvious now that copper can thus circulate innocuously, that we are liable to forget that it was not so always. The truth is that the admission of copper to the well defined position which it now occupies in our monetary system was, in the days of Smith and Steuart, of very recent occurrence indeed.

The echoes of the controversy over "Wood's halfpence " had then hardly died away. It is probable enough that Swift himself knew very well that he was talking nonsense when he described the attempt to put into circulation some 40,000l. worth of copper in halfpence, at twice or three times its intrinsic value, as an attempt to turn Ireland " into one large poorhouse," to lay its " cities and churches in ruins," and to make it a " desert for wild beasts and robbers." The surprising thing is that his eloquence, instead of provoking general amusement, raised

[1] Works, vol. iii. p. 130.

him to an extraordinary height of popularity, and caused him to be regarded, even by many sane and clear-headed people, as the saviour of his country. It is all the more surprising in view of the fact that the money was the best copper money that had up to that date been issued in the country, and, strangest of all, that there was no forced currency in connection with it. Every one was at liberty to take the half-pence or refuse them as they pleased.

Swift owed the success of his agitation in part no doubt to the eagerness of the Irish and Anglo-Irish, at the time, to find anything in the nature of a grievance against the English government. In part however also he owed it to the ancient and deep-rooted sentiment that condemned the use by the state of anything but the precious metals as money.

The urgent need for some smaller change than the silver penny had caused, at an early date, a circulation of private tokens of some inferior metal. Such tokens were no doubt the *plumbeos Angliae* to which Erasmus alludes. They are known to have circulated as early as the days of Henry VII. Various ordinances forbidding their manufacture and use were, from time to time, issued, but, as they supplied a want that was very urgently felt, they had in practice to be tolerated. Like paper money in the seventeenth and

eighteenth centuries, and like coined money itself
—as M. Babelon thinks—in Greece and in Lydia
before 700 B.C., they had their origin in private
enterprise, and only in the second instance was it
that they were taken over by the state.

In 1574[1] the question of taking them over was
for the first time seriously considered by Elizabeth's government.   An issue of billon was
proposed, but the "Queen would by no means
give ear to embasing the coins again," An issue
of copper tokens, or "pledges" as they were
called, was decided upon, and was arranged for
in all its details.   Nothing came of it in the end.
Probably the government dropped the project
from the fear of popular prejudice. The city of
Bristol however was authorised to supply its own
requirements in the matter.

In 1613[2] the first patent for the authorised
issue of tokens was granted. They were of a
distinctly fiduciary character. Provisions that
seem adequate were made for their redemption in
sterling money, and their tender was limited to
2d. Still it turned out that the dangers anticipated in connection with the project were not
altogether imaginary. Though the tender was
limited, the far more important provision of
carefully limiting the quantity issued was not

[1] Ruding, *Annals of the Coinage*, vol. ii. p. 161.
[2] *Op. cit.*, vol. ii. p. 210.

understood. On the contrary, the patentees were allowed to resort to the practice of selling 21s. worth of the tokens for 20s. A class of middlemen at once sprang up who made it their business to buy them at the smaller figure, and to push them into circulation, whenever they could, at the greater, and thus the labouring classes appear to have been, to a large extent, practically forced to take them in considerable sums in payment of their wages. In 1644, we are told " that there was no change for the farthings." The patentees would take back none that could not be clearly shown not to be counterfeited, and there was often great difficulty in demonstrating this. Rumours too that they were about to be decried caused great consternation among the poor. The city of London and the home counties were " mightily pestered with them," so much so " that in many places there was no silver or gold coin left, but all were farthing tokens." Here indeed we have all the phenomena of a serious depreciation.

In 1665[1] an issue of tokens was made which became famous as " Lord Lucas's farthings." They bore the curious inscription on the reverse, " *Quatuor Maria Vindico.*" Lord Lucas had occasion to make a speech in the House of Lords on the evil state of the times, especially as regarded

[1] Ruding, *op. cit.*, vol. ii. p. 338.

the scarcity of money. " The milled money
issued by his Majesty," he said, "had all
disappeared ; nothing was left for common use
but a little lean coined money of the late three
former princes. And what supply," he asked, " is
preparing for it my lords ? I hear of none,
unless it be of copper farthings ! And this is the
metal that is to vindicate, according to the inscription on it, the dominion of the four seas." Lord
Lucas's speech was burnt by the hand of the
common hangman ; but " *Quatuor Maria Vindico* "
did not appear on the next issue of farthings.

The first remedy that suggested itself for the
evils above described in connection with the
copper issue was, as might have been expected,
to bring up the weight of the metal, when coined,
to its intrinsic value ; and this was actually done
with regard to the issue of 1672.[1] That system,
however, did not last long. Twelve years later
we find tin halfpence issued, on which there was a
profit of 40 per cent.

The evils appear gradually to have cured
themselves. During the eighteenth century, in
England, we hear of no serious trouble in connection with the matter. The temptations to
over-issue ceased with the cessation of the system
of granting a monopoly to patentees, and once
the danger of over-issue was done away with,

[1] Ruding, *op. cit.*, vol. ii. p. 344.

the copper, though issued much above its intrinsic value, readily circulated at par with the gold and silver. Thus, by Lord Liverpool's, time the problem of establishing a well regulated subsidiary coinage of silver was already half solved by the solution of the same problem with regard to the copper.

CHAPTER VI

In the historical chapters that have preceded, the facts brought to light have not been drawn from any recondite source. Most of them indeed must have been already familiar to many of my readers. At the same time, their significance has undoubtedly been very generally missed. There is no English writer, so far as I am aware, who does not take it for granted, without further inquiry, that silver was the standard money both of England and of all Europe up to the beginning of the eighteenth century. In France the case is somewhat different. M. de Vienne, one of whose brochures has already been mentioned, points out that ever since the fourteenth century "gold is employed in all those payments in which transmission to considerable distances is necessary, in international treaties, in the ransoms of nobles, the dowries and jointures of princesses, and the

purchase of territories."[1]   Gold thus became, he
thinks, "the international metal"—a fact which,
as he says, "secures for it a stability that silver
did not then possess, and creates in its favour a
veritable monopoly.   Thanks to this fixity of
value, gold becomes, for the great families and
for those who essay to imitate them, the *réserve
mobilière* destined to meet all important contingencies. . . . Gold is the only metal in question
in heritages and in partitions of landed estates.
It is the sole constituent in the fortunes of ladies
of high degree.   It alone is used in challenges,
in wagers and in loans."

While however M. de Vienne thus points out
the importance of the part played by gold at these
periods, I do not understand that he would admit
that it would be accurate to describe it as having
then become, strictly speaking, the standard metal
either of France or of England.   He holds to the
principle that that medium and that medium
only, in which computations are generally made
can rightly be described as the standard.

This principle at first sight seems an obvious
one.   If, however, we endeavour to adhere to it
rigidly it will not fail to land us in difficulties.
The medium in which computations are generally
made will undoubtedly, in any age and country, be

---

[1] *Des Anciens Prix et des difficultés inhérentes à leur évaluation
actuelle*, p. 28.

the popular standard, but it seems necessary to recognise the fact that it may not for all that be the true standard.

In our own experience, in England, we had for a time a popular standard in operation which every one now admits to have been not the true standard.   When the Bank of England was "restricted" from cashing its notes in 1797, it for some years managed its issues with much care and much wisdom.   No gold was in circulation, but gold for transmission to foreign countries could be bought with Bank of England notes at figures that varied very little from its mint price. Gradually however the issues augmented and the variation grew.   The market price of gold in 1810 went up to £4 12s. per ounce.   The House of Commons however, as we know, in that year passed a resolution, by a majority of over two to one, asserting that the rise in gold was not, as Ricardo and the Bullion Committee asserted that it was, due to the over-issue of the notes.   Their resolution was based on the assumption that these notes were the real standard of value in the country, and that the gold, as measured in them, might fluctuate precisely as any other commodity might.   The idea, no doubt, was a "fantastic" one, as Fox remarked, that printed promises to pay gold could serve as a standard by which the value of gold itself could be measured.   People however had come to think in notes as money, and if the fact that the bulk of the community thinks in any given medium as its standard is to be taken as an infallible proof that that medium is really its standard, then Vansittart was right, and the notes, not the gold, were the standard of England in 1810.

The co-existence of a popular but illusory standard with an unseen but real one was strikingly brought out in connection with the currency of the island of Java, in the evidence given before the Herschell Committee[1] in 1892. Java, with its mother country Holland, had then been on a gold basis for more than twenty years past; yet this is the account which a Mr. Kensington, an Anglo-Indian gentleman, who had recently visited the island, gives of his experiences there. He had been told that, though the country was a gold standard country, the people there neither knew nor saw anything of gold; so from curiosity he obtained a few ten-guilder gold pieces, the legal tender of the island, and proceeded to experiment with them. He found that they were accepted at railway stations without demur, that they were accepted, but with exclamations of astonishment, at a Dutch shop in the principal street of Batavia, and that they were altogether declined at a bazaar 200 miles up country. It

[1] See Question 1,425.

seemed clear to him that "the great mass of
the people neither knew nor felt the existence
of the gold standard in any way." Was the
gold standard in Java therefore nominal and
meaningless? Assuredly it was not. The
whole character, not only of the internal and
external trade, but of the internal currency as
well, was revolutionised by it, though the majority
of the people who used it were quite unaware
of the fact. It saved the country from the
trouble, the anxiety, and the disastrous loss
which the depreciating rupee entailed on India.;
while the peasant and the wage-earner could
lay aside their savings in the ordinary currency
of the country, with the same security against
its value becoming a vanishing quantity as the
labourer in Sussex or Middlesex, who lays aside
his savings in sovereigns, is entitled to feel.

In an early chapter I had occasion to allude
to Harris's contention that in England in his
time, the middle of the eighteenth century,
silver was still the standard of values.[1]   " Make
what laws you please," he said, " the money in
which wages are paid, and in which consequently
retail purchases are made, will always be the true
measure of values." The argument has a convincing sound, yet we know that gold was
already the unquestionable standard in Harris's

[1] *Essay on Coins*, part ii. p. 94.

day.   Where then does the flaw in his reasoning
lie?   Unquestionably he was so far in the
right that the silver in his time was, in the
conception of the great bulk of those who used
it, still the measure of value.   It was *their*
measure of value at all events, and if they were
the majority why was it not beyond question
the real and undoubted measure of value for the
country generally?   Simply for this reason, that
its own value was entirely dependent on its
relation to something else.   The shilling was
maintained steadily as the twenty-first part of
the guinea, though intrinsically only worth
some amount that varied between the twenty-
fifth and the fiftieth part of it, solely because it
was always possible to get a guinea in exchange for
twenty-one shillings.   It is because silver possesses
a derivative value only that at the present
moment no one reckons it the standard money,
and the case was precisely the same in Harris's day.

We see thus that the process of counting noses
is one that is quite irrelevant in regard to questions of currency.   Money is not a phenomenon
that illustrates the democratic idea.   Rather
indeed it seems to be one that illustrates the
"great man" theory.   The large dealers, who
accept no money without having regard to its
intrinsic value, are, as Sir James Steuart says,[1]

[1] Works, vol. ii. p. 372.

those who "regulate prices and so determine all values." It might thus very well be the case that, for the innumerable millions of India, the rupee was "the one fixed point in their universe," and that the gold which they bought in the bazaars was something that, in their eyes, fluctuated in value from day to day, like wheat or like cotton shirtings. That might certainly be so, and yet the whole appearance might be a mere illusion. The true fixed point might still be the gold ; and the fancied fluctuations in this gold might be due to nothing else but the real fluctuations in the silver, just as the apparent motion of the trees that fly past us as we sit in the railway carriage is due to no alteration in their own position, but to the real movement of ourselves.

Mr. Bagehot has occasion to remark, in a passage in *Lombard Street*[1] on a fact that is familiar enough to us all in the practical world, though it has not assumed as yet the position that its importance warrants in the theoretical treatment of the subject, the fact, viz., that it is virtually in the wholesale trade alone that prices are really fixed ; or, as Sir James Steuart puts it, that it is the large dealer who really determines all values. The retail seller, as a rule, as Mr. Bagehot remarks, merely takes the prices as they reach him, and

[1] *Lombard Street*, p. 138.

adds a uniform percentage. Where that is so
—and it may be said to be so universally—it is
evident that the medium of wholesale transactions,
whatever it may be, must become the real measure
of values. There may, then, in any given country,
be one metal everywhere in evidence, the
medium of retail and internal trade, and another
little seen except by the large dealers, the
medium of external and wholesale trade ; and yet
the money everywhere in evidence may be token
money, while the money that is hardly visible
may be the true and only standard of values.

We found Garrault in the sixteenth century
very much alive to this truth of the differentiation
of traffic and of money into two branches, the
régnicolle, and the *étranger*.[1] It formed the basis
of all his arguments for the adoption of the
gold crown as the official standard in his age.
Among modern writers, Tooke is the one who has
dwelt most upon the same truth, and made most use
of it. He points out,[2] for instance, with regard to
large bank notes and small, that their functions are
altogether different. Large bank notes do not
circulate at all from hand to hand as small ones
do. They cannot properly be regarded as currency. If they were done away with by legisla-

---

[1] Garrault, *Recueil des Avis, &c.*, A iiii–B. ‹
[2] *Enquiry into the Currency Principle*, pp. 21, 27,

tion, it is not by metallic currency that their place
would be taken, but by bills of exchange. This
difference is due to the fact that large payments
are as a rule the payments of trade, while small
payments are the payments of consumption.

Tooke quotes too a significant passage from
Adam Smith bearing on the point.[1] " The circulation of every country," says Smith, " may be
considered as divided into two branches—the
circulation of the dealers with one another, and
the circulation between the dealers and the consumers." " The circulation between the dealers,"
he goes on to say, " as it is carried on by wholesale,
requires generally a pretty large sum for each particular transaction ; that between the dealers and
the consumers, on the contrary, as it is generally
carried on by retail, frequently requires but very
small ones." There is thus a difference between
large and small payments, that is, in the main, not
one of degree only, but also one of kind, and it
is in the distinction, and at the same time in the
interaction between the two that we have to
look for the true theory of the standard.

It may perhaps be possible to assist the imagination of my reader by a diagram illustrative
of the course of the wholesale and retail circulation. I must only premise, as Sir Michael
Foster does of his diagram in the science primer

[1] *Wealth of Nations*, Book II. chap ii. ed. 1811, vol. ii. p. 71.

on physiology illustrating the circulation of the blood, that it is intended to be a diagram, not a picture.

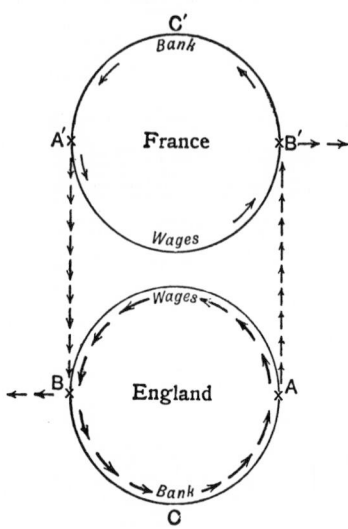

If we look generally at the trade and commerce of two countries, say of England and of France, we see at once that the internal currencies of each country make their rounds continually within the bounds of each, while the goods imported by the one from the other are, very often at any rate, paid for by the goods that it exports to the other. For the present let us confine ourselves to the consideration of the case in which this is so. Let the upper circle be taken to represent the

internal currency of France, the lower the
internal currency of England. The arrows on
the right pointing upwards represent the stream of
commodities passing from England to France,
balanced by the stream from France to England,
represented by the downward arrows on the left.
Starting with the French stream, consisting perhaps of silk, wine, gloves, etc., we find it pass
into the English retail market at B, after being
subjected to more or less manipulation in England.
There it is taken up by the demand stream of
currency, nine-tenths or more of which consists of
wages, which is represented as circling round
within English territory. The imported commodities are exchanged at B for the currency, and
pass off into consumption. They are represented
by the arrows that shoot out leftwards, indicating
that they have passed finally out of the sphere of
our diagram. The stream of currency thus exchanged for the retail commodities takes its circulating path onwards, not however without having
undergone an important modification in its character. As the takings of shopkeepers and so on,
it is now no longer in driblets, but in considerable
sums—twenties, fifties, and hundreds of pounds
sterling ; and, in that shape, it passes into the
banks, and swells for the time being the amount
of the reserves. It would perhaps be not altogether fanciful to say that, whereas the circulation,

before passing through the retail market, was venous, it has now become arterial.

We have now the currency in the banks. The question is, what becomes of it next, how does it find its way into the retail markets again? The stream of imports from France (A' to B) is, as explained above, supposed to be balanced by the stream of exports to France (A to B'). Let us suppose the factories, mines, etc., where the English exports are produced to be concentrated at the point A, which we will call the English export produce market, situated on the right hand of the lower circle. The stream of currency is next used to finance all this production. The manufacturers and the colliery companies, say, turn out so many yards of shirtings, worth, at the current market rate, so much per yard, and so many tons of coal, similarly worth so much per ton. For every hundred pounds' worth that they send to France, let us suppose that they draw a bill on their French correspondents for £100. These bills they sell to the banks for gold, or notes, or small change, the very same gold, notes, or small change—supposing the amount of the reserves to remain approximately unaltered—that we have seen the retail shopkeepers deposit there. The main use that the manufacturer or the mining capitalist has to make of this gold and these notes is to pay the wages of future production. Thus

the currency becomes venous again.   It is recon-
verted into driblets, and in driblets it finds its way,
mainly through the channel of wages, into the
retail market, to be again consolidated into
balances at the banks, and again to buy bills of
exchange, and yet again to be converted into
wages, and so on *ad infinitum.*

There are some aspects of the circulation of
course that it is not possible to make the diagram
represent or even indicate.   So far it is not made
clear how the cycle of exchanges between the two
countries is completed.   We have left the bills
drawn against the stream of English exports in
the hands of the bank at C.   If we suppose a
similar amount of bills drawn against the French
exports to be in the hands of the French bank at
C', and the two banks to have a subterranean connection corresponding to the post office, along
which the two streams of bills are continually in
transit each way, parallel to the two streams of
commodities, we are able in some imperfect
fashion to picture to ourselves the system under
which, in the modern world, commodities pay for
commodities, while the currency of each country
makes its endless rounds within its own territory.

It need hardly be said that the England and
France of the diagram represent a purely ideal
England and France, and that their relations in
the real world are vastly more complex.   Account

is only taken, in the first place, of the movements of commodities supposed to balance each other, and none whatever is taken of the movements of accumulated capital.   In the second place, in the real world it is never a case of two countries trading with each other only that we have to deal with, but of each trading with all or most of the other countries of the world ; and in addition to this the wholesale and retail trades of each centre within a country must be regarded as typified by the international and internal trades of the countries themselves.

Allowing for all this, however, I think that the view presented of the wholesale and retail circulation is calculated to bring home to us the conception of it as possessing a greater degree of organic regularity than we might have been prepared to anticipate.   There does not appear to be any place whatever in it for those alleged variations in the rapidity of circulation which are described by Mill and others as playing so important a part in connection with the determination of prices.   The pace of the circulation on the contrary appears to be determined mainly by the periods of wage payments, and that certainly does not vary between good times and bad. The essential difference between the two is not that the currency is circulating more quickly in the former than in the latter, but that there is, at any given moment, more of it in circulation, that the rate of wages being higher and the demand for labour less limited, the amount of gold and notes and small change in the hands of the spending classes is for the time being increased.

This theory of the rapidity of circulation is one which, it seems to me, by bringing in a fictitious cause to account for certain of the phenomena of money and prices, tends to obscure our view of the causes that really explain them.   It may be as well perhaps therefore at this stage to scruti- nise it somewhat more minutely.   " The value of money," [1] says Mill, " is, the amount of goods and transactions being the same, inversely as its quan- tity multiplied by the rapidity of its circulation." Elsewhere he tells us that it is inversely as its quantity simply ; and that, it seems clear, is the precise truth.   If, for example, we suppose the amount of goods to be a hundred quarters of wheat, the smaller the quantity of coin that will buy this hundred quarters the cheaper the wheat must be ; or, in other words, the greater must be the value of the coin in relation to it.   If 150 sovereigns will buy it, the value of a sovereign in relation to it will necessarily be greater than it would be if it took 170 sovereigns to buy it, and still greater than if it took 200 sovereigns to buy

---

[1] J. S. Mill, *Pol. Econ.*, People's ed., p. 300. Cf. p. 299 : "The value of money. . . . varies inversely as its quantity."

it. If you suppose the coin required to be increased, then precisely in the proportion that you increase it, must you suppose its value to be diminished. What then can be the meaning of the additional qualification, "multiplied by the rapidity of its circulation"? The value of money cannot both be inversely as its quantity simply, and inversely as its quantity multiplied by some indefinite numeral that may be anything from two to infinity. Again, we are told that "each pound or dollar must be counted for as many pounds or dollars as the number of times it changes hands" in order to buy the goods in a given market.[1] It is not of course intended to be asserted that a pound which has changed or is about to change hands fifty times in a week is worth fifty pounds, while a pound that has made, or is about to make, only one purchase in the same time is worth only one pound. If not this, however, it is not easy to discover what is intended to be asserted. The truth is there is no analogy whatever between variations in the power of simultaneous purchase on which variations in value depend and variations in respect of the fact of being about to make, or in the respect of the fact of having made successive purchases. If a pound or a million pounds could buy more of everything purchasable at one *coup* to-day than it could yesterday, then plainly it

[1] J. S. Mill, *op. cit.*, p. 300.

would be more valuable to-day than it was yesterday; but if it only buys more because it has been used in a greater number of exchanges, it is surely plain enough that that has nothing to do with its value. A foot rule is not more than a foot because you have measured a mile with it in instalments. "Two eggs are not three because there be one and there be twain."

Mr. Mill himself discerns some weakness in the theory. The phrase "rapidity of circulation," he says, requires some comment. It must not be understood to mean the number of purchases made by the money in a given time,[1] but the "number of purchases made by any given sum to effect a given pecuniary amount of transactions." Let us try this revised version by a concrete instance : say that the sum that is supposed to make the purchases is £1, and that the given pecuniary amount of transactions is £10. Is it not plain that the number of purchases that that pound must make to effect that amount of transactions will, in all possible circumstances, be neither more nor less than ten? The rapidity of circulation, under this new definition, is something that absolutely cannot vary. If the pound had changed hands eleven times, then the value of the goods that it would have bought in successive purchases would have been £11. By no sort of

[1] *Op. cit.*, p. 301.

twisting and turning can any valid signification whatever be attached to the theory.

It owes its origin, I imagine, to Locke. " There must be," he remarks,[1] " some proportion between money and trade, but what that proportion is it is hard to determine, because it depends not barely on the quantity of money, but the quickness of its circulation." Make the circulation more rapid, therefore, and by that means the money of the country will be made to go further. To his conception of "making the circulation more rapid," Locke at any rate attached a perfectly distinct meaning, though it may strike us, as applied to modern conditions, rather as quaint and curious than as appropriate.[2] " Here, by-the-by," he says, " we may observe that it were better for trade, and consequently for everybody, for more money would be stirring and less would do the business, if rents were paid by shorter intervals than six months. For supposing I let a farm at fifty-two pounds per annum. If my rent be paid half yearly, there are twenty-six pounds to be employed in the payment of it in one entire sum, a great part whereof must necessarily lie still before it come out of my tenant's chest to my hands ; if it be paid once a quarter, thirteen pounds alone

[1] *Considerations of the Lowering of Interest and Raising the Value of Money*, Locke's Works, ed. 1823, vol. v. p. 22.
[2] *Op. cit.*, p. 27.

do it, and less money is laid up for it and stopped
a less while in its course ; but should it be paid
every week one single twenty shillings will pay
the rent of fifty-two pounds per annum, whence
would follow this double benefit : first that a great
deal less money would serve the trade of a country,
and, secondly, that less of the money would lie
still." Locke's specific for economising money
has not been adopted by the world, and, failing
its adoption, the rapidity of circulation appears to
be entirely determined by custom, and not at all
by trade conditions, and does not seem to operate
in any conceivable manner as an agency in raising
prices.

When we look at the expression as used by a
writer versed in affairs, like Gilbart, we find it
again signifying something that bears no resemblance to its signification in the hands either of
Locke or of Mill. The introduction of banking
facilities into new countries or into new districts
is, in Gilbart's view, equivalent to an increase in
the rapidity of the circulation, and thus, to all
intents, to an increase in the quantity of money.
He illustrates his position by the example of an
Irish butter merchant who buys £100 worth of
butter in Cork, discounts his bill, and, with the
funds thus obtained, buys another £100 worth, and
so on. What takes place in these circumstances
may perhaps be called an increase in the rapidity

of circulation, but it has nothing about it analogous
to Mill's increases in the rapidity of circulation,
which are supposed to take place somehow
without an increase in the quantity of goods and
transactions. Gilbart's increase moreover has
no tendency to raise the price of commodities, as
Mill's is supposed to have. If it tends to raise
the price of butter in Ireland, by augmenting the
demand, it tends proportionately to depress it in
London, by augmenting the supply. Gilbart's
own view indeed is that its general tendency is
to lower prices by doing something to cut down
the cost of production, including in that term of
course the cost of distribution.[1]

Another interesting truth, if not one of the
very first importance, which the diagram brings
into a clear light is the nugatoriness of the law
which in England limits the legal tender of the
silver coin. The satisfactory working of the
whole mechanism of business and commerce is
seen to depend on the fact that practically silver
is legal tender in altogether unlimited amounts.
Mr. Leonard Courtney brought out this fact in
a striking manner in his evidence given before
Sir Henry Fowler's Committee on the Indian
Currency. " I never heard,"[2] he said, " of any
banker objecting to receive from his customer,

---

[1] *History and Principles of Banking*, p. 107.
[2] Reply to Question 13,003.

in the way of business, any amount of silver that
that customer brought to him, and if he receives
silver indiscriminately, and honours the cheques
that are drawn against that silver, it is only a
case of carrying the silver to the bank and drawing a cheque, and the banks will say 'How will
you have it?' Then you take what you get in
exchange for that cheque and pay your creditor,
so that, although the creditor may absolutely
refuse to take from you more than £2 in silver,
you always, without any limit so far as I know,
use your silver through that one intermediary in
the payment of any debt whatever. Consider,"
he went on, " what kind of an account an institution like the Crystal Palace would keep with its
bank. My earliest practical years were spent in
a country bank. There we received from our
trade customers what they had received over the
counter, a large proportion of which was silver.
Silver, notes, or gold, it is all one; it goes
in without any discrimination to your credit."
What can be more certain than that there is
not a place of amusement, there is not a railway company, there is not a retail shop, large or
small, that could carry on its business for a day
if the public took seriously the legislation which
limits the legal tender character of our silver
coin? In 1774 it was that the limitation was first
introduced ; the tender was then limited to £25.

The measure, however, was tentative, and so the limitation was not made perpetual.[1] A few years afterwards it expired, and the legislature forgot to renew it. Nobody was a penny the worse. It was all along, and is still, an absolutely dead letter.[2]

To revert to the question which engaged our attention in the earlier part of this chapter, the question what are the characteristics in virtue of the possession of which we may without hesitation set down any given description of money, in any given country and at any given date, as standard money ; we may of course leave the question of ubiquity on one side. There is very little gold commonly seen in Scotland or in Canada at the present day, yet no one doubts that gold is the standard in these countries. We find too that we must leave out of account the inquiry as to what is the medium in which computations are currently made, as a final and conclusive test question to determine what is the standard ; otherwise we should be forced to conclude that notes and not gold were the standard in England in the beginning of this century. There remain then only the questions, What is the money that passes by weight ? and

---

[1] Lord Liverpool, *Coins of the Realm*, p. 128.

[2] It must be said however that it may have an indirect effect of importance in removing the temptation to unlimited issues.

What is the medium of external trade? In
England and in all Europe to-day, gold, and gold
alone, passes by weight, and gold, and gold alone,
is the medium of external trade, and it is, beyond
question in virtue of its possessing these characteristics, that we describe gold as the standard
metal now.

At the same time, while it cannot be admitted
that the answer to the question, What is the
current medium of computations? also decides
the question, What is the standard? it must be
said that there is an important difference between
the state of things in which the principal metal,
nowadays gold, is not the medium of computations and the state of things in which it is.
Current phraseology commonly describes the
transition from the former state of things to the
latter as "the adoption of a gold standard" or
as "the transition to gold." At the same time
we must bear in mind that this is only the final
and by no means the most important stage in the
transition. It might perhaps be possible to mark
the distinction between the two states of things
by describing the first as a condition in which
gold is the latent standard, and the second as
one in which it is also the overt and official one.
In either state of things however it is the only
real money. All other is subsidiary, or fiduciary,
or both.

In the fourth and fifth chapters I have adduced a good deal of evidence to show that, as far back as the middle of the fourteenth century, the principal medium of all large international transactions was gold. In the sixteenth century, as Garrault tells us, the bankers made all their remittances in marks, ounces, grains and pennyweights of gold. The conclusion that gold was the medium of external trade of necessity carries with it the conclusion that it commonly passed by weight. There is some independent evidence on that point, however, that is worth noticing. We found Rice Vaughan remarking that it passed by weight in his time, 1675. In 1632, in and about London and Westminster, most people carried scales in their pockets [1] to weigh gold on all occasions, and they obtained them "at the office for that purpose erected." The office [2] referred to was established by James I. in 1617; and at the same time a proclamation was issued enjoining on all men to refuse such gold coins as were deficient in their legal weight by more than a few grains allowed as remedy. This proclamation merely reinforced the injunctions contained in a similar proclamation of Elizabeth in 1587. [3] In the latter every borough,

[1] Ruding, *Annals of the Coinage*, vol. ii. p. 245.
[2] *Op. cit.*, vol. ii. p. 220.
[3] *Op. cit.*, vol. ii. p. 172.

city and town corporate was required "to prepare
and to keep, for the use of all, upright balances
and true weights for the weighing of every
several piece of gold lawfully current within
the realm." The provision reminds us of the
exagia solidi [1] provided for the principal towns
of the Roman Empire by Constantine. The
proclamations of Elizabeth and of James I. introduced no new enactment, but merely enjoined
compliance with provisions which were embodied
in the statute book, at least as early as the
time of Henry V., and which if they had never
been enacted would still have tended to become
customary law of themselves. It is interesting
and significant to find that in the time of John,
when silver was still real money, an office similar
to that referred to in James I.'s proclamation in
regard to the gold was in existence where " penny
poizes " could be obtained for weighing the
silver. [2]

When gold passes by weight it is evident that
a state of things exists in which there is the perfect equivalent of free coinage as regards it. In
such circumstances the uncoined metal in bars

---

[1] Mommsen, *op. cit.*, vol. iii. p. 156.   An office for weighing the
gold florins was established in Florence in 1294.   Orsini, *Storia
della Moneta della Republica Fiorentina*, p. xviii.

[2] Ruding, *op. cit.*, vol. i. p. 342.   Ruding remarks in a footnote
that this was the last occasion on which provision was made for
the weighing of silver.

and ingots ordinarily becomes the money of large transactions.   It became so in Rome in the time of Sulla, and again in the time of Constantine, and has become so again in all civilised nations to-day.   The whole stock of the metal, however great it may be, in these circumstances becomes available as standard money.   The universal acceptability of gold is thus of very old standing in the world, and we find in this fact the real reason why the Bank of England as well as every other bank in Europe can always accept it without a moment's hesitation at £3 17s. 10½d. per ounce.

The question whether copper, silver or gold was real or was merely subsidiary money at various dates in the history of the Republic and the Empire is one that is continually engaging Mommsen's attention in his great work on Roman money, and the tests which he applies in order to decide it are precisely those above enumerated. If, in the third century B.C. for example, he finds the copper circulating at a conventional value, and thus manifestly passing by tale, while the silver is the money of international commerce, and thus must pass by weight at its intrinsic value, he sets down the silver as the real money of that epoch and the copper as the subsidiary. Again, if during the later centuries of the Empire, he finds the silver the subject of continual depreciations, while the gold throughout maintains its quality and—after Constantine at any rate—its weight, unimpaired, while at the same time the silver or rather the billon, as evidenced by the localities in which it has been discovered, is found to have circulated within the Empire only, he then concludes that the transition from the silver to the gold standard had by that date been definitely effected.   If we too decide the same question by the same tests as regards the modern world, we shall be forced to conclude likewise that in it a similar transition took place at least five hundred years ago.

CHAPTER VII

THE ORIGINATING CAUSES OF TRANSITIONS

In the first and second chapters of this part I have endeavoured, in connection with the history of the transitions of standard in England and in Rome, to show how it was possible that such changes could take place unconsciously. The question remains to be considered, What are the originating causes that gave rise to them in the world?

We shall find, it must be said here, that the subject-matter of a chapter devoted to this question bears a very close affinity to the subject-matter of the previous chapter on the criteria of the standard. Almost anything indeed that seems to fall naturally under the one heading would fall equally appropriately under the other ; and this is what we might expect when we reflect that whatever from one point of view can be set down as the cause of a transition may from another point of view be set down as evidence of its having taken place.

As regards the usual proximate cause of such transitions in any particular country, there can seldom be any question. We who have seen Germany adopt the gold standard in 1872, and have seen almost every other state of Europe adopt it before the close of the decade, will hardly deny that the cause of a transition in any particular country, as regards its final stage at any rate, is likely to be found in the influence of neighbouring countries. The contention that "the foreign trade of a country is a thing hardly to be considered in connection with its internal money" [1] is one that surely, to say the least, displays a singular love of paradox.

If, again, we go a stage further back in the history of the great modern transition from silver to gold, we find that we have to give due weight to the fact that, by the close of the eighteenth century, England had definitely and manifestly adopted the gold standard, and that at the same time London had become or was rapidly becoming the centre of the world's finance. The cottons of New York when shipped to Canton, and the teas of Hong-Kong, when shipped to Amsterdam, were all alike paid for by sterling bills on London. The money therefore which the merchant found

---

[1] Sir R. Giffen, in *Economic Journal*, Sept. 1898, p. 305.

that he must have, whatever his business was or in whatever part of the world it was conducted, came to be either sterling money itself or money that was readily convertible into sterling. Hence it was that, long before the German demonetisation of silver, it had become already observable that when gold supplanted silver in the coinage of France there was nothing but satisfaction felt at the change ; but when on the contrary, ten years later, silver began to supplant gold, the case presented itself in a very different aspect. It was felt then that this was a change which it was entirely impossible for the country to tolerate.[1]

Viewing the subject historically, suppose that we put the question to Mommsen : When we see a change of standard taking place in any country, where are we to look for the cause to which it owes its origin ? We find that he would answer at once : You will find it in " the impulse from without." [2] He regards it accordingly as impossible to give an intelligible account of the development of Roman money without prefacing it by an account of the monetary conditions antecedently ruling in the world outside Rome ; and thus the first division of his work treats of the Greek and

[1] See Prof. Erwin Nasse, *Second Report Gold and Silver Commission*, p. 261.
[2] *Op. cit.*, Preface, p. xviii.

Asiatic monetary systems under the influence of which the Italian coinages were developed. The second deals with the issues of Italy itself and of Sicily, at the epoch which immediately preceded the Roman domination ; and he makes it abundantly clear that the transition to silver in Rome was due to the necessity felt by the citizens of the Republic of conforming their standard to that of the commercial nations around them. The earliest denairi bore on the reverse the image of the Dioscuri [1] on horseback, galloping, the lance in rest. They were the tutelary divinities of the Greek sailors, and their images were thus, as Mommsen says, in the highest degree appropriate on the coins which the richest and most warlike city of Italy struck, with a view particularly to its maritime commerce, and by which it assimilated its monetary system to that of the Hellenic world about it.

We have what might almost be described as a laboratory experiment illustrating the manner in which standards change, recorded for us by a highly competent observer, under whose eyes the change took place, in the evidence taken before the Indian Currency Committee of 1898.[2] The committee had occasion to inquire into the circumstances attending the recent adoption of the British rupee, in the place of its own rupee,

---

[1] See Title page.   [2] Question 12,026.

by the native state of Kashmir. Mr. J. E.
O'Connor, the able head of the Indian Statistical
Department, thus explains the causes that led up
to this event. " I happen to know exactly what
happened in Kashmir," he said, "for I was in
Kashmir myself for two months in 1897.
Kashmir formerly was practically almost inac-
cessible to Europeans, but a road was recently
constructed which enabled people to go from
Rawal Pindi to Srinagar with ease in three days.
There has since been an increasing crowd of
visitors to the state who come with British
Indian rupees. A branch of the Punjab Bank
was established there, which also did its business
in British Indian rupees. Soon everybody, even
the natives of the country, refused to take
Kashmir rupees, and the state treasury was
filled with the local coin presented in payment of
taxes. The safes of the bank were also filled
with Kashmir coins which its customers declined
to take. The state found itself loaded with a
great sum of rupees that were practically bullion,
and application was made to the Government of
India for advice and assistance. The Government was ready to prevent the state from falling
into serious financial difficulty, and an arrangement was made under which the government took
over all the Kashmir coin at a value materially
above its bullion value, British Indian rupees

being given in exchange.   Of course it had to safeguard itself by requiring that the state should not coin more native rupees."   There is no question here, it will be seen, of the worse money cutting out the better, which, we are often told, is the one cause to which changes of the standard must always be attributed.   So far from its being here the worse money that cuts out the better, it is, on the contrary, the better that cuts out the worse.   Every one was naturally anxious to get rid of the native rupees and every one naturally discharged his outstanding obligations in them, as debtors under the operation of Gresham's Law are held to do with the cheaper money.   That fact however did not even suffice to maintain the rupees in the position they already occupied as the money of the country, much less could it have achieved such a position for them.   They conformed to the ideal of an automatic currency ; but the trouble was, as with silver in India itself, that, while there was an unlimited automatic inflow of them, there was no automatic outflow.[1]   The Maharajah therefore had to close his mints to the coinage of them, for the very same reason for which Europe, in the seventies and India at length in 1893, had to close her mints to silver.

[1] Cf. Question 10,326, Indian Currency Committee, 1828.   Mr. Le Marchant asked : "Would not one of the conditions with the word ' automatic ' in currency be freedom in flowing out ? "

It is worthy of notice, in this Kashmir case, that the change of standard was an accomplished fact before any action was taken by the government of the country in the matter. All that legislation could do was to conform itself to the state of things that it found in existence. This is a point not without interest in its historical applications. That such changes can take place without the intervention of the legislator is a fact that must be taken into account in interpreting the ever-increasing tendency towards centralisation manifested by the money of antiquity. The cause of the cessation of their own local coinages by the allies and dependencies of Athens has been the subject of some discussion ;[1] the more so as it is not known that Athens ever took any definite action to bring it about. We can see now however that it might very well come about of itself without any such action. Again, it was very probably, as Mommsen thinks, the settled policy of Alexander and his successors, as well as, in a later age, of the Romans, to make their own coinage supplant the local coinages of the subject peoples ; but, even if this had not been so, we can see that, once the expanding use of the central money had acquired a certain degree of momentum, there would necessarily be an impulse continually at work, which, apart from any action on the part either

---

[1] See G. F. Hill, *Handbook of Greek and Roman Coins*, p. 83.

of the Hellenistic or Roman governments, would tend to push on the process of consolidation.

The discussions of the previous chapter should, I think, have thrown some light on the rationale of the connection between the foreign trade of a country and its internal currency. This connection, we have found, seemed obvious enough to Garrault in the sixteenth century. It was not the wholesale trade alone, as he pointed out, that was affected by the rise in the value of the gold crown. The merchant who made his purchases abroad, wholesale, had to sell his goods at home, retail, and had to get from his retail customers a description of money that he could send away without loss to the wholesale seller abroad, and thus the price of everything in the country, down to the charge for a man and horse by the day, was affected.

We have, in the fact of this interaction and interdependence between wholesale and retail internal prices, the link that connects foreign trade with internal money. The wholesale importer, say, of calico from England, who is resident in France, will plainly have to pay for it in money which will be acceptable in England ; that is, in this case, in gold by weight, or, if the seller is willing to take them, in documents conveying the right to such gold on demand. To be able to do this he will have to get gold, or its equivalent,

for the calico goods which he manufactures and
sells.   Every exporter is thus, whether he will or
not, engaged in a ceaseless propaganda of the
standard of his country abroad ; and the standard
of the country which has most of those things to
export which the inhabitants of neighbouring
countries want, is plainly the one which is likely
to prevail and predominate generally in the end.
In regard to the goods sold at home, the purchase
money will have ultimately to be obtained from
persons who get their earnings in an innumerable
variety of employments, and to none of them can
the producer afford to sell his goods, unless either
they pay him in full-weighted gold or its perfect
equivalent, or unless—supposing that to be out of
their reach—they make up for the deficiency by
giving him a greater quantity of the light coin or
over-issued paper than they would have to give
otherwise ; and as this greater quantity will be precisely proportioned to its lightness or to the degree
of its depreciation by over-issue, it is evident that
the full-weighted coin is still the true measure of
values. The exigencies of importers and exporters
thus exert their influence in respect of every
internal payment, from the purchase of the week's
groceries to the fee of the lawyer or the salary of
the *prima donna.*

This proximate cause, the influence of neighbouring nations, it may be as traders or it may be

as conquerors, or as both, is no doubt sometimes the only cause which it is possible for us to assign for a change of the monetary standard. The primeval cause, in such cases, is hidden in impenetrable prehistoric mists. That, for instance, is the case with regard to the change from gold to silver in Europe in the eighth century. It is not however the universal, nor indeed even the usual, case.

Adam Smith, having observed that in his own day the silver shilling had become nothing else but a token representing a fractional part of the guinea, possessing no independent value of its own, but being manifestly held up in value by the gold coin, and varying with its variations, and knowing moreover that this state of things had come about altogether spontaneously, formulated a general law applicable to the situation, to the effect that, when two metals are circulating together at a fixed ratio, the value of the most precious of the two "will regulate the value of the whole coin"[1]; in other words, that the most precious metal will, in such circumstances, assume the position of standard money, to the exclusion of the less precious.

The question whether there are any exceptions to this law is one that will engage our attention presently. In the meantime, it may be said that

[1] *Wealth of Nations*, ed. 1811 (Edinburgh), vol. i. p. 54.

it is a principle which we have already found to be very widely operative.   In the Roman Republic, the Roman Empire, and, again, in mediæval and modern Europe, we have seen the more precious metal supplant the less precious, in the first instance as standard, and eventually also to a great extent as currency.

It remains for us to endeavour to follow out the steps by which the change takes place, and to try to comprehend the true nature of the process. The formula known as Gresham's Law has been erected into a theory of the transition of standards.   Mr. Mill for instance says : "When there are two legal standards, that one of the metals will always be the standard of which the real has fallen below the rated value" ; that is to say, that in a state of things in which we find the silver the subject of depreciation, we shall find it also assuming the position of standard money. This law may be tersely expressed in the words, "the worse money cuts out the better," and there is no doubt that there are circumstances to which it is applicable, and in regard to which it expresses an important truth.   At the same time, we see it here apparently confronted with a law which directly reverses it, the law that the better money, like the better merchandise, cuts out the worse.

Gold, we know has supplanted silver as the standard in modern Europe, and there is no possible sense in which it can be regarded as having been the worse money. In England it has been the metal that has been normally on the rise in value, as measured in the other metal, at any rate, since the reign of Stephen ; and consequently it has been the metal whose real value has usually tended to rise above, and not to fall below, its rated value. We must not however take the mere fact of its being the more precious metal, and identify that with the fact of its being for the purposes of the present inquiry, the " better money." There is no obvious reason in the nature of things why fifteen pounds of silver, let us say, should not be coined into as good a money, for every possible purpose, as one pound of gold. Circumstances are at any rate conceivable in which the silver might be the better money of the two, and indeed in the Græco-Persian period appearances seem to me to favour the conclusion that it then was so.[1]

If we follow Professor Ashley [2]—as we justly may—in regarding the use of money as a store of purchasing power as its primary and essential use, we will then have to esteem that description of money as the best which best subserves that end. This being premised, I think the process by which the gold has supplanted the silver can most readily

[1] See below, pp. 209–212.
[2] *Introduction to Economic History*, vol. i. p. 164.

be understood if we regard the change of standard as taking place in two stages. First, the introduction of the gold into a circulation previously consisting exclusively of silver so operates as to impair the efficiency of the silver as a store of purchasing power, and, secondly, the gold itself necessarily becomes the only reliable store of such power in the country, and thus it comes to occupy the position formerly occupied by the silver.

But how, it will be asked, can the introduction of gold into the circulation so operate as to impair the efficiency of the silver as a store of purchasing power? The manner in which it does so is not free from complexity. What takes place, in the first instance, is the differentiation of the money of the country into its two branches, the wholesale and the retail, the one passing by weight, the other passing by tale only. It is noticeable that the differentiation can take place even when there is only one metal in circulation. We have a curious instance of it in Holland in the eighteenth century, when practically the whole currency consisted of silver. Sir James Steuart [1] tells us that the silver currency of that country in his day was of two sorts, " the bank species and the current species." The one was habitually bagged and passed by weight, and was consequently always up to about its full standard weight ;

---

[1] Works, vol. iii. pp. 124 and 129.

the other was not bagged, and passed by tale, and thus, like the English shillings and sixpences of the same period, circulated at a value that was entirely conventional. Like the English silver too it was very scarce, and it therefore showed no tendency to fall to a discount.[1]

When gold and silver are both in circulation, the rôle of wholesale money most naturally falls to the gold, while that of retail money falls to the silver. Supposing this accomplished, we have next to look at the position of the state in reference to the matter. The fixing of a ratio between the metals, it must be observed, may be quite unintended and unconscious; it appears at any rate to be always quite inevitable. In Locke's opinion, the wisest course for the government of his day to have pursued with regard to its money would have been to have fixed no ratio between the silver and the gold, but to have left the price of the guinea to be determined by the market; and indeed the guinea, in Locke's day, is often spoken of as if it had conformed to that

---

[1] The "gross gelt," as it was called, consisting of 3-guilder, 30-stiver, and 20-stiver pieces, was put up promiscuously in the same bags and passed by weight. The bags were of 600 florins each. The smaller silver was not bagged or weighed. The use of bagged money in large payments is a phenomenon that has frequently repeated itself in monetary history, *e.g.* the Follis in the later Roman Empire, and the Fiorino di Suggello in Florence in the thirteenth century (see Orsini, *Storia della Moneta della Republica Fiorentina*, p. xviii).

ideal.   We saw however that, by the limitation
of the amount for which it should be received at
the Exchequer, a perfectly effective ratio between
the gold and the silver was as a matter of fact
fixed, a ratio, too, which, like other such artificial
ratios, was subject, to a large extent, to control
by the government.

M. Lenormant,[1] in dealing with the coinage of
Alexander, warmly praises it for having been
based on this principle, which, following Locke,
he regards as the only sound one.   A gold stater,
we are told, was issued of the same weight as the
silver didrachm, and the two were then allowed to
find their own value without government inter-
ference.   They found it at a ratio of one to ten.
This might have been the original intention, and
probably it fairly describes the system at its
inception.   It seems impossible however to
believe that the state could have maintained an
attitude of neutrality in the matter for any length
of time.   As soon as ever it became necessary to
enact that a fine or a tax payable in so many
drachms would be received in so many staters, the
ratio would be, to all intents and purposes, fixed
by the state.   Mommsen is thus perhaps right
in thinking that already in Alexander's time the
ratio 1 : 10 probably over-valued the silver.[2]   If the

---

[1] *La Monnaie dans l'Antiquité*, vol. i. p. 179 ff.
Mommsen, *op. cit.*, vol. iii., p. 44, footnote.

state indeed had steadily determined not to fix any rate at which receipts due to it, or payments to be made by it, in drachms should be accepted or made in staters, the result would most likely have been that the staters would never have got into circulation at all. It is only a theory-ridden government, however, that could ever have dreamt of adopting such a course. Our own government did indeed adopt such a course with regard to the sovereign in India in the middle of the past century, and the result was that it did not circulate. A similar attempt was made, a good many years earlier, in Germany, with regard to the issue of a coinage of gold crowns. The result then again was that the crowns, as Mr. Shaw says,[1] " never struggled into existence." Money with which no fines could be paid, no stamps could be bought, and no government obligations of any sort could be liquidated, would be deprived of so important a part of its functions as money as probably to render it altogether unavailable for use in the internal currency. At any rate, in every instance in which currency has come under contemporary observation and of which intelligible records have been kept, we see the two metals rated to each other at some figure.

The case of Rome in the fourth century A.D., and the centuries that immediately succeeded it,

[1] *Hist. of Currency*, p. 212.

is in some ways a significant one. When Constantine undertook the reform of the coinage, it appears to have been undertaken, in the first instance, in a spirit animated by some such principle as that of Locke and Lenormant. A gold piece was issued which was the $\frac{1}{72}$ part of the pound of gold in weight, and a silver piece which was the $\frac{1}{72}$ part of the pound of silver. The rating of the gold to the silver was, however, plainly not to be avoided in the end. By Julian's time, at any rate, we find the silver again circulating above its value. The ratio between the uncoined metals was then 1 : 14, while the monetary ratio was 1 : 12.[1]

If we suppose then that a ratio is fixed between gold as the wholesale, and silver as the retail money, the principle of " quasi redemption " next comes into play. The attitude of the state with regard to its money is too often dealt with from the point of view of its disciplinary and penal powers only, and the fact of its being a great economic entity is overlooked. The failure of innumerable sumptuary laws, laws of the maximum and such like, to effect their purpose, has indeed abundantly proved that governments have very little control over the value of anything in virtue of their powers of reward and punishment. It is a familiar fact, however, that the Bank of England

[1] Mommsen, *op. cit.*, vol. iii. p. 160.

has a great control over the rate of discount, without possessing any powers of reward and punishment at all. It has this control in virtue of its being the greatest dealer in cash and in securities. The state has similarly a large measure of control over the value of the subsidiary currency in virtue of its immense receipts, and no less immense expenditure. In England, a sum that is nearly equivalent to the whole stock of coin in circulation passes through the hands of the government, in the shape of revenue, every year. I have dealt already, however, in the fifth chapter, at some length with this principle of "quasi redemption," as illustrated in English monetary history in the seventeenth and eighteenth centuries, and it is not necessary to go over the ground again. We have, in the operation of the principle, an explanation of the singular analogy, or, it might be more rightly called, identity that exists between subsidiary money and money that is, from the beginning, strictly speaking fiduciary. The dollar in America, and the five-franc piece in France, may now be regarded as promises engraven on silver to pay so much gold ; but it is surely a remarkable fact that they should have become so, as they did originally, owing to the mere fact of the closure of the mints to silver. One would have thought it entirely impossible that they could have assumed such a character without a distinct pledge having been taken by the governments of these countries to treat them as such. Without any such pledge, however, our own shillings and sixpences as well as all the over-rated silver of Europe, America and India have fallen spontaneously into a condition in which they possess all the characteristics of fiduciary paper, and consequently, in all discussions of the monetary situation, are treated as being, for practical purposes, identical with it.

We find Mommsen too, in treating of the money of Rome, using the terms fiduciary and subsidiary as synonyms. It was possible, he thinks, whether rightly or wrongly we need not inquire, to maintain the parity between the two metals that were in circulation for longer periods in the ancient world than is possible nowadays. At the same time, when a change took place in their respective values, and when the equilibrium was thus destroyed, the coins, he says,[1] "which did not consist of the standard metal disappeared rapidly, whenever their real value rose above their nominal, or, on the other hand, *became mere fiduciary money*, as soon as it sank below it." The generalisation is a very important one, and one to which I shall have occasion to revert. We can only comprehend the fact of the Roman copper becoming, as it were, spontaneously fiduciary money, on the

[1] *Op. cit.*, Preface, p. xxvi. See also vol. iii. p. 46.

introduction of the silver, when we remember that
the state could not avoid practically redeeming
the first in the second, as soon as a ratio was
fixed and taxes were collected. The same prin_
ciple, in a later age, applies to the silver and the
gold. By "standard" of course must be understood what I have called the latent standard.
There can be no question of using the word
in any other sense in regard to the money of
antiquity.

If it may be considered now as sufficiently
explained how it is that the mere introduction of
gold into the circulation tends to convert the
silver into fiduciary money, some progress has
then been made towards showing how it tends to
impair its efficiency as a store of purchasing
power. Once the silver becomes fiduciary, its
descent into the condition of money that is
altogether bad and unreliable has, in most periods
of history, been only too easy and rapid. As I
have pointed out in the chapter on the French
currency, the great and irrecoverable shock which
the public confidence sustains may often be
delayed till the first steps towards reform are
taken. It needs little imagination to conceive
what a shock the public confidence in the silver
of Edward VI. must have sustained when the
shilling was, all of a sudden, cried down to nine-
pence. This crying down was not in itself a

crime, it was the inevitable result of previous crimes. It reminds us, however, of the first reduction in the value of the Mississippi Company's paper, which led immediately to its total collapse. If the government could reduce it 20 per cent. to-day, people began to ask, why should they not reduce it 50 or 100 per cent. to-morrow? And so they made haste to get rid of it at any price. So great was the alarm caused by the reduction of the shilling, says Ruding,[1] "and such various rumours were spread concerning it, that it was found necessary to endeavour to put an immediate stop to them." The means adopted to effect this end were to issue a proclamation denouncing the "lewd persons" who "of their own light heads had imagined that because His Highness had some-what abated the value of his said coin, therefore he should yet more abate it," and threatening them, in the event of their continuing to "devise any such manner of tale, news, or report," with fines, imprisonment, the pillory and the cutting off of their ears. For all that, within a month of the date of the issue of this proclamation, the shilling was cried down to sixpence. "The loss,"[2] an old chronicler tells us, "mostly fell on the poor ; the richer sorte," he says, "partly by

---

[1] *Annals of the Coinage*, vol. ii. p. 110.
[2] Quoted by Ruding *op. cit.*, vol. ii. p. 111.

friendship, understanding the thing beforehand, did put that kind of money away, partly knowing the baseness of the coin, kept in store none but gold and old silver that would not bring any loss."

In depreciations, ancient and modern, the sequence of events is usually the same, The government debases the coin and leaves a considerable margin between the nominal and the metallic value. Then the illicit coiner comes in to share the plunder, or the recklessness of the government itself knows no bounds, and the quantity of the subsidiary coinage is increased far beyond any possible outlet for it ; finally it has to be cried down, or, as with the Roman government of Elagabalus, to be refused at the exchequer altogether.[1] When this happens, the public are of course forced to resort to the use of the metal that has not been tampered with, if there is such a metal in circulation, as the only trustworthy medium for the storage of their purchasing power.

Among modern English and American economists, Mr. Edward Atkinson is the only one, so far as I am aware, who has pointed out the fallacy that is involved in giving an unrestricted application to Gresham's Law, to the doctrine that "the worse money cuts out the better." In the evidence which he gave before our Commission

---

[1] Mommsen, *op. cit.*, vol. iii. p. 142.

on Agricultural Depression in 1897 he had occasion to point out that in that sphere to which the influence of legal tender laws could not extend the opposite was the principle that applied. His words are worth quoting:[1] "I want," he said, "to put in one important point in my judgment. You have the Gresham Law, that the poorer money, which is legal tender, drives out the good money. I think I am right in saying that, in that commerce to which no legal tender Act has been or can be applied, the good money which is not legal tender drives all the poor money out of circulation and in that way the standard or unit of all international commerce has become exclusively gold."

The truth is that the much talked of Gresham's Law is not a law applicable to money generally, but only to subsidiary or fiduciary money. Without taking the principle of "quasi redemption" into account the law cannot be understood. When we know, however, that a clipped and worn shilling has a legally appointed use in the fulfilling of which it is absolutely on a par with a full-weighted one, it becomes comprehensible at once why the worst coins should monopolise the circulation. If such shillings as are only the weight of sixpence yet count as shillings in paying taxes, it is surely what we might anticipate when we find

[1] Reply to Question 33,176.

that the heavier shillings are used for other purposes, in the fulfilment of which they have an
advantage over the lighter ones proportionate to
their greater weight.

Gresham's Law, it is worthy of notice, has no
application to money that passes by weight. The
weight of real money may be, to almost any extent,
irregular, and yet the lighter coins will not cut out
the heavier ones.   In the latter half of the third
century A.D. the weight of the aurei that were in
circulation together varied in the most extraordinary manner, and the same was the case with
the libral asses that were in circulation together in
early Rome.   The latter varied between twelve
ounces as the heaviest and eight as the lightest.
Heavy and light however are found buried in the
same hoards, and no doubt they were buried, as
they circulated, together.

It is in regard to retail payments alone that
Gresham's Law operates, and the reason is obvious.
The shopkeeper who accepts currency for his
wares thinks, and is ordinarily justified in thinking,
that, whether the money that he takes is liable to
depreciation or not, the chances are greatly against
its so depreciating, while it is in his possession, as
to affect his interests.   He has too to face the
competition of other shopkeepers whose goods are
for sale at the same price as his own.   In such
circumstances, it is the buyers' money, whatever

that is, that tends to become the general medium
of exchange, so far as the transactions to which it
is applicable go.   With the payments of wholesale
trade the case is altogether different.   Being large
sums, their intrinsic value comes to be all important to those who have to accept them.   A
great many of such payments are the payments
of foreign trade, and the money to be paid must
of course in that case have a value not in one
country only, but in any part of the world, otherwise the vendor stands to lose directly and immediately by taking it.   Even when that is not so,
the man who receives a large sum knows that he
may have to keep it by him for a long time, and
therefore will not accept a description of money
that is liable to fall in value, unless indeed he
compensates himself by asking more of it than he
would accept of the sound money.   Thus, whatever sort of money it is that actually changes
hands, the bargain is sure to be made in the most
trustworthy medium.   It is in the wholesale trade
however, as I have already observed, that the
prices of commodities are all really fixed.   The
retail seller, as a rule, merely takes the prices as
they reach him, and adds a uniform percentage ;
and thus the medium of wholesale trade, being
that in which values are determined, cannot fail to
become the true standard of value.   The main
channel which connects the two branches of money,

the retail and the wholesale, is to be found in the weekly payments of wages to the labourers engaged in production, and if there are two sorts of money in a country, a worse and a better, the wage-earner is quite certain to be paid in the worse. It is no doubt greatly against his interests in the long run to accept the worse, but it does not appear to be so in regard to any individual transaction. The masses indeed, as a rule, in any state, are ordinarily found to be in favour of " cheap money," as they call it, unless it chance that they have had a bitter experience of its working, and have become intelligent enough to connect cause and effect. The wage-earner, at any rate, usually accepts the worse money without demur, and it is through his expenditure that it finds its way through all the retail circulation.

We have seen already that the doctrine that the worse money ousts the better is historically without warrant. We can now see further that, as a principle of real money, it is theoretically impossible. It takes for granted that it always lies with the debtor class in a community, the class that has payments to make, to dictate what the money of a country shall be. That this should be so is contrary to all experience. It is the creditor class, the class who have payments to receive, who in such matters are, in the end, always masters of the situation; and for this there is a very obvious reason, viz., that the money in which payments for goods are to be made, or in which money lent is to be repaid, is ordinarily fixed before the creditor becomes a creditor at all, and while the goods are still in his warehouse, or the loan money is still in his till.

It will seem perhaps somewhat less surprising that a law which is applicable to subsidiary and fiduciary money alone should have been so frequently treated as applicable to money generally, if we reflect, what a widespread and conspicuous phenomenon in the world this subsidiary and fiduciary money is. The whole visible circulation of Java and of India is at this moment subsidiary. During the English Bank Restriction the pound notes were so exclusively visible that, as we found, the great majority of a highly capable and business-like House of Commons came to the conclusion that they alone were true money. In the Roman Imperial period—in the time, say, of Caracalla—all the money that the mass of the people saw anything of must have been subsidiary. It was all billon circulating at a conventional value. We have heard a good deal of late of the objections to "a managed currency"; but a subsidiary currency, it must be remembered, must always be a managed one. Our own silver currency is of course managed. The Bank of

England lets the Treasury know when more silver coin is wanted, and about how much, and silver is issued accordingly.

One broad fact that confronts us, whenever we cast our glance over monetary history, is this : that in those ages when we find only one sort of money in circulation in the world, or in some great and practically self-contained section of it, we hear nothing of depreciations of the currency, and nothing of the worse money cutting out the better. There the same principle applies to money that applies to every other commodity, that the best brand cuts out the inferior. The purity and "truth to name" of the Athenian "owl" made it, in the fifth century B.C., acceptable all over the known world as far as India, and was no small factor in creating the commercial pre-eminence of Athens. So well aware, too, were the astute business men of that republic of the fact that they carefully guarded the identity of its type for some three hundred years ; so that, at the close of the period, its archaic rudeness presented a curious contrast to the artistic perfection of the contemporary coinage of such cities as Syracuse. In Tarentum the "nomos" played a similar part in connection with the over-sea commerce of that city, and when it was suppressed by the Romans the Tarentine trade is said to have suffered a blow from which

it never recovered. In Rome,[1] in Cato's time, the
" victoriat," a coin three-fourths of the denarius
in value, had come into universal use. It owed
its success apparently to the fact that, being a
foreign coin which could circulate only at its
full intrinsic value, it was necessarily always of
full weight; and, at the same time, being an
Italian replica of the small drachm of Corinth,
and of Massilia, it was the most suitable medium
for the transmission of funds both to Greece,
Egypt, and Asia Minor in the east, and to Gaul
and Spain in the west. It was subsequently
absorbed in the system of the denarius. These
are all instances of moneys that gained and retained
their positions, not in virtue of their badness, but
in virtue of their goodness. We can add to the
list the sterling money of the twelfth and thirteenth centuries, and again the sterling money of
to-day.

Another broad fact that can hardly be overlooked by the most casual observer is the fact
that, while silver has been continually subjected
to debasements and depreciations, gold has been
so but rarely. In England the debasement of
the silver in the last years of Henry VIII.'s
reign was certainly also accompanied by a debasement of the gold. The standard of the latter

---

[1] Mommsen, *op. cit.*, vol. ii. pp. 89–103. Also *Observations sur
l'Origine du Victoriat*, by M. de Blacas, pp. 104–107.

was reduced from 24 carats, first to 22 and then to 20. It is worthy of notice,[1] however, that while Edward VI.'s government continued and even carried still further the debasement of the silver, they almost at once proceeded to reform the gold. In the French era of depreciations the experience was similar. Philippe le Bel, reckless as he was with regard to the silver, never ventured to tamper with the gold. Philippe de Valois and John certainly tampered with it. The standard during John's reign was brought as low as 18 carats.[2] Under Charles VI., however we find it pure again, and after the close of his reign it was never debased. Similarly in the Roman world, even in the worst times of monetary confusion, the quality of the aureus was always fairly well maintained, and, after Constantine, it remained almost unaltered in weight and quite unaltered in standard for more than eight hundred years. Cosmas,[3] a traveller who found his way as far as India in the reign of Justinian, tells us that then the Roman gold piece, on account of its excellence, "was used in the commerce of every nation and was received from

[1] Lowndes's Report, containing an essay for the amendment of the silver coin, p. 46. By the 3rd of Edward VI. the standard of the gold was raised to 22 carats, and by the 4th the old standard was restored, while by the 5th the silver was made three-fourths alloy.

[2] Le Blanc, *op. cit.*, Tables, p. 318.

[3] Mommsen, *op. cit.*, vol. iii. p. 128.

one extremity of the globe to the other," and this remained true of it down almost to the period when gold coinages again became general all over Europe.[1]

The contrast, in this respect, between gold and silver is surely a fact that calls for an explanation of some sort. Granted that the cupidity and shortsightedness of kings and governments have continually driven them to debase their moneys, why should this cupidity and shortsightedness have acted so much more effectively on the money made of one metal than on that made of another? The explanation is evidently to be found in the fact that the differentiation of money, together with the operation of the principle of quasi-redemption, has very frequently made the debasement of the cheaper metal, for a time, easy and lucrative, while the debasement of the principal metal has always, when attempted, been

---

[1] The solidi issued from Constantinople appear never to have been debased before the sack of the city by the Latins in 1204, though the Isaurian emperors seem to have issued some base gold in Italy, as our Elizabeth, while she kept the English coin pure, issued base money in Ireland (see Sabatier, *Monnaies Byzantines*, pp. 51–61). The debasement of the Bezant by the *Palaeologi* (see Sabatier, *op. cit.*, p. 241) was no doubt one cause of the great and rapid success of the Florentine florin (cf. Gibbon, *Decline and Fall*, ed. Milman, 1838, vol. xi. p. 336). It probably dealt a blow to the stability of the Greek Empire hardly less severe than the disaster of 1204 itself. It is regrettable to find that the first debaser seems to have been the capable and vigorous John Vataces.

followed at once by the loss of credit, and by manifold embarrassments.

The question whether there are any authentic instances of the circulation of gold at a conventional value, which was greater than its intrinsic value, is one of some interest. The lines of Aristophanes, in the *Frogs*, in which he recognises the operation of Gresham's Law, are sometimes cited as referring to such an instance. They run as follows :[1] " I have often thought that the attitude of our city towards the noble and good among its citizens is just the same as its attitude towards the time-honoured currency and the new gold. We make no use of the former, though the coins are free from alloy, and are the finest of all, being I think the only ones that are rightly struck and tested among either Greeks or foreigners all the world over. Instead of this, we use these wretched bronzes, struck but a day or two ago, and with the worst of stamps." It will be observed that Aristophanes describes the coins, whatever they were, which had supplanted the silver, in the first half of the passage as gold, and in the second as bronze ; and whether they were really gold which, by way of vituperation, he described as bronze, or whether, on the other hand, they were bronze which, by way of irony, he described as gold, it

[1] Line 717 ff.

is not altogether easy to determine.   Eckhel, the
famous founder of the science of numismatics,
thinks that they were bronze, and in this opinion
Lenormant follows him.   There are some reasons
however, into which I need not enter, for thinking
it possible that they were really gold ; and if this
was the case it seems, further, that they were not
debased gold, but gold which was in truth of the
finest quality.   A few of the pieces which are
believed by some eminent authorities to be
samples of the very coinage referred to are still
extant.[1]

Whenever such money has been issued in the
modern world, it has always been the money
which men have been eager to secure and to
retain, and never that "worse money" which
they are usually desirous of passing on to their
neighbours, and which in consequence becomes
the prominent feature in the circulation.   How
then could things have turned out so differently
in Athens?   M. Babelon's [2] explanation is ingenious and interesting, if not thoroughly and
fully convincing.   The coinage referred to, he
remarks, took place during the Peloponnesian
War, and at a time when the Athenians were
cut off from their famous silver mines at Laurium,

[1] Three in Berlin, three in Paris, one in London, and one in
St. Petersburg.
[2] *Les Origines de la Monnaie*, p. 337.

and when silver must have been abnormally
scarce, and, it is presumed, in consequence, abnormally high in value as compared with gold.
Even apart moreover from this abnormal state
of things, gold, it is certain, had for some generations been falling in value as measured in
silver, and continued indeed so to fall for some
generations afterwards.   Some accounts which
remain relating to the purchase of the gold used
by Phidias in the construction of the statue of
Athene for the Parthenon, 438 B.C., show that
the market ratio between the metals then was
1:14.   A hundred years later, under Alexander
the Great, it had become 1:10, and the fall seems
to have been continuous during the whole period.
In such circumstances, if the monetary ratio
between the two metals was fixed, at any given
date, in accordance with their respective intrinsic
values, that ratio would be likely to be found
at any subsequent date to be one that over-
rated gold, and that consequently made it operate
as the worse money in cutting out the better,
silver.

This explanation is at any rate a possible one.
The relations between gold and silver in the
Græco-Persian period present other problems
that still await solution.   It is contended, and
the contention is supported by very strong evidence, that for the two hundred years during

which the empire of the Achemenides lasted, the ratio between the coined gold and silver within that empire remained fixed at the precise figure of $1:13\frac{1}{3}$. It is quite incredible that the relations between the market values of the metals them-selves could have remained thus stable to a fraction during such a period. It would be like nothing else seen in the world before or since. Outside the bounds of the Persian Empire too, at the very same date, the ratio, we know, was conspicuously variable. The phenomenon, how-ever, would be explicable if we suppose that one or other of the two metals was circulating at a conventional value ; and, if either was, it certainly was the gold. That which unfailingly maintains the identity between the monetary and the in-trinsic value of gold among ourselves is of course the fact that the mint is always open to its free coinage. Greece and the Greek cities of Asia Minor had, as regarded silver, an effective sub-stitute for our free coinage in the fact that any silver that one city might conceivably be indis-posed to coin could be sent to another and could be coined there, and that the coins of all, as in Europe in the Middle Ages, circulated every-where. The Athenian silver was as acceptable universally as the English gold is now ; while [1] at the same time we come across such a pheno-

---

[1] G. F. Hill, *Handbook of Greek and Roman Coins*, p. 70.

menon as the electrum of Phocæa and Cyzicus, with regard to which the rate of exchange varied from city to city. The poet Persinus,[1] for instance, found that he could change his *phocaides* on better terms in Mytilene than in Atarneus.

As a matter of fact, we know from Xenophon that the Athenians never had any hesitation about coining every ounce of silver that they could get from the mines of Laurium. Silver was the one thing in the world, as he remarked, that never varied in its value, no matter to what extent you increased its supply. With gold it was different. The cities under the suzerainty of Persia were not permitted to coin it, and the most important of the Greek cities apparently had no desire to do so. The principal gold coinage of the Græco-Persian world therefore consisted of the darics of the Great King. Vast stores of gold bullion were accumulated at Susa, and darics were issued according to requirements. It seems quite possible, thus, that the Persian government had learned the necessity of limiting their issues of gold if they wished to maintain their monetary value. The very fact of their possessing such stores of it is evidence that they were not a spendthrift or bankrupt government, obliged to coin all that they could lay their hands on. The monetary ratio, which had been 1 : 13⅓ in the days of Hero-

---

[1] *Ibid.*, p. 70, note 3.

dotus[1] and of Xenophon, was still it seems $1 : 13\frac{1}{3}$ in the earlier days of Alexander's campaigns.[2] When Persia was conquered, however, and the treasures of Susa were dispersed, then this apparently artificial ratio could no longer be maintained. Then, at last, the metals seem to have reached bed rock values at a ratio of $1 : 10$.

The conclusion to be drawn from the above, in as far as it is possible to draw any conclusions from facts so remote historically, and in regard to which our information is necessarily so imperfect, is that during a protracted period in which the value of gold is tending downwards the two metals may circulate together in the world without gold showing a tendency to oust silver from its position as the standard money; and that of course is the result that we might look for on *a priori* grounds. That money will always tend to become the standard money which is felt to form the most reliable medium for the storing of purchasing power; and in as far as there was, from one generation to another, a perceptible fall in the value of gold, its trustworthiness in that respect would necessarily be impaired.

If then there are any exceptions discoverable

---

[1] Herodotus says $1 : 13$, but is believed to speak only approximately. Xenophon's information is precise.

[2] Babylon, *Les Origines de la Monnaie*, p. 323.

to Adam Smith's law that the more precious
metal always assumes the position of regulator of
the value of the whole coinage, in other words
of the standard, these, we find, are not exceptions
to the more general principle on which it depends,
that the better money in the long run, as
standard, ousts the worse. If silver held the
position of the standard metal, to the exclusion of
gold, in Greece, during the fourth and fifth
centuries before Christ, it did so because it was
then the better money, the more reliable medium
for the storage of purchasing power.

We can see now the importance of the question,
What, at any given date was the trend of the ratio?
We are often told by writers who deal with the
money of antiquity that the ratio between gold
and silver in the old world generally averaged
1 : 10, or that during the Roman Imperial period,
say, it averaged 1 : 12. This savours of the
conception that " all the ancients lived at once."
Such general statements are necessarily of little
interest. What is, however, of great interest is
to learn which metal, during any particular epoch,
was on the rise as measured in the other, how
long it had been rising, and how long it continued
to rise. The period in Rome, for instance, which
witnessed the displacement of silver by gold was
a period during which the latter was all the time
on the rise. The monetary ratio at the fall of the

Republic was 1 : 11·91. By Diocletian's[1] time it had risen to 1 : 13·88. From Constantine[2] to Theodosius it ruled from 1 : 13·88 to 1 : 14·40, and appears in that epoch to have been still rising.

As regards modern Europe, again, in England, in Henry III.'s time, when gold was first issued, it was regarded as overrated at 1 : 10. A hundred years later it had become highly acceptable at 1 : 11 and something over it. Thenceforward, for 250 years to the close of Elizabeth's reign, there were minor fluctuations continually, but little alteration of the general average. Another seventy years however—from the accession of James I. to the tenth year of Charles II.'s reign—brought its value up to a point very close to the celebrated modern figure of 1 : 15½. Again, a period of approximate stationariness succeeded. The earlier years of the eighteenth century saw a tendency indeed, both in England and in Europe generally, to a rise in silver. About the middle of the century, however, the tide turned. In 1761[3] Sir James Steuart significantly observed that the late war—the Seven Years' War—had established a marked rise in gold. By 1774 the market ratio had

[1] Mommsen, *op. cit.*, vol. iii. p. 154.
[2] G. F. Hill, *op. cit.*, p. 75.
[3] *Works*, vol. ii. p. 406. See also vol. iii. p. 112.

reached Newton's ratio of 1717 and threatened to pass it, and the result was the legislation which, for the first time, put a limitation on the legal tender power of the silver coin.

The course of events as regards the ratio in England typifies pretty fairly their course in Europe generally. From the survey of it there are two conclusions that suggest themselves. First, the existence and the steady operation, throughout, of such causes as the superior suitability of gold for foreign trade and for reserves, which always tended to send it up at the expense of silver ; secondly, the existence of some counteracting cause that during long periods rendered the action of this first cause ineffective. We find the latter, I think, whenever we look for it throughout the whole period, in the conditions of the Eastern trade.

In quite recent years, in the sixties, silver went up to 5s. 2d. per ounce. We are told that this was due to the abundance of the gold found in Australia and California. Those who tell us this, however, so far as I am aware, never attempt to trace the connection between the two phenomena. On the other hand, we have an obvious and clearly traceable cause for the rise in silver, in that instance, in the fact that the European supply of cotton from America was cut off by the Civil War, and that Europe had therefore to get its cotton from India, and had to pay for it largely in silver bullion. A great and unusual demand for silver was thus created, and the metal naturally rose in the market.

Again, in the eighteenth century, we find Newton[1] regarding such rises as took place occasionally in silver in his time as being always due to an increased demand "for the Indies"; and Rice Vaughan,[2] in the seventeenth century, anticipates Humboldt's generalisation in the nineteenth. "So fareth it with silver," he says, "that all countries which do draw from Spain do necessarily set a greater price upon it by how much they are remote from thence, and this is the reason why the sphear of silver seemeth to roll from the west unto the east, where it seemeth to fall into a gulph. But of gold it is not so, because that cometh in as great abundance from the east as from the west." In Turkey, he remarks, silver was higher than in Western Europe. In Persia it was higher than in Turkey, and so forward into China. In Japan, in our own day, before the great revolution that brought that country into line with the rest of the world, the ratio was about 1 : 8. Altogether, throughout the East, the ratio appears for many centuries to have been more favourable to silver than it was

---

[1] Newton's Report as Master of the Mint in 1717.
[2] *Discourse on Coyn and Coynage,* p. 171.

in Europe ; and thus any increased activity in
the Eastern trade always operated to check the
downward tendency of that metal in the West.
The discovery of the Cape route, which brought
us into closer trade relations with India, was
almost simultaneous with the discovery of America,
which so greatly increased our supplies of silver.
In the Stuart period however the American
supplies became apparently far too great for the
Eastern trade to absorb, and then we see silver
falling rapidly.   This is an aspect of the matter
that has not been sufficiently attended to by those
who think that a readily traceable connection is
to be found between fluctuations in general prices
and fluctuations in the supply of the precious
metals.   In as far as the increase in the quantity
of silver in Europe between the close of Elizabeth's reign and the Revolution was discounted
by the fall of 40 per cent. in its value, it would
plainly have had no tendency at all to raise prices.
It is surely, on any theory, not the increased
weight of the metal in use, but its increased
purchasing power that would be effective in that
direction.

Such a survey of the situation is calculated to
tempt us into speculation in regard to the future.
When we see that the influence of the Eastern
ratio is a spent force, while the causes that made
for the rise in gold as compared with silver are

more active than ever, we cannot help asking ourselves, Are we to look for still further diminutions in the value of the white metal? It is noteworthy, too, that, in the ancient world, the secondary metal, when supplanted as the principal money, showed more than once a tendency not only to fall steadily in value, but even to disappear as money altogether. The copper disappeared in the age of Sulla, to reappear indeed again, but only as token money, under the Empire. Later on, the end of the third century A.D. saw the complete disappearance of the silver. By the time of Severus it had become no better than billon, and by the time of Aurelian it was pure copper.[1] When Diocletian undertook his great reform there was absolutely no silver in circulation. Diocletian coined silver afresh, and the succeeding emperors never debased it as the preceding ones had done. At the same time,[2] in A.D. 368, we are told that the commerce of the Empire was conducted exclusively in gold and in bronze. In the fifth century, at any rate, bronze had become so exclusively the medium of internal trade that it had arrogated to itself the name of " pecunia."

It is conceivable, though at present no doubt it seems very far from probable, that history may in this respect repeat itself, and that the world

[1] Mommsen, *op. cit.*, vol. iii. p. 86.
[2] *Op. cit.*, vol. iii. p. 133.

at some distant date may again witness a disappearance of silver as money.   Its monetary value
has now ceased altogether to depend on its metallic
value, and in these circumstances it is always. possible that a cheaper medium may supplant it.

It must be observed that, though it is the case
that a fall lasting during many generations might
tend to impair the reputation of the more precious
metal as a store of purchasing power, and might
thus tend to prevent it from assuming the position
of the standard money, it would not do to
conclude that a sudden fluctuation downwards at
any particular date would be likely to be attended
with any similar consequence.   We might, for
instance, regard the rise in silver in the sixties as
a fluctuation downwards in the gold ; and that
we know was an event which, instead of standing
in the way of the adoption of the gold standard
in Europe, was the very agency which achieved
its final completion.   Similarly, the rise in the
silver in the eighteenth century no doubt assisted
in effecting the transition to gold in England, and
the rise in silver, or the fall in gold, whichever
we choose to consider it, in Cæsar's day in
Rome appears to have led up towards a parallel
result.

In dealing with Gresham's Law we came to the
conclusion that one of the reasons why a principle
which is plainly applicable only to subsidiary

money should have been so frequently treated as a principle applicable to money generally, and should have thus been erected into a theory of the transition of standards, was to be found in the fact that the subsidiary currency itself has so often filled the whole visible horizon as money the real money of the epoch being hardly seen by the bulk of the population. Another reason is to be found in the fact that phenomena such as those above alluded to have often been erroneously taken for instances illustrating the operation of that law.

But "why erroneously?" it will be asked. "Are they not instances of the cheaper metal ousting the dearer?" That may be so, but they are certainly not instances of the worse money ousting the better. If gold was a worse money than silver in France in the sixties, why is it that we have such unanimous testimony to the satisfaction with which its growing predominance in the currency to the exclusion of silver was witnessed by the public at the time? And why is it that the general sentiment with regard to that fact was undoubtedly so different from the sentiment with regard to the displacement of the gold by the silver, then become the cheaper metal, during the next decade?

The truth is that the current view which regards any two metals which may be circulating together in any age and country at a bimetallic parity as necessarily occupying positions which are precisely the equivalent of each other is an unsound one. If there is anything in the reasonings of the previous chapters, then the one metal may in such circumstances already be the standard, while the other has already become mere token money; and this, although the law recognises no difference between them, though both are open to free coinage at the mint, and are still unlimited legal tender in all transactions. That, as we have already seen, is the view which has impressed itself on Mommsen's mind in regard to such situations, as the result of a comprehensive survey of the money of antiquity. He takes it for granted that in such cases there is already a standard and a non-standard metal in existence, and goes on to distinguish between the results that will ensue in the event of a fluctuation upward or downward in either of the two respectively. Mill tells us quite generally that in the event of a fluctuation downwards in either of two such metals the one that fluctuates downwards will become the standard. Mommsen on the contrary says if the metal that fluctuates downwards is not already the standard, the coins that are made of it will sink into the condition of token money. Which view is most in accordance with the teachings of history? That is an issue the verdict on which may now, I think, be left to the reader.

PART II

THE ORIGIN OF MONEY AND THE NATURE OF THE STANDARD

Crescit amor nummi quantum ipsa pecunia crevit.
—Juvenal, *Sat.* xiv. l. 139.

Tale è la natura delle ricchezze, che, crescendo elle, piu ne cresca la sete.
—Petrarch, Memoir of himself prefixed to his Latin works (14).

CHAPTER I

THE ORIGIN OF MONEY

In the preceding chapters the attempt has been made to disentangle the laws which are applicable to subsidiary money alone from those that are applicable to real money. Subsidiary money circulates, we have found, as the medium of exchange in virtue of its convertibility into real money. In virtue of what is it that real money itself circulates? The standard commodity is, after all, but one commodity out of many. How is it that it attains a position and a character so different from that attained by any other? Let us get rid, once for all, of the idea that it attains it owing to its "adoption" as money by any "convention," tacit or explicit, entered into with each other by the members of primitive communities. We should scout at once, as an unhistorical absurdity, this conception of "conventions" if applied to the origin of language or

of government ; and it is certainly no nearer
the truth when applied to the origin of money.
Those who speak of conventions, in such a
connection, would probably tell us that they do
not mean to be taken literally ; they merely mean
to say that something was done, or somehow
came about, which was tantamount to the adoption
by an early convention of some metal or some
other commodity as the medium of exchange.
Whether they mean to be taken literally or not,
the use of such language is mischievous. It seems
to afford some sort of explanation of the phenomenon, and thus tends to set at rest the inquiries
as to the real explanation that would otherwise
be inevitable and might be fruitful. It was not
till students of the science of language had got
rid of the idea of conventions that philology came
into existence, and not till the notion of social
contracts was finally discredited that the scientific
treatment of the origin and growth of civil government became possible.

Let us glance, in the first instance, at the current
explanation of the origin of money, as put into
shape by Adam Smith. It runs, it will be remembered, somewhat as follows.[1] The division of
labour having been established, the power of
exchanging commodities must frequently have
been embarrassed by the difficulty which a would-

[1] *Wealth of Nations*, B. i. cap. 4.

be exchanger would often feel in finding any one who happened to possess a superfluity of the commodity that he wanted, and who at the same time would take what he had to dispose of. "To avoid the inconveniency of such situations the prudent man would naturally endeavour to have by him a certain quantity of some one commodity or other *such as he imagined few people would be likely to refuse in exchange for the produce of their industry.*"[1] . . . "Many different commodities it is probable were successively both thought of and employed for the purpose." In the end, however, "irresistible reasons" led all civilised nations to give the preference to the metals, and eventually to the precious metals. The "irresistible reasons" were of course the high value in small compass, the homogeneity, fusibility, divisibility, and so on, of these metals.

On this explanation, the criticism at once suggests itself that, if the prudent man could find any commodity that few would refuse in exchange for their products, then money was already virtually established. The very thing that we want to know is, How did first one commodity, then another, and finally gold and silver, attain such a degree of universal acceptability as ensured their being refused by none in exchange for their products?

Professor Walker, whose discussion of the

---

[1] The italics are mine.

subject in his *Money, Trade and Industry* (p. 6) is, within limits, most lucid and enlightening, after defining money as that which every one receives without the slightest reference either to his own need for consumption or to the credit of the person who offers it, remarks, "When an article reaches this degree of acceptability it becomes money, no matter what it is made of, and no matter why people want it." This conception of an article as "becoming" money spontaneously as soon as it has reached a certain required degree of "acceptability" is certainly much nearer the truth than Adam Smith's conception, which seems to assume that the prehistoric communities first decided that the establishment of money would be desirable, then experimented with a variety of commodities as money, and finally, for irresistible reasons, fixed on the precious metals.

Supposing the attainment of this required degree of acceptability by any commodity—say, by gold — successfully completed, Professor Walker goes on to show how it then comes to measure the values of all other commodities. The passages in which he does this are to my mind among the most important of recent contributions to economical science. "Given the fact," he observes,[1] "of a general desire for one article of uniform quality which is susceptible of easy and

[1] *Op. cit.*, p. 38

exact division, we have all the requirements of a common denominator in exchange satisfied. The effort of every dealer to obtain as much as possible of this one article for each and every part of his stock, the wish of every producer to bring to market the product involving the least labour which will purchase a given quantity of this article—these must result in ranging all commodities, according to the cost of replacing them, upon a scale of prices the degrees of which shall be expressed in terms of this one article, money." The mode in which commodities range themselves in a price current on the basis of the standard is given in a more concrete form as follows :[1] " At first we will suppose wheat, corn and oats exchange for equal amounts of gold ; but the farmers soon find that they can raise oats more easily than corn, corn more easily than wheat ; and consequently many farmers bring oats and much of it, few farmers bring corn and little of it, no farmers at all bring wheat. Why should they ? Hence, as the existing stock of wheat begins to disappear, more and more gold is offered for wheat, until the point is reached when the farmer gets as much gold for a day's work in raising wheat as in raising oats " ; and, in a manner similar to this, the scale of values for all commodities comes to be settled.

All this is perfectly comprehensible once we

[1] *Op. cit.*, p. 34.

make the important supposition that gold has attained such a degree of "acceptability" in the community that no one will refuse it, no matter in what quantities it is offered. Suppose however, for a moment, the contrary ; suppose that, while the process of constructing the scale of values is yet only half complete, the farmers should find that they had got enough gold, and suppose that they consequently declined to take any more of it ; it is evident that the measuring of values is at once at an end. It was the " acceptability" of the gold alone that made the measurement possible, and now that the "acceptability" exists no longer, the measurement too ceases.

This obvious truth has not impressed itself so clearly on Professor Walker's mind as could have been wished. He is of opinion that gold, or whatever other commodity we suppose to have become the standard, will owe the attainment of its "acceptability" to the fact that it has been constituted money by the government of the community. If the government make paper legal tender, there is no reason, he thinks, why paper should not measure values as well as gold itself. It is evident however that here it is original value, not such derivative value as this, that we are concerned with. Whatever truth there may be in the view that fiduciary money can measure values, it is plain that it can have no application

to the prehistoric period in which money originated. Undoubtedly it is true that once any
commodity has become established as money, the
fact that it has become so established will react in
an important manner on the demand for it ; but
we cannot use the fact of this reaction to explain
how it became money. We must recognise, once
for all, the truth that we can look to no fancied
convention for the cause that has, in various ages
and countries, converted such commodities as
cowry shells, copper, silver and gold into the one
material which every member of the community
is bending all his energies to obtain in unlimited
quantities. We shall find this cause, if we find it
at all, in some qualities that appertain intrinsically
to the material, qualities that have adapted it so
to operate on human springs of action as to
elicit universal effort for its acquirement. The
monetary standard can be no vague or dim abstraction.[1] It must be some individual, concrete
substance, which has something about it which
causes vast numbers of men and women to make
its possession the final goal of the concentrated
effort of their lives.

In endeavouring to solve the problem what are
these qualities—in other words, what are the
characteristics which enable one commodity to
distance others in attaining the position of money

[1] Cf. such as an " Exchange Standard."

—it may be worth while to take note of those characteristics which render a commodity conspicuously unfit for its attainment. The eminent German historian whom I have had occasion to quote so often already may be quoted again in this connection.[1] "The commodity that becomes money," Mommsen observes, "must above all things not be one that is indispensable for the supply of the most urgent material needs. It is for this reason that in no country has corn ever been used as the comparative measure of the value of other merchandise; and that mankind after having, from the most remote antiquity, successively and in various countries employed as money cattle, iron and copper, have uniformly ended with silver and with gold."

Why is it, we are impelled to ask, that corn and such like necessaries of life have never in any country become money? It is plainly because the desire for them is dependent upon bodily appetites, and is therefore liable at any moment to satiation. Wheat assuredly could not circulate. If a man had not more than enough of it to satisfy present hunger, he would not part with any of it. If, on the contrary, he and the rest of the community of which he was a member had enough of it for present wants, together with such provision for future needs as they regarded as

---

[1] *Hist. de la Monnaie romaine* (Blacas), Preface, p. xiv.

adequate, then any man who had a superfluity of it would not be able to barter away any of it on any terms whatever. No one would take it off his hands. The only circumstances in which wheat could conceivably assume a position anything like that of money would be in the event of there being an export outlet for it. It is possible indeed that it did, from that cause, assume the position of money, for a time, among the Greeks of Southern Italy.[1] Any fairly homogeneous substance for which there is a steady export outlet can, it seems, temporarily become the local money of the community that exports it. We have the well known instance of the tobacco money of Virginia. "Since,"[2] as Professor Walker explains, "tobacco was in unfailing demand for shipment abroad, it was always readily taken at the country store. The colonists, knowing that there was this outlet for it always open, passed it from hand to hand among themselves as a medium of exchange. It acquired thus the degree of acceptability requisite to convert it into money."

We gather, then, that the first requisite for the commodity that is to distance other commodities in attaining the position of money, is that there should always be an outlet open for it, an "auto-

---

[1] Cf. Ridgeway, *Origin of Metallic Currency*, p. 327.
[2] *Money, Trade, and Industry*, p. 5.

matic outflow." [1] When however we take the world as a whole, or any self-contained section of it, like Europe in the early Middle Ages, there can evidently be no outlet constantly open for any commodity, so far as the conditions of Space are concerned. There may however be an outlet in Time. That is to say, the whole surplus of some commodity which is not required to supply present needs may be absorbed for the purposes of provision for the future ; and this, as a matter of fact, is what happens with regard to the monetary commodity. The origin of money is thus essentially connected with that stage in human development when men begin to " look before and after." In regard to every form of wealth that, in the varying circumstances of innumerable communities, has become the medium of exchange, this condition will be found to hold good, that it was, at the time, the commodity that was, of all others, the one that was best suited to serve as a provision against future contingencies.

In the earlier stages of industrial development, when a man's food and clothing were produced mainly or exclusively by his own labour or that of his household, this provision for the future would be direct, and little, if at all, dependent on the operation of exchange. In these circumstances, the ideas of wealth and money would naturally be

[1] Cf. *supra*, part i. chap. vii. p. 181.

most closely associated with cattle and sheep, from which the tribal supplies of food and clothing could be drawn ; with slaves, whose indispensable services would be always at command ; or, again, with the implements of cookery, of agriculture, or of the chase.   Among the early moneys of many nations, thus, there figure, after cattle and slaves, or it may be contemporaneously with them, such things as knives and fish-hooks, hoes, tripods and caldrons.

A further stage is reached when, for such implements and utensils, comes to be substituted the material out of which they are made, and from which, when lost or worn out, they can be replaced.   Homer gives us a glimpse of the light in which a mass of pig iron presented itself to the husbandmen on the islands and coasts of the Ægean.[1]   At the games in honour of Patroclus, Achilles lays down a mass of iron as the prize for hurling the quoit.   In describing its value to the winner, he says : " Even if his fat lands be very far remote, it will last him five revolving seasons.   For not through want of iron will his shepherd or his ploughman go to the town, but it will supply him."   " Among the Madis of Central Africa," says a recent traveller,[2] " the nearest approach to money is seen in the

---

[1] *Iliad*, xxiii., 826.

R. W. Felkin, quoted by Prof. Ridgeway, *op. cit.*, p. 43.

flat round pieces of iron, which are of different sizes, from three-quarters to two feet in diameter. and half an inch thick. They are much employed in exchange. This is the form in which they are kept and used as money, but they are intended to be divided into two, heated and made into hoes." We can see from such an example as this how iron and bronze might naturally—as they did—assume the position of money in the countries bordering the Mediterranean. It is a fact worthy of notice that the earliest bronze money of Italy consisted of precisely the same alloy of copper, tin and zinc as did the utensils which had preceded it as the medium of exchange.[1]

When the division of labour had made some considerable progress, then provision for the future would largely cease to be of this direct and simple character, and the commodity which would then best secure a man's future sustenance and well-being would not be so much the commodity best adapted for immediate utilisation by himself or his dependants as the commodity which would be most efficient in securing for him the services of his neighbours or of strangers unconnected with him.

We find now moreover, and not without surprise, that the two classes of commodities, those which possess the greatest direct utility and those

[1] Mommsen, *op. cit.*, vol. i. p. 75.

which are most securely to be relied upon in pro-
curing for us the services of others, are very far
indeed from being identical. A great and striking
fact that meets us everywhere as the world pro-
gresses is the substitution of ornament and the
metals of ornament, for instruments of utility and
the metals used in their construction, as the stores
of purchasing power, and consequently as the
media of exchange. Referring to the use of
copper in Italy as money, while silver was
used in Greece, and gold in the Persia of the
Achemenides, Mommsen remarks: "The West
thus had chosen for its monetary instrument the
useful metal, and the East the metal of ornament.
The experience of centuries has proved that of
the two the East was the better inspired." [1]

[1] *Op. cit.*, Preface, p. xvii.

CHAPTER II

ORNAMENT AND MONEY

THERE is surely something surprising and paradoxical in the fact that substances such as gold and
silver, which could have been so very well done
without by the human race without any sensible
diminution of their comfort or even of their luxury,
and whose intrinsic value seems to depend upon
feelings and desires that are to so great an extent
merely fanciful and frivolous, should in the end
have distanced all other commodities in the attainment of the monetary status. It seems to indicate
that the fanciful and the frivolous occupy a greater
share in the moulding of human destinies than our
too prosaic economical science is accustomed to
allow to them.

M. Babelon is struck by the paradox.[1] " Everywhere," he says, " wherever we come across man
on the surface of the globe, we find at the same

[1] *Les Origines de la Monnaie*, p. 248.

time that it is the superfluous which by instinct
seems to him the most necessary ; man has
scarcely learnt the use of clothes before he
hangs on to his neck, his arms, his legs, his
ears, necklaces, bracelets, rings and pendants of
every shape, in the manufacture of which the
precious metals are always and everywhere preferred. Ever since the beginning of the world,
among the prehistoric peoples as among the
savages of to-day, the pursuit of gold and silver
dominates everything ; ages before the invention
of money and the appearance of the legislator
nations made war with each other for the possession of the precious metals, organised for their
acquisition long and perilous expeditions, which
have left their memory in history and in fable,
such as the expedition of the Argonauts in search
of the Golden Fleece, the adventures of Hercules
in the Garden of the Hesperides, and the voyages
of the ships of Tyre and Sidon to the country of
Tharsis."

Nor are gold and silver the only substances
whose main or whose exclusive use is the decoration of the person, which have, for a time, had an
extensive range as money in the world. Polished
shells, which were used by prehistoric man as ornaments in the neolithic age [1] are used to-day both
as ornament and as money in the East Indies, in

---

[1] Ridgeway, *op. cit.*, p. 14.

Siam, and on the east and west coasts of Africa. Marco Polo found the cowry in use as money in China in his day, and there is reason to believe that it subserved a similar purpose in ancient Nineveh. The earliest Chinese book extant uses the expression "a hundred thousand dead shell fishes" as an equivalent for "riches."

It must be remembered too that the metals that have been spoken of as the useful metals are also very largely used for purposes of ornament, and it may have been after all mainly to their fitness for that purpose that the iron of Sparta and the bronze of Italy became, in these countries, the media of exchange.

It is not rare among primitive peoples to find the combination of the monetary and ornamental uses manifested in the very shape and texture of the ornaments. "In Calabar, for example," says Professor Ridgeway,[1] "they formerly employed bunches of quadrangular copper wire as currency. Each wire was about twelve inches long, and they were, of course, meant to be made into necklets and armlets." They were also meant however to be cut off in the required lengths to make payments with. The well-known wampum money[2] of New England is another instance in point. The wampum belts "consisted of black and white shells rubbed down, polished

---

[1] *Op. cit.*, p. 40.   [2] *Op. cit.*, p. 14.

and made into beads, and then strung into belts and necklaces, which were valued according to their length, colour and lustre, the black beads being the most valuable." More recently, among the Karoks of California,[1] we are told, a similar description of money was in use, which consisted of strings of the dentalium shell; and curiously enough, when it was supplanted by the American silver, it at once came natural to the Karoks to use the new money for the purposes which had given its intrinsic value to the old. " The young bloods," says a recent writer, " array their Dulcineas for the dance with lavish adornment, hanging on their dress 30, 40, or 50 dollars worth of dimes, quarter-dollars and half-dollars, arranged in strings. " This shows," remarks Professor Ridgeway, " that the new currency of silver is treated by them in exactly the same way as the old shell strings, both of them deriving their value as media of exchange from the fact that they are the objects most universally prized as ornaments for the person."

As regards the natives of India the fact has become familiar to us that the peasant's hoard naturally seems to take the shape of bracelets, bangles, and ear-rings for his wife and daughters; and the peasant himself seems usually to regard them in the double light of decorations conferring

[1] *Op. cit.*, p. 15.

social prestige and of provision for future needs. A native gentleman, Mr. Romesh Dutt, who was examined by Sir Henry Fowler's committee, had some things to say on the subject which are worth rescuing from the dust-heap of the Blue-books. Referring to the vast amounts of money spent annually by the natives on silver ornaments, he was asked by one of the members of the committee,[1] "Would not the country have been benefited if that money had been employed, instead of being allowed to lie idle?" "I do not think it lies idle," replied Mr. Dutt, "because it serves the purpose of ornament and savings bank." "As regards savings banks," went on his interlocutor, "is it not very much more economical and better to put your savings into some interest-bearing security than to tie them up in a bag?" The reply was very much to the point:[2] "If an Indian cultivator," said Mr. Dutt, "had 200 or 300 rupees in the bank, it would disappear in the course of a year or so; but, if it is in the shape of his women's ornaments, he will keep them until he is compelled by famine to part with them. You must take into consideration the customs of the country in considering these questions. Silver ornaments are a far safer and more lasting investment for the Indian than deposits in banks."

[1] Mr. Campbell.   [2] Question 10,857.

Because it comes natural to the business man nowadays to save all he can out of his surplus earnings, he is too liable to think that it would come natural to people in other and lower stages of civilisation to do the same. The lesson is slowly learnt that, in endeavouring to interpret the mental operations of more primitive peoples, we must avoid transferring to them in thought our own moral and intellectual apparatus all developed and complete. There are tribes of savages in whom the power of making any provision for the future is almost as completely dormant or non-existent as it is in the horse or in the ox. The Shoshons of North America are said at the close of every winter to be always on the verge of starvation ; yet the approach of the next winter finds them no more provident than the last had found them. The very power of making provision for the future is something that the human race have had to learn slowly and with difficulty ; and even among civilised peoples a great proportion of the population have made little progress as yet in that branch of mental discipline.

We do not need to search in any field more recondite than our own school-day remembrances to recognise how strong a social sentiment there is always at work that makes against saving. Among schoolboys, among sailors and

and among our heedless youth generally, if any one is known to have a pound or a shilling in his possession, he is liable to be regarded with a certain amount of coldness or even of dislike if he is not willing to spend it straight away for the benefit of all. The most reckless, in money matters at any rate, is likely to be the hero of the hour. This sentiment, so strong still to-day, would assuredly among the earlier generations of mankind have carried everything before it, and would have rendered all attempts at saving impossible, if it had not been met by something that could make a stronger appeal to the passions and impulses that sway untutored humanity than could be made by the counsels of far-seeing prudence.

This want of a counter impulse was supplied by the desire of personal decoration. There might be something mean and contemptible in general opinion in putting a hundred rupees away in a bag, and refusing to lavish them at the marriages and the funerals of your relations. It was a different story when they were used to make your womankind outshine their neighbours in the glories of bangles and earrings. We are not to suppose that the Indian who expended his rupees on such ornaments had ordinarily the *arrière pensée* in his mind that some day they might be available to meet an urgent need ; though, with the experience of

generations, that view of the matter too might
begin to enter into his calculations. His primary
impulse, however, and all along his most potent
one, would be the desire for the social distinction
that such ornaments would confer. If we view
the matter aright we should regard this desire for
ornament, for prestige, for distinction as the
instinctive impulse which animated his individual
action, while the provision for future contingencies,
which has the appearance of accidentally accom-
panying it, must be regarded as the thought of
that wider and greater Intelligence which was
guiding his destinies.

This intimate association between the monetary
and the ornamental uses of gold and silver is very
far from being an exclusively Hindoo characteristic. If we go back a few centuries, we find it
conspicuous enough in Western Europe. Indeed
it is only within the last two hundred years that it
can be said to have become altogether a thing of
the past. No doubt plate and money, in our
thoughts now, have completely parted company.
It would not occur to us to regard the £2,000,000
worth of plate, which is said to have been dis-
played at Windsor, on the occasion of the
German Emperor's visit last year, in the light
of a reserve for emergencies, or to anticipate
the possibility of its being some day coined into
sovereigns. Even in the later Stuart period,

however, such a thought would have occurred to any one quite naturally. The conversion of plate into money by the Crown, in its time of need, was then a recent event, and money and plate had in those days an intimate connection in popular thought which was by no means shared by other forms of wealth. A proclamation[1] of Charles II. in 1661 describes the English nation as having, in former times, been "renowned for its plenteous stock of money and the magnificence of its plate," as if the two were very much the same. It is interesting, again, to find Sir Dudley North assailing the policy of a recent law, forbidding the use of plate in taverns, by the argument that "if every one had plate in his house, the nation would then be possessed of a solid fund in these metals which all the world desires."[2] A goldsmith's trade is now a very different sort of trade from that of a banker; but, in the seventeenth century, they seemed naturally and inevitably the same. No one would dream of converting old silver plate into bullion nowadays, as the plate is worth, perhaps, about £5 per ounce, while the bullion is worth about 2s. 4d. Then however the "fashion," as it was called, made quite a trifling difference to the value of the material. Jean Bodin alludes to a proverb that was current in France in his time,

---

[1] Ruding, vol. ii. p. 322.
[2] *Discourses upon Trade.* Reprint 1822; postscript, p. 3.

that,[1] " in plate, one loses nothing but the fashion."
Lord Burleigh's will leaves his plate to be distributed among the legatees by weight just as if
it were so much bullion.

The farther back in our history we go, the more
obviously intimate and the more generally recognised does the connection become. We know
that it was from plate, mainly of the religious
houses, that Richard I.'s ransom was obtained.[2]
We find Edward I. enacting that no one should
sell his wool, or leather, or lead, or tin, to go out
of the realm, " except for good and true sterlings,
or for silver plate assayed and marked at the
King's great exchange "; and, some years later,
though apparently no gold was as yet in use as
coin, the Parliament nevertheless regarded it as
within its province to regulate the description of
gold which the goldsmiths should employ. None
of it was to be " worse than the touch of Paris."
We have seen that similarly, in Rome, in the
age of Sulla, the quality of the gold was the
subject of regulation by the state before gold, as
coin, had entered into the currency system of the
Republic ; and we have in such a fact a fresh indication of the importance attached, in all former
ages, to the maintenance of a state of things

---

[1] *Discours sur le rehaussement tant d'or que d'argent*, &c., t. iii.
(not paged).

[2] Ruding, *Annals of the Coinage*, vol. i. p. 385.

analogous to that which existed up till recently in India, where gold and silver ornaments were always readily convertible into gold and silver money, a state of things the necessity for which, however, the modern world has now definitely outgrown.

At the dawn of mediæval history, the connection between ornament and money is found to be so intimate as to merge into virtual identity. The gold armlets with which the Anglo-Saxon noble delighted to bedeck himself were, like the earrings that Abraham sent to Rebekah, made on a definite scale of weight and standard of purity, and apparently were also so made as to be readily divisible into portions of a definite weight. The *scillingas*, from which our word shilling is derived, were originally pieces cut or broken off from these armlets,[1] and were eventually at any rate equated with the weight of the Roman solidus. A "ring-breaker," both in the Anglo-Saxon and Norse languages, came to be used in the sense of "a distributor of treasures, an attribute especially given to princes." In "The Traveller's Song," a prince, whom Mr. Hodgkin identifies with Alboin,[2] is described as being "the man who, of all mankind, had the lightest hand to win love, the most generous heart in the distri-

---

[1] Keary, *op. cit.*, p. viii.
[2] *Italy and her Invaders*, vol. v. p. 176, Note D.

bution of rings and bracelets." "In Beda," says
Mr. Keary,[1] "there are passages which seem to
point to the circulation of ornaments as a sort of
currency. For instance, when King Raedwald,
king of the East Angles, was tempted by the
threats and promises of Aethelfrid, king of
Northumbria, to betray the fugitive Eadwine, his
wife dissuaded him from this act of treachery,
"*admonens quia nulla ratione conveniat tanto regi
amicum suum optimum in necessitate positum auro
vendere, imo fidem suam, quae omnibus ornamentis
pretiosior erat, amore pecuniae perdere.*" To the
mind of the father of English history *ornamenta*
and *pecunia* were plainly one and the same.

[1] Keary, *op. cit.*, p. x., footnote.

CHAPTER III

THE GROUND OF THE CONNECTION BETWEEN
ORNAMENT AND MONEY

IT may perhaps tend to diminish the surprise with
which we discover that superfluities seem inevitably
destined to distance necessaries in attaining the
position of the medium of exchange to reflect
that it was with superfluities that exchange began.
The early groups of families that formed the first
village communities were, as regards necessaries,
always self-sufficing. All their labour was forced
labour—if such an expression can be rightly used
in regard to a state of things in which such labour
was looked upon as part of the order of nature
—and the distribution of its results was made
by the strong hand. It was the desire for superfluities, merging later into the desire for money,
which acted as the solvent that ended the old,
and produced a new order of things. The lord
must outshine his neighbours in the display of

armour or of horseflesh ; his wife must be arrayed
in silks and jewels ; and so the villain's service
was commuted for a money payment, and
villainage disappeared from the face of the earth.
The Church did something towards its suppression, the *auri sacra fames* did infinitely more.

There is one aspect of the connection between
superfluities and the measurement of values that
did not escape Adam Smith. It is true that, in
some passages in *The Wealth of Nations*, he
attempts to erect corn into a standard of value.
At the same time there are others in which he
expressly recognises the fact that the price of a
necessary of life cannot serve as a measure of
national wealth, while the price of a superfluity,
to some extent, can. The prices of necessaries
do not rise as wealth increases in a country, or
fall as it diminishes, as the prices of superfluities
do.[1] " When we are in want of necessaries," he
says, "we must part with all superfluities, of
which the value, *as it rises in times of opulence
and prosperity, so it sinks in times of poverty
and distress.*[2] It is otherwise with necessaries. . . .
Corn is a necessary, silver is only a superfluity."

This fact of the rise in the price of necessaries
as the wealth of a nation increases is a very
familiar one to us nowadays. We are struck
every day almost, as we glance over the news-

[1] Ed. Edinburgh, 1811, vol. i. p. 265.   [2] The italics are mine.

papers, at the values reached by orchids, by old china or by old silver plate, by chairs of antique pattern on which no one would willingly sit, or couches on which it would be impossible to lie with comfort. The fact is plainly dependent on the same causes as those which give rise to the automatic outflow, the continuous absorption of the metals of ornament in proportion as their supply increases, as contrasted with the liability to glut in necessaries; and to this again, as we have seen, is due the fact that ornaments, not necessaries, have become the media of exchange,

It has been too hastily taken for granted that an increase in the supply of any commodity whatever must, of necessity, result in a diminution of its value. Increase of supply cuts down values in so far as it satiates demand, but in so far only. By Mr. Jevons and the Austrian school of economists this important qualification seems to have been, to some extent, overlooked. They accordingly set forth the proposition as an absolutely universal one, that, for every successive increment of supply there is of necessity a successive diminution in the " utility," that is to say, in the " wantedness " of the thing supplied, till presently this " utility " altogether vanishes.

This conclusion, it seems to me, has been arrived at owing to an over concentration of attention on the most simple cases, and a neglect of the more complicated ones. If we regard the supply as being furnished to one individual standing alone, and as consisting of food or clothing, then no doubt the more he gets of it the less will he want. But let us take a slightly more complicated case. Suppose the supply to be furnished to a group of warlike tribes, such as the earlier traders found in possession of New Zealand eighty years ago, and the article supplied to be gunpowder. It is evident that, for a considerable period at any rate, the increase of supply is likely, instead of being attended with a diminution of demand, to be attended with a demand that is always increasingly urgent. The very fact that one tribe has secured a supply of gunpowder makes it a matter of vital necessity for others to secure a supply likewise. The more that each obtains, the more must all the others have. If, again, we extend our view to the world generally, and conceive the article supplied to be some arm of precision or armour of defence, or the material of which one or both are made, it is difficult to place any limit to the period during which increase of supply may not be necessarily attended by a proportionate or more than proportionate increase of demand.

Rivalry and contest, however, come into play not alone in the struggles of actual war. Mr.

Darwin has exhibited to us the animal world as one continuous scene of emulation and strife. He has shown us too that, in that sphere, emulation and ornament are two branches springing from the same root ; and it will be found that the same economic consequences which we have seen flowing from the fact of the existence of war in the world flow also from the peaceful rivalry of men and women in the race of life. There too the increase in the supply of all that conduces to success, to distinction, to the outshining of our neighbours, or to our security from being out-shone by them, is inevitably accompanied by an increase in the demand for it.

The phenomenon of "progressive desire" in man has attracted some attention on the part of recent writers on economics. The satiated bullock or the satiated tiger rests from its labours till the pangs of hunger come again to stir it to exertion. With men, in the pursuit of wealth, there is ordinarily no satiation. A multimillionaire loses a few of his millions, and takes his loss so much to heart that he blows his brains out. Yet perhaps the one-thousandth part of what he had left would have supplied all his material needs for half-a-dozen lifetimes. Such a case, it will be said, is an extreme one. Leaving then such cases out of account, one may ask : Does not all current literature and all

common experience show us men with incomes
of five hundred a year just as keen in the pursuit
of fresh wealth as men with incomes of two
hundred—men again with incomes of a thousand a
year just as keen as men with incomes of five
hundred? Is there any proportion discoverable
between the amount of money that a man possesses and his desire for more? Does not, on the
contrary, every man find, as he grows richer, that
his wants and those of his wife and children
expand, at least as rapidly as his means? If
any proportion is discoverable, it is an inverted
one. It is the poor most frequently who lead the
happy-go-lucky, heedless lives, careless, comparatively speaking, about adding to the amount of
their savings, ready on the contrary to lavish
them on present pleasure ; while it is their well-
to-do neighbours, who are bent steadily, day in
day out, on making such additions and often with
ever increasing assiduity.

Is this phenomenon of " progressive desire " an
ultimate fact in human nature, or does it admit of
anything in the way of explanation? What is it
that men and women really want, once all
material needs are satisfied? They want, it will
be answered, not only to satisfy present needs,
but to make some provision for the satisfaction
of future needs ; and that answer is both true
and to the point. At the same time, if it is

provision for future material needs alone that is
to be taken into consideration, the motives of
action throughout very vast spheres of human
exertion will certainly be left still unaccounted
for. I had occasion a few pages back to quote
M. Babelon's picturesque observations on the
passion of primitive peoples for the ornamentation of their persons. Scarcely has early man,
as he remarks, learned the use of clothes than he
begins to hang on to his arms, his legs, and his
ears bracelets, earrings and pendants of all sorts.
Indeed, for that matter, he often learns to bedeck
himself with ornaments without having learned
the use of clothes at all. What is true of
primitive man remains, with modifications, very
largely true of his civilised brother. It is true
even with regard to ornament in its most literal
sense. We do not, however, often realise how
wide a place ornament, in its more extended
sense, occupies in all our lives. Nine-tenths
probably of the expenditure that we look upon as
expenditure on necessaries and comforts is in
reality expenditure upon little else than ornament.
In an individual case of course expenditure on
ornament may really be expenditure on the
absolute necessities of life. The clerk, with an
income of a hundred a year and a family to
support, must nevertheless array himself in a
frock coat and a shining silk hat. If he appeared

in the more comfortable dress of a sailor or a
navvy he would lose his situation, and with it his
means of livelihood.

Let us endeavour to picture to ourselves a state
of things in which the world, male and female,
became suddenly blind, yet in which otherwise
life continued to go on as it does now ; or let us
endeavour to think out the equally impossible
supposition that we and our neighbours became
all at once altogether indifferent in every respect
to appearances.   One of the first results would
be that the present yearly expenditure on clothes,
even of an economical middle-class man, would
be found sufficient to last him for a lifetime.
The patched coat and trousers of twenty years
standing most of us would then find actually
preferable to the new array from Poole's in all its
glories.   If Emerson had to admit that the fact
of being well dressed was more efficient in maintaining a man's self-esteem than the possession of
a good conscience, we need not be ashamed of
owning up that we too are all the slaves of
appearances.   At any rate, ashamed of it or not,
the fact is there ; and it is one of the great facts
of life, and one that it is idle for the economist
to ignore.

Extend again the conception of ornament from
the ornamentation of the person to the ornamentation of the environment.   What is all our

expenditure on large houses, parks and gardens, and so on, but expenditure on ornament? As Goethe said, none but those born in palaces can ever find themselves quite at home in their atmosphere. Put appearance out of the question, and most of us would find more comfort in a cottage, with glowing fires in winter and pleasant verandah space in summer, than in any castle or villa that ever was built.

When we think of the Hindoo peasant with his bracelets and his bangles, we must remember that these are to him the equivalent of all that fineness of texture and elegance of cut in dress, as well even as suitability of residence, are to the men and women of the European world. The peasant is driven, no doubt often by a social necessity as urgent as any physical necessity, to acquire and to wear these bracelets and these bangles, and can no more forgo the necessity of wearing them than the average Englishman or Englishwoman can forgo the necessity of dressing himself or herself in a manner which those about them regard as becoming to the station in life that he or she occupies.

In examining the nature of the forces that moulded the destinies of the lower world, Darwin found himself led to the conclusion that the struggle for existence was not everything. It had to be supplemented by the principle of sexual

selection, by the struggle between the males to
outdo other males in attractiveness in the eyes of
the females, and the struggle between the females
to outdo other females in attractiveness in the
eyes of the males.   But if the struggle for existence, that is, in economical language, the industrial effort devoted to the supply of material
needs, is not competent to explain everything in
the lower world, much less can it explain everything in the sphere of human development.
There too sexual selection, in its literal sense,
plays a part of the first importance, and one of
which, if literature has taken abundant account,
economics has taken but little.   Sexual selection
itself however may be regarded, in man, as but
one manifestation of a more extensive law, the
operation of which among ourselves attains a
far wider scope than it does among less advanced
forms of life.   Mr. Mill remarks somewhere with
point and truth, that, if we reflect what it is that
we are all really striving after, once the necessities
of the body have been satisfied, we shall find that
it is, in one shape or another, the favourable
opinion of those about us.   We must take
of course opinion in its most general sense.
What we strive for may no doubt be moral
approbation, but, on the other hand, it may not.
Our aspiration will, at any rate, be to be looked
up to, to be admired, perhaps to be envied.

There is, it may be assumed, a certain degree of consideration in the eyes of those about us which we all of us possess to begin with ; a certain " position," as we call it, which has been conferred on us by the circumstances of our birth, or which we have attained by our own exertions, and it is to the maintenance and to the improvement of this " position " that nine-tenths of the exertion of civilised man is directed. Nor must we suppose that such exertion is, necessarily, selfish in its aim. Its main stimulus, on the contrary, comes from its unselfish side. We none of us come into the world isolated. All of us, when we enter it, enter it as members of some group. There is the family group, first and foremost, then the wider groups of kinship and connection. As life advances, a man, again, may enter another group than his own, perhaps become the head of another group by marriage and by the begetting of children. In whatever he does or fails to do in life, his fortunes are bound up with those of the group to which he belongs. He cannot lapse from his position in the eyes of the outside world without the position of those dependent on him and those closely connected with him sustaining more or less of reflected injury. Nor will it readily happen that his position will be signally improved without theirs being, in a measure, improved also. The young man entering on life, going abroad, it may be, to seek his fortune, will have his eyes bent, in the first instance, on the opinion of this group. What he will look to will be the approval of the father and mother, the brothers and sisters, left at home. To win that approval will ordinarily be the goal of his first efforts ; and the surest road to the attainment of that end, he knows, is to be found in the improvement of his own position in the eyes of the world generally. Presently perhaps he meets the woman of his choice, and finds that to be seen to be " getting on in the world " is the likeliest, most often indeed the only, way of winning her. After marriage it will probably become his aim, yet again, not to disappoint the reasonable expectations of his wife, and it may soon become the aim of both of them to give their children "a better bringing up than his had been, or hers."

This ceaseless universal eagerness to get on, to pass others in the race of life, presents itself often in an unamiable aspect, and its excesses are a favourite subject of moral denunciation. Mr. Mill, among others, is " not charmed with the ideal of life held out by those who think that the normal state of human beings is that of struggling to get on." " The best state for human nature," on the contrary, in his opinion, " is that in which, while no one is poor, yet no one desires to be

richer." Even supposing that to be so, one may
of course answer that we have to take the world
as we find it. All, however, has not been said
when this has been said. Mr. Mill, in the middle
of the century, looked out on a world in which, as
as it seemed to him, following Malthus, population was pressing hard upon the means of
subsistence, and was about to press upon them
yet more hardly. There seemed to him to be
little hope for the improved prosperity of the
masses in England unless it might be by their
following the French example and practically
ceasing to increase their numbers. The facts of
the last fifty years have happily, to some extent,
at any rate, falsified this gloomy anticipation.
The population of England has vastly increased,
but the pressure on the means of subsistence,
instead of having been intensified, has been, to
an amazing extent, lightened.

The truth is, I think, that we have to recognise
in the creation of wealth, as in everything else
throughout the whole sphere of life, the operation
of a double purpose—the purpose of instinct and
the purpose of reason; the immediate purpose of
the individual, and the wider purpose that under-
lies it. Von Hartman tells us that we are all "the
dupes of the Unconscious," and it may be that
it is so, if we can conceive of That as unconscious
which is capable of thus making dupes of us. At

all events, the scene that seems to present itself to any one who endeavours to watch the game of life from the position of an outsider is a world in which men, in every rank, are toiling and straining to increase their command of gold, to distance each other in the race of life, while the net result of it all is that, from decade to decade, the masses are becoming better clothed, better housed and better fed, that they have more leisure and more enjoyments, and that they may, within reason, and without danger of imminent misery, go on multiplying and replenishing the earth.

We have come to learn that "the evolution of improved machinery is found to be attended by a continual increase in the product, a fall in piece wages, and an increase in the weekly earnings." Improved machinery is seen indeed "as the direct cause of high wages and short hours." The Edisons, the Siemenses and the Bessemers are thus, it appears, greater benefactors to the working classes than all the Fabian socialists and all the Liberal administrations. Yet we know that philanthropy has very little to do with the inspiration of their efforts. It is because men are everlastingly in pursuit of position and distinction, and because in this pursuit satiety is in the nature of things impossible, that private wealth continues to be produced in ever increasing quantities. Once produced, economic forces take possession of it, and soon it finds its way through every fibre of the social organism.

If the struggle for existence had been the only or the main stimulus to human exertion, if men, like cattle, had found their only spur to effort in the desire to satiate material needs, we should be left without any explanation of the progressive well-being that has characterised in so marked a manner our recent history. It would be hard in that case to conceive of anything that could have stood in the way of the fulfilment of the Malthusian prediction, that nothing but vice and misery could check the increase of population. The fact of the existence of a " standard of living " which is rightly regarded as occupying the position of a buffer between the forces that tend to the increase of population and the deluge of misery which their unimpeded play would inevitably bring about, means nothing else but this, that the pursuit of position, of distinction, of consideration in the eyes of one's fellows extends to all classes of the population, more or less, even to the lowest. It is noteworthy that while the moralists denounce such springs of action as unworthy, the practical philanthropist, when he finds them absent or dormant, makes it his first business to endeavour to waken them into existence. The author of *Darkest England*, for instance, has occasion to remark that the tramps who resort to the

twopenny department of the Salvation Army's
shelters resent the introduction among them of
"dirty fellows" from the penny department, and
the fact that they do so he regards as of hopeful
omen for their future.

This "position in life" then of which men
think so much, on what is it dependent? No
doubt to a great extent, it is dependent on the
circumstances of birth, also on character, on manner, on strength, on beauty, on ability. These
latter however are not acquirable and not transferable. For our present purpose it is only the
transferable means of maintaining and improving
"position" that concern us. The briefest glance
at the world in any age will show us to how great
an extent it is dependent on expenditure on
superfluities, on things that are in the nature of
ornament. Unwritten laws create for all of us
social necessities for expenditure that seem hardly
less urgent than provision for bodily health and
comfort. The conception of a certain position in
life is liable thus to attach itself in the first instance
to a certain scale of expenditure, and from this it
readily transfers itself in the second instance to
the fact of possessing the reserved power of
making such expenditure whenever we please, to
wealth, in short, to command over the medium of
exchange, whatever it may be.

We seem thus at length to be in sight of the

explanation of the intimate connection between ornament and money, as well perhaps as the explanation of the causes which make the demand for gold always go on increasing *pari passu* with the supply, and thus render the value of the standard commodity at the least approximately invariable. There is at bottom a discernible identity between the impulse of the primitive savage or of the Hindoo peasant, whose aim in life appears to be to bedeck himself with ornaments of gold and silver, and that of the millionaire who, it may be, thinks of little else but of making fresh additions to his millions. With both the thought is the same, to stand out of the crowd, to distance others, not to be left behind in the race. The Hindoo aims at being more highly ornamented than his neighbours, the millionaire at being able to draw his cheque for a larger sum.

With the average civilised man a kindred impulse is ever present. Very often indeed it is in its negative aspect that it presents itself. The hope of becoming more wealthy and more important than those about us, in youth, no doubt, gilds the future for most of us. As life goes on, the aim becomes ordinarily rather that of maintaining the position already achieved. We are haunted by the dread of going down in the world, perhaps of seeing those dear to us forced to fall back on a scale of living and on a description of

occupations that we have come to regard as associated with a lower *couche sociale* than our own ;
and the one thing that, in the world as we find
it, can fulfil the hopes of youth and can dissipate
the anxieties of middle life is increased command
of gold, of the medium of exchange.   What wonder then that the demand for gold appears to be
altogether incapable of satiation.

It may seem to some of my readers that in the
prominence that has been given to the maintenance
and improvement of position in life, and its intimate association with the power of expenditure
on superfluities, a state of things that may be true
of modern Europe has been depicted, but yet one
that is neither deep-rooted nor permanent in the
world.   I think however that the consideration
of the one fact of the universality with which the
two metals whose only use practically is ornament
have ousted other commodities in attaining the
degree of general acceptability necessary to convert them into money, will be calculated to modify
that opinion.   What is the secret of it all?   Why
was the world of Xenophon so like our own?   To
what springs of action in Rebekah's nature did the
rings and bracelets that Eleazar brought her
appeal?   Why did men in the Babylon of Sargon
and the Egypt of Sesostris, in ages long before the
coinage of money had been dreamt of, toil and
strive and engage in perilous expeditions and in

sanguinary wars for the possession of gold and
silver? Was it their colour and their brilliancy
alone that exercised this marvellous fascination
over mankind in every age? In a sense it
was, but if we look to the æsthetic sentiment
alone, we should leave the desire of possession
unexplained. The love of beauty alone in
men would be as much gratified by the sight
of ornaments worn by others as by the sight
of those worn by themselves. The true impulse at the root of ornament wearing lies in
this, that they convert, or are thought to convert,
the wearer himself or herself into something not
only beautiful, but uncommon. If any one could
obtain the ornaments without difficulty, no one
would prize them. They are prized on account
of the distinction they confer. Gretchen first
fully appreciates her ill-fated jewelry when she
finds herself taken for a grand lady. Wheat is
bought eagerly no doubt when it is scarce, because
people dread being left without enough of it to
satisfy hunger ; but its utility is not dependent on
its scarcity. Of gold and silver it is true, on the
contrary, that their utility, that is to say their
adaptation to meet the want which causes them
to be desired, is absolutely dependent on their
scarcity. Make wheat as common as water, and
still people would use at least as much of it as
they do now. Make gold, on the contrary, as

common as iron, and no one would use any of it at any rate for those purposes that constitute its main use at present. If the possession of it and the display of it conferred no distinction, its present utility would be absolutely gone.

CHAPTER IV

THE NATURE OF THE STANDARD

If we revert now to the line of reasoning with which we began the first chapter of this part, it will be remembered that, accepting Professor Walker's exposition of the manner in which the standard substance measures value, it was seen to be, above all things, necessary that it should be a commodity which every one would be always willing to accept in exchange for his produce, in whatever quantities it might be offered ; and that therefore a commodity which was in any circumstances liable to glut could never serve as the standard. Whatever commodity on the contrary distanced all other commodities in attaining this universal acceptability became forthwith the money of the community in which it existed.

It seems necessary, however, at this stage to inquire more carefully into the precise meaning of the word "acceptability." It is evidently used in a special, if not indeed in a technical sense. The highest degree of acceptability is plainly not to be identified with the highest degree of exchange value. There are at the present moment innumerable substances that possess a higher degree of exchange value, weight for weight, than gold, though gold surpasses them all in "acceptability." We have perhaps a synonym for it in the modern commercial term, "liquidity." The value of two commodities may be approximately the same, and yet the one as an asset may be to any extent more liquid than the other. A finished pair of boots, although their cost was much greater than that of the leather used in their manufacture, might be, as an asset, much less liquid ; the reason being that the market for boots of special sizes would probably be a very restricted one, while the market for the leather would be a very wide one. It might be laid down indeed as a general rule that the less manufactured an article is the more liquid will it be. Cloth will as a rule be more liquid than clothes ; it will command a wider market, and its value will be less liable to be affected by changes of fashion, and wool for similar reasons will be more liquid than cloth.

There are thus, we can see, innumerable degrees of liquidity or acceptability among things purchasable. Next to gold itself, good three months' bills and the best class of Government securities stand highest in the list. They come next to gold in their availability for the purposes of bank reserves. Silver would now-a-days have to take a place very far down. The acceptability or liquidity of anything thus appears to be inversely proportioned to the risk of loss in holding it. In other words, the commodity which forms the most trustworthy store of purchasing power, that is to say the commodity which most approximates to invariability of value, is the commodity which may be said to possess acceptability in the highest degree.

We have thus arrived by another road at a conclusion similar to that at which we arrived at the end of Part I., in our inquiry as to the originating causes of transitions of the standard. We there found that the best money, that is to say the money whose value was least liable to fall, and which therefore formed the best store of purchasing power, ousted as standard all the money that was in that respect less to be trusted. And here again we find that the reason why, in prehistoric days, the metals of ornament ousted all other commodities as money, was precisely the same; it was because, in this very same respect, they surpassed them all.

Another of the universally postulated requisites of the monetary substance is homogeneity, or

uniformity of quality.   What is it therefore, we
have to ask, that is salient in this characteristic?
It is plain, at a glance, that simple homogeneity
is not enough.   It must be combined with the
capacity for easy and perfect reunification of the
parts when divided.   Platinum, which was for a
short time coined by the Russian government,
had to be abandoned owing to the difficulty of
melting it.   Without the facility for melting and
reunification of parts there might indeed be
uniformity of quality, but there could not be
uniformity of value.   A piece of the substance
twelve ounces in weight might then be worth
very much more than twelve times as much as
a piece one ounce in weight ; just as a diamond
weighing twelve grains is worth far more than
twelve times as much as a diamond of equal
lustre weighing one grain.   We thus see that
uniformity of quality is only efficient as a characteristic of the monetary substance in as far as it
conduces to uniformity of value.   Uniformity of
value appears to be, all through, the really salient
matter.   Locke says,[1] " The measure of commerce
must be perpetually the same, invariable, and
keeping the same proportion in value in all its
parts," and we find a clear confirmation of this
view if we return to Prof. Walker's illustration.
It is plainly the fact that the gold paid to-day for

[1] See *Coins of the Realm*, p. 114.

wheat is, or seems to be, of the same value as was the same amount of gold paid yesterday for oats or the day before for maize, that enables wheat, oats, and maize to be ranged upon a scale of values expressed in quantities of gold.

Locke had no doubt this thought in his mind when he asserted with striking emphasis, with regard to the substance which he looked upon as standard money in his time, that [1] " an ounce of silver, whether in pence, groats, or crown pieces, stivers or ducatoons, or in bullion, is, and always eternally will be, of equal value to any other ounce of silver, under what stamp or denomination whatsoever." A contemporary authority, M. Cernuschi, gives a vivid expression to the same thought with regard to gold. " Whatever may be the quantity produced," [2] he says, " it enters without question into the circulation. *Every gramme of new gold is exactly equal to a gramme of old gold. All have the same power.* The old metal is powerless to bar the passage to the new." Such a statement is all the more significant as coming from an exponent of that line of economical speculation with which M. Cernuschi was identified.

After listening to these utterances of seven-

---

[1] Locke's Works, ed. 1823, vol. v. p. 82.

[2] *Anatomie de la Monnaie*, p. 12. See Babelon, *Origines de la Monnaie*, p. 286.

teenth and of nineteenth century thought on the question, it is interesting to inquire what was the light in which it presented itself to a fresh mind that had its attention turned to it more than 2,000 years ago. Xenophon,[1] in urging on his countrymen the active exploitation of the silver mines of Laurium, after remarking that no doubt gold might be as desirable as silver as an addition to the public treasure, goes on to say : " Nevertheless this I know that when gold abounds, its value lessens and that of silver becomes greater. We say this in order to be able to insist with more confidence on the desirability of developing the silver mines. One will alway find silver, and it will never lose its value." This conception of silver as never losing its value had evidently impressed itself vividly upon Xenophon's mind. He deals further with the matter, pointing out the conspicuous difference that silver presented when viewed in comparison with other commodities, together with the causes of that difference. " Silver mining," he remarks earlier in the same chapter, " is the only enterprise in regard to which one need have no fear of increasing to any extent the number of labourers. A farmer will tell you precisely how many pairs of bullocks he needs for his land. If any one has more than he needs he makes a loss by it. But

---

[1] *The Revenues of Athens,* c. iv.

in the work of mining for silver every one wants labourers. The case is by no means the same in regard to copper mining. When things made of copper have to be sold cheap the copper miners are ruined. The same applies to iron mining. In the same manner too when there is a great abundance of corn or of wine these commodities have to be sold at a low price. The cultivation of wheat and of the vine then bring in nothing. So much so indeed that numbers of people have to leave the country and become traders, dealers, or money-lenders. The greater, on the contrary, the amount of silver that is produced the more numerous we find are the people who take to silver mining. When a man has everything that he needs to set up house with, he does not buy anything more. With silver it is different. No one ever possessed enough of it not to want more. So much so that those who have a great quantity of it find as much satisfaction in burying their surplus as in using it. This further must be said, that when states flourish it is then that every one feels the need of more silver. The men want splendid arms, good horses, fine houses, magnificent furniture, while the women set their hearts on rich stuffs and ornaments of gold. When, on the other hand, a town is suffering from famine or from war, as the ground cannot be cultivated as usual, there is

the greater need of money for expenditure on
food and on the procurement of allies."

Xenophon's theory of value undoubtedly places
itself in very marked contrast to the modern
theory already alluded to, which asserts that
every increase in supply is necessarily attended
with a proportionate diminution of the value of
the thing supplied.   Silver, he thinks, never loses
its value, and the reason is this, that no one ever
possessed enough of it not to want more.   This
happens because, as wealth and luxury increase,
every one is bent on outshining in splendour
all his neighbours.   The ultimate cause of the
contrast between the two theories appears to lie
in the fact that the modern theory assumes men
and women to be perfectly rational beings, beings
always animated by the pure hedonic impulse, the
calculated determination to obtain the maximum
of satisfaction for their wants at the minimum of
cost, while Xenophon's theory displays them as
full of all the vanity and all the frivolity of true
human nature.

In regard to the theory of the standard generally however it must be said that it is very
necessary to endeavour to keep, in thought, two
things distinct which, in their actual working, are
always inextricably involved with each other;
that is to say, to keep distinct, in our minds, the
causes that lead, in the first instance, to the

assumption by any commodity of the position of standard money, from the causes that maintain it in that position, when once it has been attained. It is in regard to the first set of causes alone that the frivolous side of human nature is conspicuous. It is to the love of display no doubt that we owe it that the metals of ornament first distanced the metals of utility in becoming money ; but if we suppose the monetary status once attained by them, then the rigidly rational side of human nature, the side that looks to self-preservation alone, will come into play also to maintain their acceptability thenceforward unimpaired.

Xenophon is fully alive to this, especially as regards national self-preservation. In time of war, as he says, then it is that silver is most urgently needed. The special exigencies that presented themselves to his mind were the need of resources for the procurement of food, in the event perhaps of the city being besieged, or for the supply of its armies when on the march, and of resources for the subsidising of allies. Exigencies not dissimilar appeal to us still. All through our mediæval history, and up to the close of the Stuart period, the same conception as to the urgent necessity for maintaining the nation's stock of actual treasure as an indispensable means towards national self-preservation, together with the im-

minent danger involved even in its temporary
depletion, occupied a very large space in the
thoughts of our forefathers ; and we should be
greatly in error if we imagined that considerations which are practically identical with these
have ceased to be of weight with us now. We
no longer lay stress indeed on the necessity for
a war-chest of eighty or a hundred millions
sterling in London, such as the Russians have
in St. Petersburg, but we are fully alive, from
the national point of view, to the urgent importance of the possession by the nation of the
greatest amount possible of solid and tangible
wealth capable of being drawn upon at need by
the State ; and in what, after all, does this solid and
tangible wealth consist but in documents or commodities the possession of which carries with it
the immediate command of gold whenever it shall
chance to be wanted ?   No wealth, in the practical
world, is reckoned as real which is not identical
with the command of gold.   Let any European
Power surpass us in the acquirement of such
wealth, and it probably will not be long before
it has a navy that can sweep ours from the
seas.   The necessity for national self-preservation
alone thus presents itself as possessing vast
powers for the absorption of the standard substance, whatever it may be ; and of not less, rather
indeed of much greater importance, from the

same point of view, is the necessity for individual self-preservation, the ordinary incentive to thrift and to the accumulation of savings.

These two desires, then, the one for distinction in the present and the other for security in the future, are the two elements in human nature that have made and that now maintain gold as the standard of values. We can recognise, however, how intimate is the connection that subsists between them, when we reflect, on the one hand, that the possession of ample means of provision for the future is itself a great and universally coveted distinction ; and, on the other, that when we think of security for the future, it is not alone, perhaps not at all, of security from the risks of hunger, or of cold, or indeed of pain or discomfort of any sort, that we are thinking, but rather of security for ourselves and for those dependent on us from the loss of that distinction, that position in life, which is ours already.

One cause no doubt which accounts for the prevalence of the view that corn or some necessary of life, or perhaps some group of necessaries expressed in index numbers, should be the standard of values, rather than a superfluity like gold, is to be found in the consideration given to the fact that most things in the nature of ornament are exceptionally liable to fluctuations in value, owing to changes of fashion : and it is worthy of notice that this view assumes that the standard is or ought to be the substance that of all others fluctuates the least. The liability to changes of fashion however, as regards the monetary commodity, soon finds itself to a great extent counteracted by the association of that commodity with the idea of wealth itself. The monetary metals soon become in common thought, as Pliny calls them, *ipsae opes*, and this fact at once immensely enhances their efficacy for purposes of ornament. The Karoks in California, we noticed, when the American coins supplanted their shells as currency, learned to use the coins in place of the shells as ornaments. In Central Africa, where calico is used as money, as cloth was in Norway in the tenth century, instances are quoted in which the wealthy decorate the tombs of their ancestors and the shrines of their gods with offerings of calico,[1] as elsewhere they do with gold and silver. The religious use, another variety of the ornamental use, has, we know, in many ages and countries been an immense absorber of the precious metals. At Athens,[2] the chrys-elephantine statue of Pallas alone used up no less than forty talents of gold. In our own day, it is noticeable that the use of gold "in the arts" appears to keep pace with the ever increasing output. When Soetbeer wrote

---

[1] *On the Threshold of Central Africa*, François Coillard, p. 165.
[2] Ridgeway, *op. cit.*, p. 220.

that use was annually absorbing about the half of
it. Mr. Senior's dictum that "the value of the
precious metals depends on their value as jewelry
and plate" is one that still expresses an important
truth.

In the practice of hoarding Xenophon finds
another cause of the maintenance of the value of
silver. "Those who have a great quantity of it,"
he remarks, "find as much satisfaction in burying
their surplus as in using it." We find the same
thought given expression to in a modern form by
an economist who wrote during the earlier part of
last century, Mr. Fullarton. "The hoards," he
says, "absorb the surplus produce of the mines
when it is overflowing, and disgorge when it is
wanted for use, so that the fluctuations [in the
quantity of gold] do not affect at all that portion
of the coin that circulates, and which alone
operates on prices, but only that portion that is
hoarded."[1] The eagerness to hoard real money,
in fact, he thinks, operates so as to cause a constant automatic outflow for it, and so effectually
prevents glut.

Under modern conditions, however, for
"hoards" would usually have to be substituted
"bank reserves"; and the operation of bank
reserves, especially of the reserve of the Bank of
England, in absorbing all the surplus gold of the

[1] *Regulation of Currencies*, p. 71.

world, and in thus preventing its action on prices, was a fact to which Mr. Fullarton was very much alive.[1]   There is a really remarkable passage on the subject in the little book already quoted, *The Regulation of Currencies.*   Referring to the provision, in the Act of 1844, to the effect that the Bank of England should buy all the standard gold brought to it, at a fixed price of £3 17s. 10½d. per ounce, he says, " It does appear to me that so long as it shall be possible to adhere to it strictly it must inevitably operate as a bar to any rise in prices whatever, as a consequence of the increased production of the mines." . . . " For what," he goes on to ask, " is the substantial effect of this regulation ?   What is it but to hold out to the world a minimum price which all persons bringing gold to the Bank of England shall be entitled to demand for it ?   How then, let me ask, with all the facilities for communication at present existing, is it possible that the price of the metal can ever fall materially below that minimum, or that, with this universal reservoir for ever open to receive it at a fixed valuation, any considerable portion of the yearly produce of the gold mines should be thrown on the markets of the world in such a manner as to occasion its depreciation ?   Gold forms a part of the circulation of almost every country of Europe, but in England alone is it the standard

[1] *Op. cit.*, p. 77.

metal, and to England accordingly all the surplus
gold in the world must centre. However large
that surplus may be, after supplying the periodical
wants of the other countries of the world for
consumption and for coinage, it is obvious that
the whole must find its way into the vaults of the
Bank of England, there to remain buried and
wholly inoperative on prices till called forth by
some new demand for additional circulation. This
circumstance, I apprehend, so long as the system
shall endure, must continue a perpetual and insuperable obstacle to any action on prices as
measured in gold coins from the increased production of the mines." This elimination of the
effect of fluctuations in the supply of the standard
metal on the prices of commodities Mr. Fullarton
appears to regard as one of the aims of Peel's
Act. " No enterprise, as it seems to me," he
says, " could be more quixotic or absurd than for
this country to engage in a struggle to maintain
the value of the precious metals (*sic*) at a higher
level than that warranted by the cost of production." [1] By a curious inaccuracy he here uses the
expression " the precious metals " instead of the
word " gold." It is however quite manifestly gold,
and gold only, that he is writing and speaking
of. " By making gold," he goes on, " take the
place of £11,000,000 of Government securities in

[1] *Ibid.*, p. 80.

the reserve, the Bank of England might be maintained for a term longer as a general sink for
draining off the superfluous produce of the mines,
and sustaining the prices of commodities in gold
at a uniform level over the world. But if the
augmented scale of production and the diminished
cost of the gold were anything more than an
accident of the day the experiment would inevitably fail in the end."

The augmented scale of production of gold, as
we know, instead of being an accident of the day,
has gone on augmenting till now the output is
about six times annually what it was when the
Act of 1844 was passed, yet the fact does not
appear to involve any struggle on the part of the
Bank of England to maintain the present value
of gold. The only struggle indeed on the part
of the Bank in connection with the matter is to
get all it can at that value.

Further than this, if Mr. Fullarton had referred
to Lord Liverpool's famous book, he would have
seen that the system under which a fixed price of
close on £3 17s. 10½d. per ounce was always obtain-
able for gold at the Bank of England, instead of
originating with Ricardo or with the Act of 1844,
was in full operation in the eighteenth century.[1]
The eighteenth century system too was only a
much older system in a new guise. What the

[1] *Coins of the Realm*, p. 150.

mint price of £3 17s. 10½d. per ounce for gold really means, we all know, is merely this, that the mint will always take all the gold brought to it, coin it, and give it back to the man who brings it. If he brings 40 lbs. of it they will return precisely 1,869 sovereigns, which weigh just 40lbs. The maintenance of the mint price depends therefore upon this alone, that all the gold brought shall be always readily and unhesitatingly received, coined and returned as coin to those who bring it.

By the 18th of Charles II. it was enacted that the mint should be always open to the free coinage of both metals. With regard to silver, however, we have seen that this provision never was and never could be anything more than nominal. With regard to gold, on the contrary, as it had for several centuries passed in practice uniformly by weight, the perfect equivalent of free coinage had, during that period, already necessarily existed with regard to it. The true reason therefore why gold could always be bought by the Bank of England for £3 17s. 10½d. per ounce did not lie in the fact that the statute of 1844 enacted it. That statute merely consecrated an existing practice. It lay in the fact, on the contrary, that gold itself, in virtue of its intrinsic qualities, had become the standard of Europe, and had thus become, like the silver of Xenophon's day, subject to the operation of causes which precluded, or at any rate appeared to the whole practical world to preclude, the possibility of all downward fluctuations in its intrinsic value.

I have, so far, endeavoured to guard myself from making the assertion that the standard substance does not fluctuate in its value. That assertion, I am aware, would be strongly repudiated by many of my readers ; and it is not necessary to the theory of value here set forth that its validity should be maintained. The position at present contended for is simply this, that gold owes its attainment of the position of standard money to its universal acceptability, and that this universal acceptability is due to the universal belief on the part of the people who use gold as their store of purchasing power, that its value does not fluctuate. If this universal belief is admitted, it is evidently itself a phenomenon of great interest in the world and one that requires to be accounted for. Its existence may, however, quite conceivably be consistent with the fact that, in some sense, gold does really fluctuate, while it yet remains the standard. The belief in its invariability of value would of course be just as effective in maintaining its acceptability, whether the whole thing was— say in the eyes of a divine intelligence—ultimately reality or only appearance.

I may perhaps be permitted at the same time to draw attention to some vulnerable points in the

opposite theory, the theory that not only attributes
fluctuations of value to the standard, but also
endeavours to make them the basis of practical
conclusions affecting the ordinary business of life.
It seems necessary, however, in the first instance
to point out that the contention as to the stability
in value of the standard substance—even as regards appearance alone—applies only to that period
during which that substance remains the standard.
When it is urged : " But if gold became as common as pot metal, would it not lose its value ? "
the answer is, " No doubt it would, but before that
happened, probably very long before it happened,
it would have ceased in one way or another to be
the standard." Xenophon of course was wrong
in thinking that silver could never fall. He may
have been right all the same in thinking that it
could not fall in Athens under the existing monetary conditions. All that is contended for is this,
that, while no distrust whatever exists in the
practical world as to the maintenance by gold of
an invariable value, those fluctuations downwards
and upwards which are alleged to take place in
regard to it are phenomena of a wholly different
character from the fluctuations downwards of
subsidiary money, or of commodities, owing to
their supply being in excess of the demand for
them, and from their fluctuations upwards owing
to the contrary cause.

As to the fact itself of the universality of the belief in the practical world in the perfect stability of gold, that will probably not be called in question. Ideally no doubt the best medium for the storage of purchasing power would be an always rising commodity; and if such a commodity could be found it would beyond question be preferred by every one as a medium for the storage of his power. Experience, however, very soon teaches us that every commodity that is susceptible of rises in its value is liable also to falls. It teaches us something more than this indeed. It shows us a tolerably exact proportion as prevailing in regard both to commodities and securities, between the chance of rises and the risk of falls. We buy Consols, not expecting to make much out of them, but at the same time feeling satisfied that we shall lose but little. If we want something even more stable than Consols we store gold, being perfectly satisfied that, if we can gain nothing by holding it, we can also lose nothing. With regard to the perfect invariability in the value of gold the practical world never entertains a moment's doubt or hesitation.

CHAPTER V

In the previous chapter I had occasion to draw
attention to the fact alluded to by Mr. Fullarton
as possessing such significance, the purchase by
the Bank of all the gold brought to it at a fixed
price. That fact itself is something beyond all
question ; and it is further beyond question, I
think, that it must operate in such a manner as
to prevent any effect from being produced on
general prices by increased supplies of gold that
is in the remotest degree analogous to that
produced by the redundancy of over-issued
paper or of depreciated silver. That great gold
discoveries produce some effect on the values of
many, perhaps of most, commodities there is of
course no doubt, but then so do vast discoveries
of coal, or iron, or petroleum ; and so unquestionably does the opening up of great fresh areas
to the culture of wheat. Every form of wealth

in the economic sphere, seems to be related to every other form of wealth very much as every particle of matter in the physical sphere is related to every other particle. Move or alter any one unit in the whole mass of either, and—though it may be imperceptibly—you necessarily move and alter every other. The conception however that has been so rife in the world as to the peculiar effects produced on prices by the increases and decreases of the supply of gold is due, I think, mainly to the observation of the phenomena of subsidiary money, and is altogether inapplicable to the phenomena of real money itself.

Mr. Fullarton's book on *The Regulation of Currencies*, from which the passage above quoted was taken, was published during the controversies to which the Act of 1844 gave rise. It aimed at supporting the views on the currency question then recently enunciated by Tooke. That truly original thinker had found the quantitative theory of money completely in possession of the field. In his own earliest writings he was himself still under its influence, and it was only gradually that he emancipated himself from it. He then became the founder of a school which embraced, besides Mr. Fullarton, Mr. Wilson of the *Economist*, and, one might add, Mr. Gilbart, Mr. H. D. M'Leod, and, up to a certain point, Mr. Mill. Mr. Mill's general opinions on money however are rather

to be identified with those which Tooke so strenuously endeavoured to refute.

The quantitative theory of money could not be
better summarised than it was in the eighteenth
century by Harris in the *Essay on Coins*. " If,
in any country," he says " the whole quantity of
money in circulation be either increased or diminished, the value of a given sum will be accordingly
lessened or increased," that is to say, the average
prices of commodities will accordingly rise or fall.
To this proposition Tooke's reply was that, if it
be meant to assert that an influx of the precious
metals into the country is always followed by a
proportional rise in general prices, nothing can be
more obviously false, as millions both of gold and
silver come into the country and go out of it
again every year without becoming part of the
circulation at all, or in any way entering into
general prices. If it be answered, " No ; what is
meant is this—that, if you increase, not the precious metals in the country only, but also the actual
monetary circulation itself, you will raise general
prices," his reply again was in effect the following :—You are depicting an imaginary state of
things, you are putting the cause in the place of
the effect, and the effect in the place of the cause.
When you are dealing with real money, you
cannot increase the circulation and thus raise
prices. That is something that never has happened

and never can happen. What does happen continually, on the contrary, is this, that prices rise from some cause or other, it does not matter what, and that then an increase of the circulation inevitably follows, or is rather another aspect of the same fact. The two phenomena are concomitant, but the rise in prices is always the cause of the increase in the circulation, and never its effect. With fiat money the case is altogether different. "Compulsory government paper, on the other hand," he says, "which is in the course of augmentation acts directly as an originating cause on prices."[1]

The particular form of the theory with which Tooke and his friends were principally concerned was the assertion that the issue of convertible notes, of the sort of notes which people who were entitled to demand gold took in preference to it, swelled the volume of the currency and thus raised prices. That they did so was maintained by Mr. Loyd, afterwards Lord Overstone, by Colonel Torrens and by many others possessing great reputations in the financial world. Sir Robert Peel indeed himself was more or less under the influence of that theory. Tooke's reply to this contention appears to be perfectly conclusive. It may be given in the words of his disciple, Mr. Wilson : "The public do not receive notes

[1] *Enquiry into the Currency Principle*, p. 19.

from a bank without paying interest for their use ; and however low that may be, they will take no more than they require, nor do they retain notes in their possession beyond what the convenience of trade requires, and therefore, if issued in excess of that quantity, and if convertible, a portion would be instantly returned upon the issuers. Nor can we conceive any means whatever by which the circulation could be so augmented." [1]

To get at the root of the fallacy it is worth while to turn to Mr. Mill's doctrine of money. There is a well-known and often quoted passage in his *Principles of Political Economy* [2] in which he lays it down, that while the price of commodities may be determined either by the actual or by the potential supply, it is the actual supply only that determines the value of money. It is necessary however to inquire what is meant by the words "the actual supply." There is no ambiguity about the matter if we look at it as regards a past transaction. If in any market 10,000 quarters of wheat are sold at 25s. a quarter, this 10,000 quarters constitute the actual supply, and any other wheat, even if it chanced to be stored in the same town, which is not sold, though its owners would have sold it if its price had gone up to 26s., is not to be reckoned as

[1] *Capital Currency and Banking*, p 83.
[2] People's Edition, p. 306.

" actual supply."   We are thus forced to conclude
that the actual supply is *something that we can
know nothing about till the price is fixed, and the
transaction is over*; and it plainly will not do
therefore to say that it is it which fixes the price.
It is clear on the contrary that that which
determines variations of prices is always and only
variations in the potential supply, together with
their recognition by buyers and sellers.   The
news of a deficiency in the crop of some
important grain-producing country, for instance,
gets wind.   Sellers raise their prices and buyers
raise their offers to meet them.   We always in
the real world look for the explanation of a rise
or fall in prices not only in quantitative variations
in some material, but in human recognition of
these variations, and in the play of well-known
human springs of action in regard to them.   The
explanation always involves psychological data.
Mr. Mill himself has occasion in one passage to
observe that the only values with which political
economy is concerned are values that are fixed by
competition.   Values fixed by custom are of
course those which he means to leave out.
When he gets to monetary questions however,
he gets to a region where his values do not seem
always to be fixed either by custom or by competition, but in some mystical automatic fashion by
augmentations and diminutions of quantity.   We

look in vain for the psychological factor. The
fallacy lies in thinking that in political economy,
which is essentially a mental science, human
beings are to be treated as algebraic symbols.

We see this very clearly when we attempt to
apply his conception of the actual supply as
affecting values to the value of money itself.
What corresponds in the case of money to the
actual supply is what is called the "circulation."
Look back at the past : we can say clearly and
definitely that, supposing the amount of goods
and transactions in any market to remain the
same, the greater the circulation, that is to say,
the greater the amount of money that is found to
have changed hands, the higher must the average
of prices have been. To say indeed in such
circumstances that the circulation has increased
is merely another way of saying that prices were
higher. To take a simple case, supposing there
to be 1,000 quarters of wheat in the market
and half-a-dozen transactions, then no doubt, if
the circulation, that is to say the money that has
changed hands, was found to have been £3,000,
prices must have been higher than they would
have been if the circulation had been found to
have been £2,000. In the first case wheat must
have averaged 60s. a quarter, in the second 40s.
But we can only speak rationally about the matter
in the "must have been "and " would have been "

moods and tenses. If you say, "Increase the circulation and you will raise prices," you find you might as well say, "Raise prices and you will raise prices." You are brought face to face with the difficulty, that, putting an increase in the number of transactions out of account, nothing but a rise in prices can possibly increase the circulation. This was the truth that was clearly seen and strongly set forth by Mr. Tooke and his friends. "Mr. Horner had laid down the principle in 1802 that if the quantity of the circulating medium is permanently augmented without a corresponding augmentation of internal trade, a rise will unavoidably take place in the prices of exchangeable commodities."[1] Mr. Wilson, in commenting on this passage, remarks that what was in Mr. Horner's mind was an increase of inconvertible paper, that you can no doubt find instances in abundance of prices being raised by excessive issues of inconvertible paper, but that they are nominal prices only. If on the contrary you attempt to raise real prices by issues of convertible notes you find that it cannot be done.

The general conclusion of Tooke and his school then we may take to be this, that while increases of compulsory government paper often act as[2] "an originating cause in raising prices," nothing

[1] Wilson, *Capital Currency and Banking*, p. 81.
[2] *Enquiry into the Currency Principle*, p. 71.

of the sort holds good in regard to increases of
real money. It is true that the form of real
money with which they were mainly concerned
was that of convertible notes. Mr. Tooke however, it must be said, quotes with approval the
reply of one of the witnesses before the committee of 1840,[1] which extends the principle to
sovereigns. It was, in his view, no more possible
to " throw " sovereigns than to " throw " convertible notes into circulation. We find also Mr.
Fullarton arriving at the opinion above cited that,
under present conditions, the purchase by the
Bank of all the gold brought to it prevented the
increased production of the metal from taking any
effect whatever on prices. Mr. Wilson on the
other hand specifically separates the case of gold
from that of convertible notes ; at the same time
the arguments which he employs to show that
banks cannot raise prices by increasing their
issues of convertible notes are every one of them
quite equally applicable to gold. The real reason,
in his view, is this, that such notes can only be
made to circulate in as far as they contribute to
the augmentation of internal trade, and that when
they do that, they balance their own increase by
assisting to bring about an increase in the volume
of commodities.[2] This however is equally true of

---

[1] *Enquiry into the Currency Principle*, p. 62.
[2] *Capital Currency and Banking*, p. 83.

gold.   Business men will no more take sovereigns
from their bankers than they will take notes,
unless they can turn them over at a profit, that
is unless they can, in one way or another, increase
the volume of commodities in the market by
means of them ; and, if business men do not take
them, they will lie in the vaults of the banks and
will not affect prices in any way.

If we turn to Mr. Gilbart's work on the *History
and Principles of Banking*, we find him maintaining
that [1] "an increased quantity of money," an expression which he uses in this instance as meaning an
increased issue of convertible notes, not only has
no necessary tendency to raise prices, but that, on
the contrary, *in the ordinary course of business*
(the italics are his own) its tendency is not to
advance but to lower prices.   His reasons for
the opinion are given as follows.   " The banks by
advancing capital on lower terms than it could be
otherwise obtained diminish the cost of production and consequently the price.   The banks still
further reduce prices by destroying monopoly.
In towns where there are no banks a few moneyed
men have all the trade in their own hands, but
when a bank is established other people of character are enabled to borrow capital of the bankers.
Their monopoly is destroyed, competition is produced and prices fall."   If this, however, applies to

[1] *Hist. and Prin. of Banking*, p. 106.

an increase in the issues of banks, there can be no reason for maintaining that it does not apply to an increase in gold, on which, in the long run, an increase in bank issues depends. On the contrary, it is certain that convertible bank notes owe this characteristic, in common with all their other characteristics, to the fact of their practical identity with gold as real money. In the case of such notes as those of the Bank of England, which are nothing else but coin certificates, this identity is beyond question absolute.

Mr. Gilbart lays down a general law with regard to increases in the quantity of money in the following terms : "If the increased quantity of money raises the demand for commodities beyond a certain point it will advance the price, but if it increases the supply it will lower the price."[1] We are here presented with a theory very different from that which affirms the necessary connection between increases and diminutions in the quantity of money, and rises and falls in prices. Mr. Gilbart's doctrine is that an increase in the quantity of money is in itself a fact from which no conclusion can be drawn in regard to prices. Before we can draw any such conclusion we must know what is to become of the new money. Its expenditure may be so directed as to raise prices, but it may also be so directed as to lower

[1] *Op. cit.*, p. 107.

them. In the modern world it seems more likely
to have the latter effect than the former. When
Alexander distributed the gold stripped from the
palaces of Susa among his soldiers, there was
perhaps little else that the soldiers could do with
their new money than to expend it on commodities already in existence, and thus to raise their
price. When the produce of African or Australian
mines comes home nowadays, the case is different.
It finds its way first into the vaults of the Bank
of England, and practically only gets drawn out
and passes into circulation in as far as it is engaged in increasing the production of commodities
and in thus balancing or more than balancing its
own increase. The broad facts of the world are
clearly in keeping with this conclusion. The
annual gold production has been increased from
two millions to over fifty millions since the beginning of the nineteenth century, and yet prices,
instead of being increased, have fallen by more
than one-half. In these circumstances it would
be rash to maintain that an increase to a thousand
millions annually during the twentieth century
would have the effect of raising them.

Much has been said about the rise in prices of
many, perhaps of most, commodities that followed
the gold discoveries in California and Australia ;
and the phenomenon has often been represented
as having been equivalent to a fall in the value of

money. It is worth while, however, to point out the contrasts which it presents when compared with the palpable and unmistakable changes that we find taking place in the value of silver or of paper that is over issued. In the latter case everything connected with the fall is clear and definite. There is no difficulty in saying what, at any given date, the precise change in value amounted to ; it can be stated to a shilling or to fractions of a shilling. In regard to the alleged change in the value of the gold in the fifties, on the other hand, not only its amount, but its existence even, appears to be all a mere matter of opinion. Jevons, for example, puts it down at 26 per cent. ; Mr. Falconer, of the United States Bureau of Statistics, thinks there was no change at all ; and Professor Nicholson, though his general line of thinking on economical questions might have led us to expect a conclusion more in accordance with the quantitative theory, inclines to the opinion that there was actually a rise in the value of the sovereign, instead of the commonly alleged remarkable fall.[1] In the crisis of 1856, at any rate, there was certainly no redundancy of gold, The wonder was what had become of it all.

The cause of the contrast is plainly this—that in depreciations of the silver or the paper there is always gold in the background to measure their

---

[1] *Money and Monetary Problems*, ed. 1893, p. 273.

amount by. In order to find it we have only to sub-
tract the gold prices from the paper prices; whereas
in alleged changes in the value of gold itself there
is really nothing whatever to measure them by.
"There are index numbers," it will be said. Let
us inquire what Professor Nicholson has to say on
that point.[1]   In England, in 1875, he tells us, the
"commodities" to which alone index numbers
can refer were £577,000,000 in value, while the
total "national inventory" was between eight and
nine thousand millions ; that is to say, that these
"commodities" were about one-fifteenth of the
whole. By their very nature such commodities
are necessarily confined to things that are quotable at so much per pound or per bushel ; and
they must therefore exclude all such forms of
wealth as land, ships, houses, railways, furniture, and such like. A rise or fall in the value
of everything purchasable, if one could anyhow
ascertain it, would no doubt be synonymous with
a counter fall or rise in gold ; but it will not
do to take fluctuations in the value of one
small fraction of this total, and argue from that
as if they implied a parallel fluctuation in the
value of the whole. The contention that the one
in any way necessarily implies the other is met by
the entirely insuperable objection that the cheapening of any one important commodity means

[1] *Op. cit.*, pp. 275, 276.

necessarily the liberation of more money than was formerly available for expenditure on others. Mr. Bagehot [1] thus traces the sharp rise in the price of the leading articles of trade that took place during 1871 to the fall in wheat which occurred in 1869 and continued during 1870. If the natural result of the cheapening of one article of consumption is to liberate money for expenditure on others, it plainly cannot be maintained that the cheapening of things that constitute one-fifteenth of the world's wealth necessarily involves the cheapening of the other fourteen-fifteenths also. Its natural tendency would be indeed the direct opposite of this. Tooke [2] remarked that when the prices of commodities were high, the prices of securities were very frequently, if not universally, low, and *vice versa.* In 1894 and 1895, owing to the lowness of the prices of commodities, we heard a great deal about the appreciation of gold. At the same time securities then touched their culminating point. Of late years, on the other hand, we know that as commodities have gone up securities have gone down. As securities ordinarily mean shares in land, in ships, in machinery, in buildings, and so on, there is no conceivable reason why they should not be taken into account quite as much as indexable commodities in attempting to determine the value of gold. All attempts in that

[1] *Lombard Street*, p. 148.   [2] Tooke, *op. cit.*, p. 86.

direction seem to be, as Mr. Mill and the late
Professor Sidgwick thought, in the nature of the
case idle. Relative values can only be determined
with definiteness when they are contemporaneous,
and the more widely apart in time that they stand
the more plainly impossible does it become to
speak of them with any approximation to definiteness. Comparisons between the respective values
of money in different periods, between which a
sufficient interval has elapsed for human wants to
change radically and for fresh forms of wealth to
spring into existence, are in the main illusory,
and at any rate are necessarily devoid of anything even remotely approaching to scientific
precision.

Another and a very salient contrast that presents itself between rises in prices due to over
issues of the subsidiary money, and rises in prices
due to great gold discoveries, is this—that the first
are caused by a fall in the value of the circulating
medium, the second are not. We shall be told, no
doubt, that the latter also must be really due to
a fall in the value of the circulating medium, although this fall is disguised ; that a rise in prices
is " other words for a fall in the value of money."
I shall have occasion to examine that contention
in the next chapter. In the meantime it may be
enough to say that, if that is so, then there are
two altogether different kinds of fall in the value

of money. There is one, the practical fall, which is a matter of immediate concern to the whole business interest of the country in which it takes place ; and there is a second, which we may call the metaphysical fall, which is understood and believed in by a select few only.

In the case of depreciations of the currency the rise in prices is due to the practical, unmistakable, definite fall that all the world comprehends and knows about. After the amount of government paper in circulation has reached a certain limit, a further increase in the issues unfailingly forces down its value. The element of distrust comes in. The circulating medium can no longer be implicitly relied on as a store of purchasing power, and therefore no one will keep any of it by him any longer than is inevitable. He hastens to pass it on, if necessary at a sacrifice, and the more of it that is issued, the more is this distrust accentuated.

In connection with the rise due, or said to be due, to the gold discoveries of the middle of this century, no one can assert that distrust of gold had any place. The doctrinaire government of Holland indeed took the step of demonetising gold, but very soon repented of it and retracted it. Some of the shops in Paris, it is said, by way of pleasantry put up notices in their windows that they would be glad to accept all the gold brought to them at par in exchange for their wares. M. Chevalier certainly raised a scare among the economists, but the outside world looked on unconcerned.

The mode in which the rise, such as it was, did come about is very well analysed by Cairnes. It was in the first instance a local rise confined to the countries where the gold was discovered. There, a large proportion of the labourers engaged in the production of all sorts of other commodities left their occupations and started to search for gold. The cost of production of these other commodities was thus necessarily raised and with it their price in the market. If the average man could make £5 per week at the diggings, it was not likely that he would long go on making horse-shoes or making bricks at prices that would yield him much less than £5 per week; so the prices of horse-shoes and bricks, and of every other sort of local product, had to rise to redress the balance. As the gold discoveries increased, the area of their influence on prices became larger, and extended in the end more or less to the greater part of the world. The principle in operation however was throughout the same. The profitableness of gold mining raised the price of commodities by raising first their cost of production.

If we suppose that, instead of great discoveries of gold, great discoveries of iron had been made, and that they had been accompanied for a considerable period by a steady demand for iron, due, let us suppose, to the construction on a great scale throughout the world of armoured cruisers, a demand so steady that in spite of vast increases of supply it maintained the price of iron at a highly profitable figure, we should then have had a phenomenon precisely similar to that presented by the gold discoveries. Labour and capital would in such circumstances have been drawn away more or less from all other industries into the iron industry, and the price of all other commodities except iron would have tended to rise, first locally in the iron-producing country, and afterwards in the world in general. We do not need to look for illustrations of the principle to hypothetical or imaginary cases. We have them wherever natural conditions create for a country a highly profitable export trade of some duration. Local wages and prices rise, and their effect must be felt in the long run all round, just as the effect of the high wages and prices of California and Australia were felt all round at the time of the gold discoveries. The main difference between the production of other commodities and of gold is this, that the tendency which the profitable production of other commodities has to raise prices is balanced, or more than balanced, in the end, by the fact that the increased production of these commodities themselves tends to bring down their own prices one by one, while the price of gold, in spite of increased production, never falls. So far is it, therefore, from being true that the rise in prices due to great gold discoveries is caused by a fall in the value of the metal, that the very reverse is the truth. The rise is actually caused by the fact that the metal does not fall. If a great city owes its existence to petroleum the consumptive demand of the inhabitants of that city will tend to raise the price of everything but petroleum, just as the consumptive demand of a great city that owes its existence to gold will tend to raise for a time the price of all other commodities but gold. The proviso " for a time " is however a very necessary one, as, in the end, large demand, by making possible large, and consequently economical, production, does not raise prices but lowers them.

As the result of this radical difference between the two classes of phenomena there are some minor points of contrast of considerable interest that present themselves. (1) In the case of the rise due to gold discoveries there is an absolute increase in the wealth of the country affected, while in the case of a rise due to the depreciation of the currency there is an absolute decrease. The poorer for instance that India became by the fall in the rupee the more effectually was the fall in the price of foodstuffs, that was otherwise inevitable, counteracted. (2) In the case of rises in prices due to a depreciation of the currency, the rise turns out in the end to have been an illusion. In the case of rises due to gold discoveries it does not. (3) In the case of the rise due to gold discoveries it is the rate of wages that is raised first, and it is the increased spending power of the wage-earners that causes the rise in commodities. In the case of depreciations, on the contrary, it is the shopkeeper who finds that, in order to come out square in his wholesale purchases, he must get more currency in his retail sales, and consequently has to raise his price. The rise in wages comes last, if at all. It is thus the wage-earner that in the last instance bears the brunt of the loss, while in the case of new gold discoveries he is the chief and the immediate gainer. When the two classes of phenomena present such a contrast their identification can manifestly lead only to confusion of thought.

CHAPTER VI

THE PLACE OF MONEY IN ECONOMICS

In a historical inquiry into the origin of money we shall find it above all things needful to be on our guard against axioms. We have, for example, the doctrine which is presented to us by Professor Walker, among others, as axiomatic, the doctrine that a fall in the price of any commodity, and an "appreciation of gold" in respect to it, are "in effect synonymous."[1] If this were valid, there could then it is clear be no conceivable case in which we could have the fall without the "appreciation." Let us take a concrete instance, and inquire by means of it whether such a doctrine can be valid. A purely hypothetical case will serve our purpose just as well as any other. Say that during one year, call it the year 1900, wheat was 35s. a quarter in London, and that during the next year it was only 30s. a quarter in the

[1] *International Bimetallism*, p. 254.

same place. We should all say that it had fallen
5s. in the interim, and most of us would probably
admit, at first sight at any rate, that gold must
have appreciated by 5s. a quarter with respect
to it. Let us suppose, however, that during the
first-mentioned year its price was 30s. a quarter
in the locality or localities where it was produced,
that it cost 2s. 6d. a quarter to land it in London,
that the London importer made 2s. 6d. a quarter
by the sale of it. Clearly, so far, no appreciation
of gold occurred. On the contrary, that particular wheat before it was consumed had appreciated
by 2s. 6d. a quarter as compared with the gold
given, in one shape or another, for it. Come
again to the next year, and let us suppose that
solely owing to some reduction in the cost of
production—to the invention perhaps of a new
reaper and binder—wheat was able to be sold at
the locality where it was produced at 25s. a
quarter, the farmer obtaining just the same profit
as he had obtained during the previous year ;
that it was again brought to London at a cost
of 2s. 6d. a quarter, and again was all sold and
passed into consumption at prices representing a
net profit of 2s. 6d. a quarter to the importer,
that is to say at 30s. a quarter. Then again
there was no appreciation of gold as compared
with wheat during the second year either. On
the contrary there was again an appreciation of

the wheat as compared with the gold given for
it.   Where then did the appreciation of gold
come in?   You answer perhaps, " No doubt gold
did not appreciate with respect either to the
special wheat of 1900 or to that of 1901, but it
appreciated with respect to wheat in general."
Is not your "wheat in general," however, something suspiciously like the "men in general" and
" things in general," the *substantiæ secundæ* of
the mediæval realists?   The truth is that the
sequence, " If wheat is down as compared with
money, then money is up as compared with
wheat " would only be axiomatically valid, if the
wheat of the second year was the *very same*
wheat that was in existence during the first ; and
it will be found that the idea that the commodities of one year are either the same as the
commodities of the next, or else that they hand
down their identity to them, like the members
of a perpetual corporation, is an idea that seems
to run continually in the minds of writers domi-
nated by the quantitative theory.   We find
Professor Walker, for instance, remarking in regard to the system of comparison by means of
index numbers : " The aggregate price of the
same articles in the same quantities in the same
market at dates earlier or later, affords a comparison which is supposed to determine with a
reasonable degree of accuracy the appreciation

or depreciation of the money used in that market."[1] But if the articles are not the same, but only the perhaps remote descendants of the original articles, does that make no difference?

In economics the great necessity always is to get a perfectly clear conception of the meanings of the terms that we are using, and to make sure that we never pass unconsciously from one meaning of a term to another. Take then the term "appreciation." If a given weight of one commodity, say gold, had, since 1870, appreciated as compared with a given weight of another commodity, say silver, it would then necessarily also be true that the man who since 1870 had kept his gold and refused to make the exchange for silver would have done better than the man who had consented to make such an exchange. But when we put "commodities generally" in the place of "silver" the sequence does not hold good. No one could maintain that the people who have kept their gold in their pockets since 1870, if there are any such people, can have come out better on the average than people who have exchanged it for "commodities generally," that is to say, than people who have invested it in any way. The truth is that if we regard the substantial identity at bottom of commodities and services, the fact that it is the same thing

---

[1] *International Bimetallism*, p. 257.

whether I buy a pair of boots or whether I pay
the shoemaker for the time spent in making
them, it seems clear that instead of gold having
appreciated as compared with commodities generally since 1870, commodities generally must on
the average in their day, that is to say, between
the date of their production and the date of their
consumption, have appreciated more or less as
compared with gold.   If it had not been so
there could have been no average rate of profit
in the world ; and then there would have been
no average rate of interest.   Commerce and production in such circumstances would long ago
have stopped dead.   An appreciation of gold as
compared with commodities generally is in truth
something that only happens during a panic.

The whole line of reasoning made use of by
such writers as Mr. Wells, Mr. Atkinson and
Lord Playfair in regard to the causes of the
fluctuations of prices is, though perhaps they
themselves have not altogether recognised the
fact, directed to the establishment of the conclusion that the standard substance does not fluctuate
in value.   If you maintain and prove that the
fall in the price of any and every commodity is
perfectly accounted for by other causes than the
appreciation of gold, you are clearly maintaining
and proving that the appreciation of gold is a
cause which must be looked on as mythical.

The explanation they give of the fall in prices which marked the last twenty-five years of the past century, if regarded as established, completely supplants and negatives the theory based on the doctrine that gold has appreciated, just as the astronomical explanation of eclipses supplants and negatives all conflicting theories, such as those based on the conception of these phenomena as portents of future calamity.

The axiom in question, it must be said further, proves too much. It is maintained that if potatoes, or iron, or silver can be said to have fallen 10 per cent., then it would be equally accurate to say that gold had risen 10 per cent. If this theory were valid it is plain that not only would we be precluded from holding that the standard substance can remain altogether stable while everything else fluctuates, but, further than this, we would be precluded from holding that the standard substance can remain in the smallest degree more nearly stable than anything else. Everything in this world would then necessarily be equally stable and equally unstable. Wheat and iron warrants, we should have to hold, would really fluctuate just as much as, but no more than, Consols or than gold itself. If, on the other hand, we feel ourselves forced to admit that one commodity may approximate more to stability of value than another, then the axiom is *ipso*

facto broken down ; then there is nothing left in
it to prevent us from accepting the conclusion,
if otherwise established, that the standard substance remains stable.

Another doctrine that is presented to us in the
light of an axiom is this : that any one commodity can measure the value of any or of all
others, and it must be admitted that at first sight
it appears to possess a remarkable degree of
cogency. We have found, however, that, so far
from its being true that any commodity can
measure the value of all others, it is the case, on
the contrary, that that commodity only can be
used as the general measure of values which has
itself become the universal goal of effort in the
community.

We shall perhaps discern better where precisely the weak point of this axiom lies after
glancing at another with which it is closely connected, the doctrine that "there cannot be a
general rise of values." [1] "All values cannot rise
together," it is said, "any more than a hundred
trees can all overtop one another." In the discussions of the practical world, however, we
assume every day that all values can and do rise
together. The doctrine, it must be noticed, precludes not only the possibility of an increase in
the value of everything that already possesses

[1] J. S. Mill, *Pol. Econ.*, People's Ed., p. 267.

some value (except at the expense of other things), but on the same principle it precludes the acquire-ment of value by anything that had no value before, except, similarly, by a proportionate dimi-nution in other values. The quantum of matter of course remains stationary; it is only the values attaching to it that change. If the doctrine were true, therefore, there could, it seems to me, be no general increase in the wealth of the world or of any given country, as the general wealth, we know, is but the name for the "sum of values." What becomes in that case, however, of such calculations as the late Mr. Mulhall's, that while the wealth of the United Kingdom in 1882 was £8,720,000,000, it had reached in 1895 £11,806,000,000? Are we to reject them as unreal, or is it the metaphysics with which they clash that must be thrown over-board?

We shall, I think, arrive at the explanation of the difficulty if we take care to distinguish be-tween those relations of value that are contem-poraneous and those that take time into account. Viewed at the same moment, the prices of com-modities do seem to bear a relation to each other analogous to the relations between the various trees in a forest. We can suppose for instance that without knowing the actual values of say half-a-dozen commodities, we knew by how much the value of each differed from the value of every

other.   In that case information as to the value
of any one of them would furnish us with the
datum needed to determine the value of every
other.   Any one of them might in these circumstances be taken as the point of departure
for the valuation of the rest.

It must be observed, however, that, in such a
case, the relations between the various values
must already have been reduced practically to
relations of space capable of being represented
by ordinates and curves, and that this moreover must have been done by the past operation
of the monetary standard.   In that case certainly
no further standard will be needed but the ordinary
standards of number and capacity.   The monetary standard itself is so different an entity from
such standards as these that Professor Walker
rightly enough demurs to its being designated
by the same generic name, and insists instead
that it should always be called the common
denominator of exchange.   What it does is to
regulate the manner in which values vary in
respect to one another, from one period to
another, and this end it achieves by attaining
universal acceptability itself, and by thus becoming capable of being always exchanged for
other commodities without loss, by acquiring in
short a value of its own which *seems* at least
to remain invariable irrespective of all alterations

in the conditions of its supply. If we can conceive of a state of things in which, while all other commodities are continually fluctuating in value, there is one which remains absolutely steady, no matter to how great an extent its supply is augmented, then we have conceived of the state of things in which one commodity has attained the position of the monetary standard.

These axioms, or pseudo-axioms, as we may choose to regard them, seem to spring from one common root, the detachment of the conception of value from its historical foundation. A question which has to be faced is this: Could even the *thought* of value have existed in a state of things in which there was as yet no such thing as money? It will probably be admitted at once that in such circumstances the thought of price could not have existed. The meaning of price is clearly the amount of money which a commodity will fetch, and it thus plainly depends on the existence of money. Our question therefore resolves itself into another one, that is, Is the thought of value a thought that can exist independently of the thought of price, or is it derived from it and dependent on it? The answer is plain. To the psychologist it is a familiar consideration that the more abstract of two such conceptions always is, and always must be, derived from the more concrete. The Tasmanians, as we know, had names for many of the special varieties of trees, but no name for tree in general, and many other parallel instances could readily be cited. The more concrete con ception can and often does exist without the more abstract one, but the more abstract one, plainly enough, cannot exist without the more concrete one. A savage can have a very clear notion as to what the price of anything means long before he is capable of forming any idea of value as distinguished from price. Man, having formed his idea of price, proceeds to construct from that his idea of value by abstraction, that is to say by denuding the first idea of its details. The price of the horse I have just bought is the sum of money I have given for it. But I may have had some special luck, and may have bought the horse below its " value," or the seller may have had a special piece of luck in coming across me, and may thus have got more than its value for it. Its value then is what the average man, neither on the one hand favoured by my special circumstances, nor on the other hampered by my idiosyncrasies, would have had to give for it. Price, it has been well said, is instantaneous value, and it is clearly from the notion of instantaneous value that the notion of value in general has been derived. How concrete both conceptions were in early Rome the Latin word for the verb "to value" shows. The etymology of *aestimo* indicates that to the Romans the very thought of value was originally bound up with the special material of their standard. The modern economist too frequently takes the conception of value, developed and only capable of being developed in a social state where some commodity had already attained the position of money, and endeavours to apply it to a state of things where by hypothesis money did not yet exist.

Of all the *idola tribus* this tendency to begin at the wrong end, to put the abstract before the concrete, is the most pervasive in its influence and the most difficult altogether to escape. Aristotle put his finger on the source of the illusion when he spoke of our tendency to put the whole before the parts, when we ought to put the parts before the whole. For many generations in natural science men were arguing from the general to the particular, and getting no further ahead, till Bacon put them on the right track. Indeed every important rectification of philosophical error seems to have taken the shape of showing that it is the individual fact which should take precedence of the general truth as a subject of inquiry. The fallacious tendency dies hard. The series of science primers issued by our most eminent authorities " for the use of children between twelve and

fifteen years of age" is thought, it seems, to
be appropriately introduced by a disquisition on
the yet unravelled and unexplained distinction
between law and cause.   We have a conspicuous
example of the influence of the tendency in the
practice still prevalent in many of our schools of
commencing the teaching of languages by teaching their grammar ; much of what they teach
under the name of syntax being really metaphysics, and erroneous metaphysics at that.   In
other departments of thought it has manifested
itself in the famous fiction of the social contract
between king and people entered into at the dawn
of history ; in the conception of the law as
something that has been handed down from god-
descended legislators, instead of being based as
it is on the recognition by the state of customary
institutions ; and in the common failure to recognise that a law which is anything more than
the recognition of an already formed public
sentiment is inevitably valueless.

We find a striking illustration of the operation
of the tendency in question when we see Mr. Mill
professing to leave the conception of money out of
account altogether in the first part of his work on
political economy,[1] and to introduce it only in
the later part.   This he looks upon as the natural
order in which the subject should be treated.

[1] See People's Ed., p. 293.

Mr. Jevons's line of thought too is not dissimilar. "In a state of barter," he tells us, "the price-current would be a very complicated document. The value of each commodity would have to be expressed in terms of every other commodity." It is difficult to attach any meaning to such words. The truth rather is that in the primitive state of barter there could have been no such thing as a price-current. There would indeed have been no word, no thought even for either "price" or "value." There would no doubt have been the subjective thought, "I will or I will not exchange my commodity for this other man's commodity"; but it is the existence of the common standard alone, of the commodity that has become the goal of effort, that renders it possible for the thought to become objective, that makes it possible for a man to say or to think, "This slave is 'worth' three bullocks," or "This bullock and this caldron are identical in value."

Similarly—to illustrate the obscure, perhaps my readers will think, by the obscurer—thought and self-consciousness themselves are developed, and are only, it would appear, capable of being developed, in a state of social intercourse. The modern metaphysician, however, comes along and puts the question to himself: How would a solitary being regard the universe? On his answer to this question he bases the structure of subjective idealism. The true answer to the question is : " A solitary being would not regard the universe at all ; he would have no thought either of the universe, or of himself, or of anything else. Such thoughts are only developed and made possible in a state of intercourse ; and it is idle to ask what shape would they assume in the absence of intercourse." Mill's intricate discussion on international values owes its obscurity, I think, in like manner to the fact that he takes the whole terminology of "cost," of "price," of "buying," of "selling," and so on, all of them words and thoughts that are dependent on a standard of value for their existence, and interpolates them into an imaginary state of things in which, by hypothesis, no standard has yet been born.

If we accept this view of the genesis of the conception of value, we shall not be able to subscribe to the doctrine that has had some vogue in its day, and is probably not yet extinct, as to the insignificance of money from the point of view of the scientific economist. "There cannot," says Mr. Mill,[1] "be a more insignificant thing in the whole economy of society than money." Rather, it seems to me, money is the pivot of everything in economics. We cannot move a single step towards the elucidation of any of its problems without first studying the nature and operation

[1] J. S. Mill, *op. cit.*, p. 296.

of the standard substance. The most rudimentary conception of value is, I think, impossible antecedently to the existence of some sort of rudimentary money, and it will probably be found, further, that our modern precise conception of it is dependent on the existence of metallic money, homogeneous, divisible and reunitable. If, further, "value and wealth are," as Mr. Senior says, "related as substance and attribute," then clearly the science of the production and distribution of wealth postulates as its preliminary some comprehension of the connection between money and value.

The conception of money as being in the world of to-day, like gold and silver among early peoples, sought after so largely on account of the distinction that the possession of it confers, if regarded as valid, will make it necessary for us to revise much that has been held to be the soundest of sound doctrine in the current political economy. It may make us less disposed than we have hitherto been to cast aside as worthless all the reasonings and investigations of our forefathers in the period antecedent to Adam Smith. Of late years we have often been told that while the adherents of the Mercantile Theory had taken it for granted that the legitimate goal of a nation's fiscal policy was to make its subjects wealthy in the sense in which wealth was

equivalent to the possession or to the command of gold, Adam Smith had rendered an eminent service to mankind by showing the futility
of such a conception of wealth as this. Since
his time, we in England at any rate had come
to recognise the truth that money was not
in any real sense wealth at all; it was a mere
tool for the transference of wealth; "it was of no
use till it was spent"; neither man nor nation
could be enriched by its increased acquisition;
all that men really wanted was more and cheaper
commodities. Consequently the whole benefit of
international trade to any country lay, it was
said, in its imports, and a balance of exports over
imports meant nothing but national loss.

The validity of these doctrines might be taken
for granted by the student when he found them
within the boards of his text-books, but the
remarkable thing was that he was likely to find
them nowhere else. In all current literature, in
all common talk, he would on the contrary
find it taken for granted that what every one
who engaged in business at home, as well as
every one who went to push his fortune abroad,
was aiming at was the making of money in the
old-fashioned sense in which making money is
synonymous with acquiring the ownership of
gold. More than this, if we look at the fiscal
policy of modern nations, if we regard the

practical considerations that recommend one line of policy in preference to another, we find that the goal that they have one and all before them is nothing else but the goal of the nations in the days of the Mercantile Theory, nothing else but the goal of the Mercantile Theorists themselves, the acquisition of the maximum degree of command over the medium of exchange for the nation itself as a body, and severally for the units that compose it. Everywhere throughout the world we find commercial communities bent eagerly on the opening up of fresh markets, nowhere on the look-out for cheap imports. If the desirableness of cheap imports is put forward at all, it is put forward as a means to an end. Without cheap imports, it is urged, and certainly with truth, profitable exports are impossible ; but cheap imports are ordinarily a concession, increased exports are always the end to be achieved. When Peel said : "We will fight protective duties by cheap imports," he found an echo no doubt in the mind of the country. But what did he mean by fighting the protectionist nations ? Nothing else but this : becoming richer than they, securing a greater command of gold than they—which indeed we have done. The seventeenth-century policy of England blundered no doubt, as Sir Thomas Mun and his friends in their day pointed out, in

aiming at the accumulation of gold and silver
within the territories of the nation itself, and
thinking that this end was to be promoted by
prohibiting their export ; but if it was a blunder
to aim at increasing for their citizens the
ownership of the precious metals, the certain
command of gold at brief notice, then all the
states of the modern world, free trade and protectionist alike, are making that blunder now.
Whatever fiscal policy a statesman has to
propound in a modern democracy, the only line
of reasoning which he can advance on its behalf
which has the smallest chance of being favourably
listened to, is the one which will aim at showing
that it is the policy that in one way or another
is calculated to inaugurate good times or to ward
off bad times ; to make business prosperous and
to make property rise in value ; to bring
enhanced incomes, in short, or realisation for
increased capital sums, within the reach of every
citizen.

In Sydney for instance, where I happened
recently to reside, it would assuredly have been
idle for a Free Trader who wished to advocate
the abolition of the duty on sugar, to point out
to his audience that if this were done they would
save a few shillings each in their annual expenditure.   They would be quite unselfish enough to
decline to purchase so nearly inappreciable an

advantage by a measure which it would have to be admitted could not be carried out without for a time largely curtailing employment and causing considerable distress. Yet the duty on sugar is being reduced and will shortly be abolished in Sydney.[1] This however has come about because the Free Traders have been able to convince the public that free trade is the policy which is most likely in the end to increase the money-wealth of each citizen. Look at Sydney, they could say, with her free trade policy in the past, and you see property rising in value, shipping increasing by leaps and bounds, every one making money in fact ; and look again at Melbourne with her protectionist policy, and you can note that the reverse of all this is happening. All through, the appeal is made by both sides to a population that thinks, and thinks only, of making money, and cares nothing about the cheapening of commodities, except in so far as this cheapening conduces to the making of money.

In the more modern economists that deal with free trade, such as President Hadley, of Yale, we hear little if anything of the desirableness of cheap imports in themselves. Their defence of it is grounded rather on the consideration that the rates of profit and of wages in a country

---

[1] The above was written before Federation.

generally must be ruled by the rates prevailing
in the export trades ; that the export trades
consequently are those which are best worth
fostering ; and that it is free trade which alone
can foster them.   Convince the American and
the colonial working man of this and no
doubt America and the Colonies will follow
the English example.   The argument however
directly reverses the old line of reasoning which
laid all the stress on cheap imports.   It lays all
the stress, as the Mercantile Theory did and as
the whole business world does still, on the income
derived from exports.

The truth is that there is the same distinction
in economics between money and commodities
that there is in physics between energy and
work.   Because the utility of money is measured
by the commodities and services that it can purchase, therefore, it is argued, money is nothing but
commodities and services.   If we take them into
account, it is contended, we may leave money out
of account altogether.   One might as well contend that because energy is measured by the
work it will do, therefore it is nothing but work,
and that if work is taken into account in the
theories of physics energy may be left out of
account altogether.   The trouble would be that
in such a case when we found the energy of sun-
light stored in the coal measures for a myriad of

ages, we should be entirely at a loss to know what to make of it. Work we certainly could not call it during its period of quiescence. On the same principle we cannot identify with com- modities that power of purchasing commodities which the possession of gold or the right to gold confers. The sale of a coat by a tailor we are told is " only half an exchange" till the money obtained for it is spent, say, in the purchase of a pair of shoes. But what about the state of things that exists while the exchange is only half com- pleted, and which may continue during a dozen lifetimes ? It is analogous to the state of things that exists when a stone thrown into the air, instead of coming to earth again in its former position, rests on the ledge of a jutting rock. The energy put into it by the impulse is not lost but remains stored up for future work. So the sale of the coat, while the money for which it was exchanged, be it in coin or in credit, is still unspent, results in the storing up of purchasing power for the seller ; and it is to the increase of this purchasing power, this potential energy for themselves, that the aspirations of men and the policy of nations are everywhere directed.

If we met with such a doctrine as the doctrine that money is of no use till it is spent, anywhere else but in a treatise on political economy, we should assuredly say : This is the maxim of the

spendthrift, not of the prudent citizen.   It is in no
conceivable sense true.   The utility of money to
an individual is not bound up absolutely with the
commodities that, either now or at any future
date, it will purchase.   It has, as we well know,
satisfactions to bestow apart altogether from the
contemplation of its expenditure, either immediate
or remote.   The speculator who clears £100,000
by a successful *coup* has surely an immediate
satisfaction from his gains, though he never spends
and never means to spend a shilling of them.   He
might have it even from the groundless reputation
of having made them.   If he does not awake to
find himself famous, he at any rate awakes to
find himself somebody.   He was formerly, perhaps, of no account in the world.   He is now the
homme arrivé quite as distinctly as the successful
general or the celebrated man of letters.   The
money not yet spent has won for him that most
universally coveted of all the objects of human
desire, increased consideration in the eyes of his
fellow-citizens.   Suppose he proceeded to spend
his £100,000, on what could he spend it?   In
ninety-nine cases out of a hundred he would
spend at least nine-tenths of it on nothing else
but on the purchase, in one way or another, of
increased consideration.   Spent, or unspent, the
money at bottom subserves the same purpose.

CONCLUSION

It will be as well, before I close, to take a survey of the ground traversed. Reviewing Adam Smith's account of the origin of money, we found it defective, inasmuch as it really presumed money to be already in existence. It presumed that the prudent man could find some commodity which no one would refuse in exchange for his products. If he could, then the commodity that he found would be money. What we want to know is how any commodity attained such a degree of general "acceptability," in Professor Walker's language, that no one would refuse it, no matter in what quantities it was offered. The nature of this "acceptability" next engaged our attention. We had to inquire what in truth it was. It was not of course the same thing as exchange value. The most "acceptable" commodity in a country might be much less valuable, weight for weight, than many others. It would be the commodity however with regard to which a man might feel

most certain that he would make little or no loss
in keeping it by him, no matter in what quantities
he held it, and no matter for how long a period.
In other words it was the commodity whose value
most closely approximated to invariability. The
function of money thus as a storer of purchasing
power, it appeared, took precedence of its function
as a medium of exchange. It was indeed only
in virtue of the fact that men were able to rely on
the standard commodity as a store of purchasing
power that they ever came to use it as a medium
of exchange. We found again that wheat, with
closed markets, could never become a reliable
medium for the storing of purchasing power,
because, if every one had enough of it, any
additional supply was liable to become altogether
unacceptable on any terms, to lose its purchasing
power altogether; and the same objection was
applicable to any commodity whose final purpose
was the satiation of any material need. Was it
not however, it would be asked, applicable to
all commodities of every sort? If the Austrian
theory of value, now much in vogue, was to be
accepted as valid it would have to be admitted
that it was. That theory taught that supply,
meaning by supply the supply of anything whatsoever without discrimination, resulted necessarily
in diminution of the utility of the thing supplied,
till at length that "utility" altogether vanished.

If that doctrine had held good, then it would have been hard indeed to have seen how money and a monetary standard could ever have come into existence. The theory, however, we found, rested on a defective analysis of human wants. Nine-tenths of human expenditure was expenditure on ornament, in the widest sense of that word. It was expenditure, at all events, on superfluities. What was the ultimate aim of such expenditure? It was distinction ; it was the outrunning of those about us in the race of life, it was the attaining of greater consideration in the eyes of our neighbours than others possessed. Taking orna-ment generally, it seemed clear that the demand for it might well be insatiable, because the more of it that one man possessed and was able to display the more would others need, in order to run level with him or to surpass him. Every special description of ornament however, it had to be admitted, was even exceptionally liable to fluctua-tions of value. The fashion that prescribed its use might change, and its value might fall to zero. The demand for it was dependent on no permanent human need ; and this fact no doubt had given rise to the prevalent impression that a necessary of life was likely to be a more trustworthy measure of values then a superfluity. As civilisation ad-vanced, however, it was found that the distinction that men covet came to be attached less and

less to the display of any special description of
ornament, and more and more to the general
power of expenditure on ornament, or in other
words on those superfluities in the use of
which the outward signs of wealth consist. The
same causes thus which would make the desire
for ornament in its general sense insatiable might
make the desire for any one commodity which
became the medium of exchange insatiable.
That commodity would indeed embody the command over ornament generally, as well as over
all that was needed for the supply of material
needs. We know accordingly that, both in the
ancient and in the modern world, the desire for
wealth, for money, for gold or silver, has appeared
to innumerable observers of human affairs to be
insatiable. If however the desire for this one
commodity is truly insatiable ; if the nature of
things is such that the demand for it must
automatically increase whenever the supply is
increased, because it is the one thing that every
man needs in order to hold his own with his rivals
in the race of life, and because, for that end, if
his rivals obtain more of it than they had before
he also must have more of it—if he can get it—
then there is surely no reason why this commodity
should fall in value whenever fresh discoveries
chance to cause an increase in its supply, but
every reason, on the contrary, why it should

remain stable in value irrespective of such increases. Gold never goes out of fashion. The demand for it for "use in the arts" seems always to grow side by side with the monetary demand, and neither of them show the smallest sign of slackening or satiation, though the generation that is now passing middle life has seen the millions of Australia piled up upon the millions of California, and the coming generation seems not unlikely to see fresh millions from the bounds of the Arctic Circle piled up upon the millions that the Southern Hemisphere, both from its eastern and western regions, has of late been disgorging.

APPENDICES

APPENDIX A

No. 21 [1]

MEMORANDUM BY MR. WILLIAM WARRAND CARLILE

THE method of dealing with the Indian Currency problem which I beg to submit for the consideration of the Indian Currency Committee is briefly the following : That the Committee should make it their first business to arrive at a conclusion as to what may now be regarded as being the probable natural exchange value of the rupee, for the ensuing year, under existing conditions ; and that point having been decided, that they should consider the advisableness of recommending that a ratio should be fixed by statute, at or very close to that figure at which both the sovereign and the rupee should be made unlimited legal tender in India, in all transactions, and that the mints should be opened to the free coinage of gold.

[1] Papers relating to India, from Bluebook of Indian Currency Committee, 1898.

In support of the above recommendation I beg to submit the following :—

(1) It was the natural and obvious course that, in the first instance, suggested itself to Lord Lansdowne's Government in 1892. Sir David Barbour's proposal then was first to stop the free coinage of silver, next, after an interval had been allowed to elapse sufficient to enable the Government to ascertain what effect the stoppage of the free coinage of silver had had upon the value of the rupee, to open the mints to the free coinage of gold, and to make gold legal tender in India, fixing the ratio between the sovereign and the rupee approximately in accordance with the value to which the latter had settled down. The conception of the true policy to be pursued was, in short, to let the public fix the ratio in the first instance, and then to stereotype this ratio by making it the official one by statute. It will be remembered further that this policy received the very emphatic endorsement of the late Mr. Bertram Currie, in a memorandum appended to the report of the Herschell Committee.[1] In that memorandum, he expressed his disagreement with the recommendation of his colleagues to the effect that an announcement should be made forthwith that rupees would be given by the Government in return for gold at the rate of fifteen to the sovereign, and recommended instead that, in the meantime, the mints should simply be closed without any such announcement, and that after an interval had elapsed sufficient to guide the Government in deciding as to what had become the natural value of the rupee under the new conditions, the ratio should be definitely

[1] Appendix to Minutes, Herschell Committee, p. 148, sec. 6.

fixed, and the mints should be opened to the free coinage of gold.

(2) This fixing of a maximum value for the rupee in 1893, while its minimum value was left unfixed, has been the source of much subsequent trouble and confusion of thought. Among others of its mischievous effects, it has had that of creating an impression that, in some sense, a statutory ratio between gold and the rupee exists already, and of thus obscuring to the public mind the necessity of fixing one before the silver currency can be expected to circulate at par with gold in the country. The present Indian Government, for instance, appear to anticipate that a state of things will come about of itself in which the sovereign will " become a recognised coin of the Empire" and in which gold and silver will circulate side by side, the one as standard money and the other as subsidiary, and they make accordingly no proposal to fix by statute the ratio between the two. Now it is possible to point to a long list of countries in which the gold and silver coins circulate together at par just as if they were different subdivisions of the same substance, and in which also one can lay his finger on the statute which fixes the ratio at which each shall be legal tender, but I think it is not possible to point to a single instance of a country in which gold and silver thus circulate at par without any statute or ordinance fixing the ratio.

(3) It will then perhaps be admitted without difficulty that, before the Indian Government's ideal can be realised, gold must be made legal tender in India, and it will further perhaps be admitted that gold cannot be made legal tender, while the rupee is legal tender also without fixing the ratio between the two. The recommendation therefore at the head of this paper recom-

mends only the doing of that at once which must plainly be done sooner or later. My contention, however, further, is that if the step recommended were taken no other step need be taken ; that the simple fixing of the ratio say at 1*s*. 4*d*., and the opening of the mints to the free coinage of gold, while keeping them closed to silver, would itself be sufficient to maintain the value of the rupee definitely at that figure.

(4) As to the mode in which such a legal tender Act would operate in bringing about and maintaining the parity between the rupee and gold, it is, perhaps, easier to follow it if we suppose that, in the first instance, an order was issued making the pound sterling, instead of the rupee, the standard of all computations in connection with Government business in India, all payments in rupees being converted, at the market rate, into payments in pounds sterling, and, henceforward, all taxes being collected in terms of pounds sterling, rupees being accepted in lieu of gold at the rate of, say, 15 to the sovereign. The total rupee circulation is estimated at about 120 crores, and the revenue may be put at about 100 crores. The fact therefore of the revenue being collected in rupees, but in terms of pounds sterling, would be equivalent to the redemption annually in gold of five-sixths of the rupee circulation. A practically unlimited market would thus be provided for the rupees at a fixed gold price. The holders of them, knowing that such a market was always open, would soon cease to have any fear of their fluctuating, and would keep them by them in the slack season for use in the busy season, precisely as if they were fractional gold pieces. This fact in itself would obviate any danger of redundancy. It was, as Professor Laughlin remarks, this virtual redeemability in gold, by its receipt in payment

of taxes at a fixed ratio to gold, that in America maintained the silver and the certificates based on it, which are not directly redeemable in gold, at par with United States notes which are. It seems certain indeed that a value for the rupee could thus without difficulty be maintained, even considerably above its present market value. On all grounds, however, both of justice and of expediency, the present market value should be as closely as possible adhered to.

(5) If, further, the ratio were fixed, it would henceforth be impossible for any one to obtain rupees from the Government at a price below that fixed on. There could be no such thing then as selling Council bills, that is, orders for rupees, at anything under 1*s*. 4*d*. per rupee (supposing 1*s*. 4*d*. to be chosen), as all bills on India would be sterling bills, though, of course, a pound sterling in India might mean either a sovereign or 15 rupees, at the option of the acceptor.

(6) It need hardly be said that if it should be thought important to avoid a change of nomenclature from rupees to pounds sterling, that change could be avoided while carrying out the above recommendation (Section 4) in all essential points. The Indian sovereign might always be described as a 15-rupee piece (Rxv. perhaps) or by some equivalent designation less awkward.

(7) In many of the discussions on the subject of the Indian currency it seems to be assumed that the parity of the rupee with gold cannot be ensured without direct convertibility between the two being guaranteed. The experience, however, of a great number of countries which possess standard and subsidiary coinages not directly convertible into each other, yet circulating together perfectly at par, is against that conclusion.

An instance which, it seems to me, has not received the attention that it deserves is to be found in the case of England itself in the eighteenth century.   During a great part of that century the worn and light shillings which were not intrinsically worth more than the thirtieth or fortieth part of a guinea circulated steadily along with it at the fixed ratio to it of twenty-one to one.   The fact that they did so is one calculated to bring the power of an Act or ordinance fixing the ratio between the standard and subsidiary money in making that ratio effective into a very strong light indeed.   The facts were briefly as follows: At the end of the seventeenth century silver was the undoubted standard in England in every sense.[1]   The guinea went up and down in value like any other commodity, and the foreign exchanges varied in accordance with the condition of the silver coinage.   When we turn, however to the middle of the eighteenth century—when next information with regard to monetary conditions is available—we find that the very state of things which exists at the present day had already come into existence.   Gold we then find to be the standard, and silver merely subsidiary money.   The state of the silver coinage had not then, we find, the smallest effect on the foreign exchanges.   The exchanges, on the contrary, were ruled exclusively by the state of the gold coin, together with the balance of trade.   So long as the guineas were of full weight, the mint price of gold ruled at £3 17s. 10½d., as at present.   The fluctuation in the value of gold coins was already a thing of the remote past.   How did this all come about?   The only thing that happened between the end of the seventeenth century and the middle of the eighteenth century

---

[1] I now think this was expressed too unreservedly.

which was calculated, in any way, to alter the situation, was the fixing of the value of the guinea in silver, in 1717. The rate fixed on virtually closed the mints to silver, as thenceforward to the close of the century it paid no one to bring silver to the mints to be coined ; the mints were thus left open to gold only. At the same time it made the silver to all intents redeemable in gold, by its availability for the payment of taxes at a fixed ratio to gold. The measure was intended to fix the value of gold in silver, but ended instead by fixing the value of the silver coin in gold. The silver was already unlimited legal tender, and was thus available for the payment of taxes, as the rupee is in India now. That alone of course did nothing to fix its value. As soon however as gold was made unlimited legal tender at a fixed ratio to it, the whole situation seems to have been at once altered. Thenceforward the silver coins seem never to have shown the smallest tendency to vary in value, however light and worn they became. We have then here an instance in which the silver, though unlimited legal tender (as it was till 1774), was made to circulate at a fixed parity with gold, by the mere efficacy of the ordinance fixing the ratio, together with the virtual closing of the mints to silver, and without any one having so much as dreamt of accumulating either a gold reserve to redeem the silver, or a silver reserve to redeem the gold.

(8) The misgivings which the Indian Government express with regard to the clauses of Mr. Lindsay's scheme, which proposes that the Government should guarantee the convertibility of the rupee to all and sundry at a fixed rate, seem to me not to be without just ground. Suppose that after the announcement had been made that the Government would accept all rupees

at 1*s.* 3¾*d.*, and would give gold for them, a rumour got wind—it might be without the smallest foundation—that the scheme was breaking down and was about to be abandoned, that the mints would be reopened to silver, and that a fall of 30 per cent. in the value of the rupee might any day be anticipated, it is quite conceivable that there might be an ugly rush for gold while it was still to be got at a fixed price. We must take into account the fact that we have a vast, ignorant populalation to deal with, exceptionally liable to unreasoning panic, that there are great interests hostile to the fixity of the rupee, and that immense fortunes are to be made by finding the weak point in any scheme that could be proposed, if it has one, and wrecking it. The Dutch Government of course take an entirely opposite stand to that suggested by Mr. Lindsay. To the question " Can persons holding silver coin require the Government or any national bank to give them gold for it ? " the clear answer is " No, they cannot," and I think the answer will have to be the same in India. It is quite certain that, in spite of their taking this stand, the Dutch Government, and many other governments similarly situated, have been able to maintain their appreciated silver at par with gold. Surely the first matter for inquiry in the Indian case is whether by the adoption of the same course it is not possible to attain the same end, before thinking of adopting a course so much more hazardous as that of guaranteeing universal direct convertibility would be. A legal tender Act fixing the ratio is not, it need hardly be said, for a moment to be confounded with a guarantee of direct convertibility. Such an Act, on the contrary, gives in express terms to all tenderers, the Government included, the option of paying in whichever medium they please.

(9) An inquiry which I have not seen set before the Committee in express terms, and yet which is, I think, one fertile in important results, is the inquiry—"What, at the present moment, is the standard of India?" It plainly is now not silver. A high authority recently tells us that it is "exchange." That however is a doctrine that can assist us little. The standard of value in a country must at any rate be a concrete substance, and cannot conceivably be an abstraction. I have endeavoured in my paper on the Indian Mints[1] to show that the standard of India is already gold—arriving on that point at the same conclusion as Mr. W. Douglas, author of *The Indian Currency*—and I think indeed that the same view is unconsciously and implicitly taken by every one who speaks of the "depreciation" of silver in India. Depreciation can only be depreciation in comparison with some standard in the background, and that standard can, in this case, be nothing but gold. If however the standard of India is already gold, the official recognition of gold as the standard by the opening of the mints to its free coinage, and by fixing by statute a ratio between it and the subsidiary silver, cannot certainly make the outside gold obligations of the country any harder to meet than they are under the present state of things. Now this much is certain, that India, somehow or other, meets her foreign gold obligations at the present moment without a gold reserve ; and the question arises, Would a gold reserve be any more necessary under the new conditions—that is to say, after the mints had been opened to the free coinage of gold, and gold had been made legal tender at a fixed ratio to the rupee—than it is at present? There is of course a theory that a fall in exchange forces a favour-

[1] *Transactions*, Glasgow Phil. Soc., 1898.

able trade balance by increasing exports and diminishing imports ; but setting aside that theory, which receives no support from statistics, which is contrary to all sound principle—involving indeed, as it would, the conclusion that any nation in financial difficulties has only to depreciate its currency to find an easy escape from them —there seems to be no reason for asserting that the accumulation of a gold reserve is a necessary preliminary to what is called the adoption of the gold standard in India, that is to say to the fixing of the ratio and the opening of the mints to the free coinage of gold.

(10) When a country possesses, as India does at present, a currency that cannot be exported, or at any rate that as a matter of fact never is exported, and when it possesses no gold reserve, there is plainly only one way in which its outside gold obligations can be met, that is by the trade balance in its favour. But suppose circumstances to arise which would tend to make the trade balance unfavourable—say a great diminution of exports owing to a famine—how then can they be met ? Plainly the true answer is that a country so situated can never let the trade balance become unfavourable to it. If circumstances are such that the meeting of her obligations directly would make the trade balance unfavourable, she must, as long as she has credit, borrow, in one shape or another, and thus keep it favourable. In the case of a country which had a gold currency and no gold reserve, it would be obvious enough that the only way in which its Government could meet outside obligations in gold which would not, in ordinary circumstances, be covered by the trade balance in its favour, would be either by increasing the taxation or by borrowing. In the case of India however, with her appreciated silver currency, it seems

generally to be assumed that there is a third method open of meeting outside obligations. She can sell her Council bills, it is said, cheaper than she would sell them otherwise, and can thus raise a larger sum than she could otherwise to meet these obligations. It is true of course that she can do this, but it is also plain that doing so is only another form of borrowing. If more bills are sold than the public want for immediate requirements, they can only be sold to people who buy them on speculation, and who intend to hold them, in the meantime, till they can dispose of them to advantage, and such sale in such circumstances is plainly equivalent to drawing on the future—to obtaining money in advance. It is, on the face of it, indeed, absurd to imagine that the fact of having a token currency gives a country an advantage, as regards meeting its obligations, over countries with a gold currency. If a gold currency country would, in given circumstances, have to meet its obligations abroad, either by borrowing or by increasing its taxation, it is quite certain that a token-currency country, in the same circumstances, will not be able to meet them in any other manner.

(11) In 1893, the maximum value of the rupee having been fixed by an edict at 1s. 4d., an attempt was made to fix the minimum, for a time, at 1s. 3¼d., by refusing to sell Council bills under that price. The amount of Council bills required to meet current obligations could not be sold, and direct borrowing had to be resorted to. This borrowing was the subject of much hostile criticism at the time, and it was accordingly decided to end it, and instead to sell Council bills below 1s. 3¼d., indeed at whatever price could be got for them. The result has been a loss of revenue amounting in all to about £8,000,000 since 1893, as compared with the revenue

that would have been obtained if the price of Council bills had been kept up. The question is, How much would it have cost India, in the shape of interest on borrowed money, to have maintained the price of Council bills ? Probably only some small fraction of £8,000,000. The mistake made by those who urged the sale of Council bills at any price lay in their failing to recognise that such a sale was merely borrowing in another form, and that a ruinously expensive one.

(12) The fixing of both maximum and minimum for the rupee in 1893 amounted, of course, to an attempt to completely fix the ratio. Why then did it not succeed ? The mistake lay in this, that while the maximum was fixed by an edict, the minimum was only fixed as a measure of policy, and the decision fixing it was known, from the first, to be liable to be changed at any moment, and was, as a matter of fact changed within about six months from the date of its adoption. In such circumstances, no one, from the first, could have any confidence in the maintenance of the value of the rupee ; no one, therefore, could safely keep rupees by him for future use ; and thus, every one being driven to force them on the market, they could not fail to become redundant. The case would be altogether different if both the maximum and the minimum had been fixed at once by a step that would be practically irretraceable, that is, by the passing of a statute opening the mints to the free coinage of gold and fixing a ratio at which both the sovereign and the rupee should be legal tender in all transactions.

(13) While it is the case that India, after the opening of the mints to gold and the fixing of a ratio between gold and the rupee, would, even without a gold reserve, be in quite as good a position to meet her outside gold

obligations as she is at present, it by no means follows that it would not be desirable to place her in a better position than her present one. The fixing of the ratio, however, instead of being looked upon as something that should only follow on the accumulation of a gold reserve, should be looked upon as the first step towards making the accumulation and use of a gold reserve possible. A gold reserve, such as that suggested in the memorandum from the Indian Government, which is not in any circumstances to be parted with, is plainly not a gold reserve in the ordinary sense at all. A gold reserve is, indeed, I think, something that can only be made available after the gold standard has been brought into full working order.

(14) If the Dutch system were imitated by making gold legal tender at a fixed ratio to the rupee, it might eventually, if not immediately, be further imitated by following the practice of the Bank of the Netherlands in being prepared always to give gold to meet a *bona fide* demand for it for export, the *bona fides* of this demand being evidenced by the fact of the exchange being against the country. The operation of the scheme would then be very similar to that of Mr. Lindsay's scheme, without, however, incurring the risk of an internal drain, which his altogether fails to obviate. With regard to that scheme it is worthy of note that while it proposes in form to guarantee universal convertibility for the rupee, it absolutely relies for its success on the anticipation that there will be no internal demand for its conversion. Mr. Lindsay, himself, describes his scheme as one that will secure " full and free convertibility for the rupee for foreign payment purposes," instead of (like the Government of India's scheme) " partial convertibility for foreign payments

combined with partial convertibility for local payments
and for hoarders." He expects thus, it will be seen, to
level up the rupee by meeting the demand for gold for
export only. If doubt should remain in the mind of
any members of the Committee as to whether the simple
fixing of the ratio would be effective in maintaining the
value of the rupee, it might still be worth their while to
consider whether, with this proviso added, that gold
should always be furnished to meet an export demand,
the plan would work satisfactorily. As the real exchange is ordinarily in India's favour, the amount of
reserve required to ensure the ability always to furnish
gold in such circumstances could not be large.

(15) It seems to me in the highest degree improbable
that the fixing of the ratio at 1s. 4d. now would lead to
an accumulation of rupees in the treasuries as, under
very different conditions, in 1893. Still it would no
doubt serve the important purpose of promoting, from
the start, public confidence in the ultimate success of the
scheme, if the Government were to arm themselves with
power to melt and sell rupees in such an event. The
Dutch, in like circumstances, armed themselves with
similar powers, but never had occasion to use them.

(16) If a gold, or partial gold, currency is the desired
eventual goal, the plan proposed is clearly the only
road to it.

APPENDIX B

THE REDUCTION OF THE AS

Since Mommsen's book was written two facts that are inconsistent with his theory of the reduction of the as, at all events in the precise form in which he states it, appear to have been definitely established by numismatic evidence which there is no gainsaying. The first is the fact that the *as libralis* was not a coin of ten ounces in weight, but one of twelve ; the second is the fact that by 268 B.C., when silver was first issued in Rome, the as had already come down to close upon two ounces in weight, not to four only, as Mommsen supposes. It was at seven and a half ounces in 300 B.C., so that the fall was more or less gradual.

The truth is, I think, that Mommsen creates unnecessary difficulties for himself by starting with the assumption that copper must have been at its intrinsic value when the denarius was issued. He is very much alive to the effect likely to be produced by the introduction of a dearer metal into the monetary system of a country, in tending to make the cheaper metal circulate at a conventional value. That, indeed,

[1] G. F. Hill, *Handbook of Greek and Roman Coins*, p. 47.

is the central idea in his interpretation both of the transition from copper to silver, and of the subsequent transition from silver to gold, as standard money in Rome. He does not, however, seem to have fully realized the facts that the dearer metal may be, to all intents and purposes, introduced into the monetary system of a country long before it has been coined by the government of that country, and that its circulation as foreign coin may produce every one of those effects which would naturally follow from its circulation as national coin. Indeed, the rigid distinction between national and foreign coin is a comparatively modern phenomenon. In most periods of the world's history the circulation of every country always embraced a large proportion of foreign coin, ordinarily circulating along with the local coin at tariffed rates.

It seems beyond doubt, therefore, that the equation between the scruple of silver and either ten or twelve ounces of copper, the tradition of which was handed down in the equation between the sesterce and the *as libralis*, was of a far older date than 268 B.C., and that it, at that much earlier epoch when it originated, had begun at once to produce its natural effect in leading to a depreciation of the copper. The sesterce seems to have been modelled on the diobol of Tarentum, which would appear to have been known as the nummus, very much as our first issue of gold in Edward III.'s reign was modelled on the florin—it was a double florin—and as the aureus was modelled on the Philippus. Mommsen himself, speaking of an early period, tells us that [1] "the emission of the nummus, equal in value to 10 ounces [of copper], of the double nummus worth 20 ounces, and of the semis

[1] *Hist. de la Monnaie romaine*, vol. ii. p. 10.

replacing the quincunx in the series of southern Italy was due to the fact that the nations used to silver money were accustomed to regard the Roman ounce as the equivalent of the lesser litra, and 10 ounces as being the equivalent of the greater litra or nummus."

The alternative hypothesis, originating with Niebuhr, that the diminution in the weight of the Roman copper was due not to a depreciation of the coins of that metal, but to a rise in the value of copper as compared with silver, which caused smaller copper coins to be the equivalent of the same amount of silver as had formerly been represented by larger ones, seems to me to be beset with insuperable difficulties. On that hypothesis, the relation between the sextantal (two-ounce) as and the denarius and sesterce would express the relation between the intrinsic value of silver and of copper, that is about 1 : 120. The sesterce, being a scruple of silver, would be thus equal in value to five ounces of copper. But then what are we to make of the fact that the sesterce was, at the same time, a synonym for the *as libralis*, of twelve ounces of copper? How could it be equal, at once, both to five and to twelve ounces? If we suppose the value of copper to have already become conventional, the difficulty vanishes. Our sovereign is now equal to about four ounces of our coined silver, and, at the same time, to about double that amount of uncoined silver ; or, to make the parallel more exact, from the present monetary point of view, the sovereign is the representative of twenty shillings, weighing about four ounces, while, from the historical point of view, it is the representative of one pound weight of silver. Fines fixed in the pounds sterling of Henry III. would, if the statutes fixing them were still in force, be payable now in so many sovereigns, just as the fines fixed in asses

aeris gravis were payable in so many sesterces. At the
same time, neither the relation between the sovereign
and the shilling nor the relation between the sovereign
and the pound of silver correspond now, even remotely,
to the ratio between gold and silver themselves ; and
it will, no doubt, be found similarly vain to look for
such correspondence either in the relation between the
sesterce and the sextantal as, or in the relation between
it and the *as libralis.*

Another difficulty connected with Niebuhr's theory
is this, that it is quite certain that the diminution in the
weight of the copper coinage *after* 268 B.C. was due to
its depreciation, and it would surely be remarkable
if we should have to assign its diminution before that
date to another and a contradictory cause. It is the
falling, not the rising, metal that is ordinarily depreciated.
The hypothesis, it may be thought, gains some support
from the fact that the ratio between silver and copper
in the coinage of the Ptolemies was 1 : 120 ; but there is
not the smallest doubt that it is there the *monetary*
ratio only that is in question.[1]

The following paragraphs from the *Historia Numorum* of Dr. Barclay Head, to which Mr. Macdonald
has drawn my attention, are worth quoting in this connection. The final one is especially interesting, as it
puts beyond question the depreciation of the as at a
very early date. If copper had been the rising metal,
we should certainly have heard nothing of ordinances
for the payment of fines in silver.

" That the Tarentine diobol exchanged for ten ounces
of bronze we gather from the fact that the obol commonly bears the mark of value . . . . . as we shall
presently see. If therefore the obol was equal to the

---

[1] *Revenue Laws of Ptolemy Philadelphus*, Appendix III. p. 205.

bronze quincunx, the diobol must have been equivalent to the dextans, which as struck in Apulia was also called a nummus.

" The name Nummus seems therefore to have applied first of all to the silver diobol, as the Federal unit of account at Heraclea and Tarentum, and probably throughout southern Italy, and then to have been transferred to its equivalent, the unit of bronze, consisting of 10 ounces and weighing consequently about 5,000 grains.

" In the Tabulæ Heracleenses, which were drawn up at the time when the bronze coins were being generally reduced, a distinction is drawn between the silver and the bronze nummus, for a fine of ten nummi, δέκα νόμως ἀργυρίω is ordered to be paid by the tenant of certain lands who shall have omitted to plant the full number of olive trees specified in his contract. The fine was 10 silver nummi for each plant πὰρ τὸ φυτον ἕκαστον ; the addition of the word ἀργυρίω was intended to secure the payment of the sum in silver, and was a necessary restriction at a time when the weight of the coined bronze was beginning to fall." [1]

[1] *Historia Numorum*, p. 55.

INDEX

A

THE END